THE INDISSOLUBILITY OF MARRIAGE

MATTHEW LEVERING

The Indissolubility of Marriage

Amoris Laetitia in Context

IGNATIUS PRESS   SAN FRANCISCO

Cover design by Roxanne Mei Lum

© 2019 by Ignatius Press, San Francisco
All rights reserved
ISBN 978-1-62164-293-0
Library of Congress Control Number 2018958977
Printed in the United States of America ∞

To Joy Levering

CONTENTS

ACKNOWLEDGMENTS

This book has its origins in gratitude for Jesus Christ's gift of indissoluble sacramental marriage, a reality that makes the Sacrament of Matrimony so precious. My wife and I have shared an indissoluble marriage for twenty-six years. The indissolubility of our marriage depends upon Christ's sacramental pledge, mediated by the Church of Christ that keeps its sacramental promises, even when the spouses fail to do so.

I dedicate this book to my wife, Joy Levering, with gratitude to Christ and his Church for the sacrament that unites Joy and me and that has borne fruit in our beloved family. The Letter of James describes my beloved Joy eloquently: "Who is wise and understanding among you? By his good life let him show his works in the meekness of wisdom.... The wisdom from above is first pure, then peaceable, gentle, open to reason, full of mercy and good fruits, without uncertainty or insincerity" (Js 3:13, 17).

In the writing of this book, I incurred numerous debts, though of course no one but me is responsible for the contents of the book. I need first to thank Mundelein Seminary, especially its rector, Father John Kartje, and its dean, Father Thomas Baima. I am deeply appreciative of Jim and Molly Perry, who generously endowed the chair that I hold at the seminary. I wish to thank Jörgen Vijgen and Piotr Roszak for the first impetus to write on marital indissolubility; the essay I wrote for them (a version of which became chapter 4 of the present book) has been published as "Aquinas on the Indissolubility of Marriage", in *Towards a Biblical Thomism: Thomas Aquinas and the Renewal of Biblical Theology*.[1] I benefited greatly from the corrections and suggestions that Jörgen provided for my essay.

---

[1] Matthew Levering, "Aquinas on the Indissolubility of Marriage", in *Towards a Biblical Thomism: Thomas Aquinas and the Renewal of Biblical Theology*, ed. Piotr Roszak and Jörgen Vijgen (Pamplona: EUNSA, 2018), 243–71.

As I began to work on this book in earnest, I received outstanding encouragement from Matthew Minerd, who read an early draft and offered insightful corrections at various points in the manuscript's gestation, culminating in his extremely helpful reading of the final draft. Perry Cahall, an expert on the theology of marriage, offered sage advice in response to queries, as did Stephen Little. Andrew Hofer, O.P., read a full draft of the manuscript and helped me, with his customary precision and charity, to prune and refine it. Daniel Lendman also read a full draft, and he strengthened the manuscript on some sensitive points. Thomas Joseph White, O.P., offered encouraging remarks as the manuscript moved toward its final form. My friend and research assistant David Augustine sifted through a few German books and provided me with helpful reading notes, and David also did the bibliography. On short notice, Christian Brugger made some valuable emendations and additions to my discussion of the Council of Trent. Matthew J. Thomas helped me to expand the patristic material in important ways, and he commented insightfully on almost all the chapters. Guy Mansini, O.S.B., provided wise counsel. Joseph Fessio, S.J., read the full manuscript and suggested a clarification on an important point. Recently, I was privileged to be present when Father Fessio said Mass at Marytown for my mentor (and our mutual dear friend, who died in January 2018) Father Matthew Lamb. Many thanks to Father Fessio and Mark Brumley, for publishing this book and for all they have done for Christ's Church.

INTRODUCTION

I hold that *Amoris Laetitia* does not change the Church's doctrine of marital indissolubility. Indissoluble Christian marriage involves permanent obligations so long as both parties are alive, including acknowledging one's spouse as one's spouse and abiding by sexual exclusivity. The origins of indissoluble Christian marriage are found in the New Testament. The Apostle Paul says, "Thus a married woman is bound by law to her husband as long as he lives; but if her husband dies she is discharged from the law concerning the husband. Accordingly, she will be called an adulteress if she lives with another man while her husband is alive" (Rom 7:2–3). Paul makes this same point in 1 Corinthians: "A wife is bound to her husband as long as he lives. If the husband dies, she is free to be married to whom she wishes, only in the Lord" (1 Cor 7:39). This insistence flows from Jesus' own teaching. Paul states that "to the married I give charge, not I but the Lord, that the wife should not separate from her husband (but if she does, let her remain single or else be reconciled to her husband)—and that the husband should not divorce his wife" (1 Cor 7:10–11).

In my view, this is the shared ground upon which fruitful ongoing discussion of divorce and remarriage should take place. Yet, some Catholic theologians consider that *Amoris Laetitia* puts a de facto end to marital indissolubility, by turning it into contingent indissolubility, that is, dissolubility. Others think that the Catholic Church has never definitively taught the doctrine of marital indissolubility, and so a change in this doctrine would not constitute a rupture undermining the Church's truth-claims in other areas. Many Catholic biblical scholars maintain that Jesus or the first Christians rejected a strict doctrine of marital indissolubility. Other Catholic scholars consider that marital indissolubility—while a noble eschatological ideal of Jesus, who believed the arrival of the kingdom of God to be imminent—has proven to be unworkable in the real world, and so the Church

11

should allow divorce and remarriage due to the "hardness of heart" (Mt 19:8) of Christians.

The present book takes such concerns very seriously. After all, they come from the preaching of mercy that is at the heart of the Gospel. In 2009, the United States Conference of Catholic Bishops published a pastoral letter titled *Marriage: Love and Life in the Divine Plan*, in which they observe that after the couple exchanges their wedding vows, it is then that "the real work of marriage begins. For the remainder of their married lives, the couple is challenged to grow, through grace, into what they already are: that is, an image of Christ's love for his Church."[1] The bishops contend that imaging Christ's love for the Church does not mean sharing romantic feelings or romantic love. It means something much deeper: the married couple must live out the vocation "of a marital communion defined by the unbreakable spousal love of Christ for his Church".[2] Living out this vocation in an indissoluble marriage "will require persistent effort", even to the point that "maintaining the common courtesies—persevering in fidelity, kindness, communication, and mutual assistance—can become a deep expression of conjugal charity".[3]

But here is the problem: if even the "common courtesies" have become difficult, then why not—given the level of distrust, disengagement, and even anger that this situation implies—allow the couple to divorce (if they wish) and start over? It would seem that, while marital indissolubility is good in theory, it is in accord with the mercy of Christ to allow Catholics to begin anew when their first marriage is broken. Can marital indissolubility and its attendant obligations become mere rules, lacking not only in common sense, but also in Christian mercy? The biblical scholar and theologian N. T. Wright comments that "the real difficulty with rules is not only that we don't keep them very well," but, more than this, the "problem is that rules always appear to be, and are indeed designed to be, restrictive. But we know, deep down, that some of the key things that make us human

---

[1] *Marriage: Love and Life in the Divine Plan; A Pastoral Letter of the United States Conference of Catholic Bishops* (Washington, D.C.: United States Conference of Catholic Bishops, 2009), 45, http://www.usccb.org/issues-and-action/marriage-and-family/marriage/love-and-life /upload/pastoral-letter-marriage-love-and-life-in-the-divine-plan.pdf.

[2] Ibid., 46.

[3] Ibid.

are being creative, celebrating life and beauty and love and laughter.... Rules matter, but they aren't the center of it all."[4] Applying this point to a marriage that has broken down, in which there is an utter absence of love, celebration, and laughter, we might conclude not only that the marriage has ended but also that, with a more suitable partner or at a more mature time of life, a divorced person may be able to find love, celebration, and laughter in a new marriage.

Put simply: if God holds his people to the *broken but indissoluble* marriage as opposed to allowing the spouses to make a new start with different partners, then how can it be said that God cares about his people, let alone caring for his people with infinite mercy? Are we not dealing with a set of rules that, in certain circumstances, is frankly incoherent? Such rules seem the very opposite of Christ's merciful sayings, for example, his words with respect to the woman caught in adultery whom "the scribes and the Pharisees"—in the role of legalistic moralists—wanted to stone. Christ says, "Let him who is without sin among you be the first to throw a stone at her," and, "Neither do I condemn you; go, and do not sin again" (Jn 8:3,7,11).[5]

The theologian Julie Hanlon Rubio has remarked that "the overwhelming majority of Americans desire monogamy and expect fidelity. And despite their ongoing experience with marriage failure, most continue to promise to stay with one other person until death."[6] But

---

[4] N. T. Wright, "Why Christian Character Matters", in *All Things Hold Together in Christ: A Conversation on Faith, Science, and Virtue*, ed. James K. A. Smith and Michael L. Gulker (Grand Rapids, MI: Baker Academic, 2018), 171.

[5] For concern about rules, see, for example, Natalia Imperatori-Lee's critique of a "church of command and obligation", which she contrasts with "a church of encounter and accompaniment"; see Natalia Imperatori-Lee, "How Is *Amoris Laetitia* Being Received? Colonialism, Conscience, and Accompaniment", in *Amoris Laetitia: A New Momentum for Moral Formation and Pastoral Practice*, ed. Grant Gallicho and James F. Keenan, S.J. (New York: Paulist Press, 2018), 3. Imperatori-Lee suggests that a focus on rules goes hand-in-hand with a romanticized portrait of real life; thus "accompaniment works against the romanticization of marriage and family that pervades our church's teaching on these topics" (ibid., 9). See also James F. Keenan, S.J.,'s argument that *Amoris Laetitia* privileges relationality over abstract rationality: James F. Keenan, S.J., "Receiving *Amoris Laetitia*", *Theological Studies* 78 (2017): 193–212; as well as Gregorio Perez de Guereñu, "*Amoris laetitia* y madurez humana y ecclesial", *Páginas* 244 (December 2016): 26–34.

[6] Julie Hanlon Rubio, *Hope for Common Ground: Mediating the Personal and the Political in a Divided Church* (Washington, D.C.: Georgetown University Press, 2016), 109. See also the observation of Joachim Cardinal Meisner: "In Cologne, a curious phenomenon has arisen. Directly behind the cathedral is an iron bridge across the Rhine River for pedestrians. Fixed

if a person fails in this promise, sometimes due to no fault (or relatively little fault) of his or her own—especially in cases where one spouse is abandoned by the other—then why should the mutually valid promise on the wedding day continue to bind the persons indissolubly? Pointedly, Rubio argues that the Church has done a poor job in welcoming and caring for "the needs of broken families" and for "those who are wounded when the ideal is no longer possible to live out".[7] Again, therefore, why should the Catholic Church hold spouses to all the obligations pertaining to a valid and consummated marital commitment that has now broken down?

The Plan of This Book

In the present book, I cannot give a full answer to the question of why the Catholic Church should hold spouses to the obligations pertaining to a valid and consummated marital commitment. Such an answer would require exploring not only the diverse components of a person's moral life, but also the relationship of indissoluble marriage to Christ's Paschal Mystery, to the self-surrendering Trinitarian life, to the marriage of Christ and the Church, to social justice and the good of children, and to other such topics. I treat many of these topics in my *Engaging the Doctrine of Marriage*, currently in preparation.[8] In the present study, however, I try to set forth an important part of

---

to the grating between the railway and pedestrian crossing are hundreds of thousands of 'love-locks'. Couples go there to attach their locks to the bridge and then throw the key into the Rhine together. The lock represents their relationship, and they throw away the key in order to say: 'We want to stay together forever.' This is, of course, not a Christian ritual, but the essential elements of the marital relationship are expressed in a secular way within it: unity and indissolubility" (Joachim Cardinal Meisner, "Marriage Preparation—The Challenges of Today", in *Eleven Cardinals Speak on Marriage and the Family: Essays from a Pastoral Viewpoint*, ed. Winfried Aymans, trans. Michael J. Miller et al. [San Francisco: Ignatius Press, 2015], 55). Meisner rightly considers this to be strong evidence that "the message of our faith in the sacrament of matrimony is not foreign even to our secular world. It answers the deepest desire of men, and we say: 'Your desire is no dream, no illusion, and no outlandish ideal. Through Christ and his bond with the Church, love and fidelity are possible, wholly and without end'" (ibid., 55–56).

[7] Rubio, *Hope for Common Ground*, 108.

[8] As the Protestant theologian Geoffrey W. Bromiley beautifully says, "No theology of marriage or of anything else arises if the teaching is abstracted from God himself, if God himself is not present at the heart and center in his own relation to the topic" (Geoffrey W. Bromiley, *God and Marriage* [Grand Rapids, MI: Eerdmans, 1980], xii).

the answer, by arguing in favor of the Catholic doctrine (indeed, the *reality*) of indissoluble marriage.

Specifically, I explore the doctrine of marital indissolubility in four chapters. In the first chapter, I examine the paths taken by Eastern Orthodox and Protestant Christians on divorce and remarriage, with attention also to the Church Fathers' viewpoints and to the question of whether historical-critical biblical exegesis can help to overcome the disagreements. Although some scholars hold that study of the Church Fathers and of historical-critical exegesis tells *against* the Catholic doctrine of marital indissolubility, I argue that the case is the opposite. Jesus strongly affirms marital indissolubility, more clearly than he does almost any other Catholic teaching. The Church Fathers support the Catholic understanding of indissoluble marriage unanimously during the first three centuries of the Church. The majority of later Fathers, too, hold to the Catholic position as it crystallized through the interpretations of Jerome and Augustine.

In the second chapter, given the efforts of some scholars to suggest that in fact the Catholic Church has never definitively taught marital indissolubility in a manner that excludes remarriage after divorce (without an annulment), I explore the relevant teachings on marital indissolubility offered by the Council of Trent, Pope Leo XIII, Pope Pius XI, Vatican II, Pope John Paul II, and Pope Benedict XVI. My conclusion is that the indissolubility of a valid and consummated Christian marriage has been definitively taught by the Church. For the Church to reject this teaching would cause a rupture that would throw many other Catholic doctrines into doubt. In this context, I explore in some detail the argument of Kenneth Himes and James Coriden that the Catholic Church has not definitively taught marital indissolubility and that the doctrine should be revised to admit that a divorce dissolves a valid and consummated sacramental marriage.

In the third chapter, I provide an overview of Pope Francis' *Amoris Laetitia*, in light of his letter to the bishops of the Buenos Aires pastoral region, and in dialogue especially with the influential interpretations of Christoph Cardinal Schönborn, Francisco Cardinal Coccopalmerio, and Archbishop Vincent Fernandez.[9] As the

---

[9] For important background to Schönborn's 2016 remarks, see Michaela C. Hastetter's "*Via Caritatis*—Pastoral Care of the Divorced and Remarried: An Ecumenical Comparison in the Context of *Amoris Laetitia*", trans. Graham Harrison, in *A Point of No Return?* Amoris

theologian Louis Cameli states, "*Amoris Laetitia* ... assumes doctrine, moral teaching, law, and basic pastoral care concerning marriage and family life. There are no changes, despite claims to the contrary."[10] Cameli insists that "the famous chapter 8" of *Amoris Laetitia* "does not

---

Laetitia *on Marriage, Divorce, and Remarriage*, ed. Thomas Knieps-Port le Roi (Berlin: LIT Verlag, 2017), 206–10. She draws attention to Cardinal Schönborn's *Die Freude, Priester zu sein* (Freiburg: Herder, 2011), 144–57. As she says, Schönborn proposed and implemented a five-point plan for the care of the divorced and (civilly) remarried. The five points of the plan are as follows: (1) focusing on the "poor" in this situation, namely, the children; (2) focusing on those who, after divorce, are lonely because they do not or cannot find a new partner; (3) addressing the issue of guilt for the break-up and encouraging the divorced couple to forgive each other; (4) paying attention to marriages that endure through difficult times; and (5) attending to the pastoral care of the divorced and remarried by refusing simply to invite *all* divorced and remarried persons to Eucharistic Communion. Hastetter also draws attention to the 2012 Freiburg "Memorandum on Admitting Divorced and Remarried Persons to the Sacraments" (*Memorandum "Wiederverheiratet Geschiedene in unserer Kirche"*). Additionally, she notes the 2013 publication by the Archdiocese of Freiburg of guidelines for liturgical services for the blessing of divorced and remarried couples, including for their reception of the Eucharist (Erzbischöfliches Seelsorgeamt Freiburg, *Handreichung für die Seelsorge zur Begleitung von Menschen in Trennung, Scheidung und nach ziviler Wiederverheiratung*, https://www.kfd-bundesverband.de/fileadmin/Bilder/Nachrichten/Widerverheiratet_broschuere_handreichung_09_2013.pdf). The Archdiocese of Vienna, under Cardinal Schönborn's leadership, now offers "a whole range of liturgical celebrations for the divorced and remarried: there are three different models of blessings, blessings for people with a broken love-relationship, in addition to two models for a service of thanksgiving for a civil marriage" (Hastetter, "*Via Caritatis*", 209–10). After appreciatively surveying *Amoris Laetitia*, Hastetter concludes that its "openness to new liturgical forms could mean that, in the future, with the liturgical 'Siamese twins' (services of blessing for the divorced and remarried, and their admission to holy communion), the Catholic Church could draw closer to the Protestant individual liturgical services (*Kasualgottesdienste*) and the Orthodox practice of official solemnization of second and third marriages. As reception of *Amoris laetitia* widens with the passage of time, this convergence could become more prominent than heretofore" (ibid., 214). See also Michaela C. Hastetter, "Ehe- und Familienpastoral von Benedikt bis Franziskus: Krise oder Kontinuität?", *Ambo* 1 (2016): 84–115. On Austrian Catholic liturgical services of blessing for second (civil) marriages, see Franz Harant, "In a Second Marriage before God and before Others: New Paths of the Church and in the Church in Austria", in Knieps-Port le Roi, *Point of No Return?*, 260–63; Franz Harant, "In zweiter Ehe neu beginnen: Segensfeier bei Wiederheirat", *Diakonia* 33 (2002): 31–37.

[10] Louis J. Cameli, "How Is *Amoris Laetitia* Being Received?", in Gallicho and Keenan, *Amoris Laetitia*, 25. Cameli has in view the *dubia* put forward by cardinals Raymond Burke, Carlos Caffarra, Joachim Meisner, and Walter Brandmüller in a letter to Pope Francis dated September 19, 2016. See also Raymond Cardinal Burke, " 'Amoris Laetitia' and the Constant Teaching and Practice of the Church", *National Catholic Register*, April 12, 2016, http://www.ncregister.com/daily-news/amoris-laetitia-and-the-constant-teaching-and-practice-of-the-church/#ixzz46HheGSQ6/. For cognate concerns, see Robert Spaemann, "Ein Bruch mit der Lehrtradition", interview by Anian Christoph Wimmer, *CNA Deutsch*, April 28, 2016;

deviate from doctrinal or moral teaching".[11] In accord with Cameli, I emphasize that not only does *Amoris Laetitia* affirm the indissolubility of marriage, but also, and equally importantly, the interpreters whose views have been explicitly commended by Pope Francis as indicative of his intentions in *Amoris Laetitia* have all emphasized that the Catholic Church's traditional teaching on marital indissolubility has not been changed. At the same time, I note that the pastoral strategy advanced by the Argentine bishops and by cardinals Schönborn and Coccopalmerio does cause a tension: namely, what has happened to the obligations of the indissoluble marriage, such as the obligation of sexual exclusivity?[12] Although I agree with those who are concerned about this tension in the new pastoral strategy, my argument in chapter 3 is simply that fruitful discussion of this topic should focus upon the *shared* ground of the Catholic doctrine of marital indissolubility.

In the fourth chapter, given that a fundamental issue for marital indissolubility is whether it actually serves the good of believers in the merciful Lord Jesus Christ, I undertake a *ressourcement* of the philosophical, exegetical, and theological teachings of Aquinas on marital

---

English edition: "Interview with Robert Spaemann on Amoris Laetitia", by Anian Christoph Wimmer, trans. Richard Andrew Krema, *CNA*, April 29, 2016, https://www.catholicnewsagency.com/news/full-text-interview-with-robert-spaemann-on-amoris-laetitia-10088; Mariusz Biliniewicz, *Amoris Laetitia and the Spirit of Vatican II: The Source of Controversy* (London: Routledge, 2018). For a helpful explanation of the *dubia*, see Thibaud Collin, *Le mariage chrétien a-t-il encore un avenir? Pour en finir avec les malentendus* (Paris: Artège, 2018), 161–72.

[11] Cameli, "How Is *Amoris Laetitia* Being Received?", 25. In Cameli's view, *Amoris Laetitia* is rightly read through a "formational lens"; it offers "spiritual and moral formation by helping and preparing people to live out their commitment as disciples of Jesus Christ and to grow in it in the context of marriage and family life" (ibid.).

[12] As Camillo Cardinal Ruini puts it, the problem is that the solution of "holding firm the indissolubility of ratified and consummated marriage" while also allowing the divorced and civilly remarried "to receive sacramental absolution and the Eucharist under precise conditions but without having to abstain" from sexual intercourse logically "implies an exercise of extra-marital sexuality, given the continuation of the first marriage, ratified and consummated. In other words, the original conjugal bond would continue to exist, but in the behavior of the faith and in liturgical life, one could proceed as if it did not exist. We are therefore facing a question of consistency between practice and doctrine" (Camillo Cardinal Ruini, "The Gospel of the Family in the Secularized West", in Aymans, *Eleven Cardinals*, 85–86). For the insistence that *Amoris Laetitia* does not justify such a pastoral practice—and for reflection on the grace by which people who have civilly remarried but who are bound by a prior indissoluble marriage choose to live as brother and sister (abstaining from sexual intercourse)—see Angel Perez-Lopez, "Conjugal Charity and the Pastoral Care of the Conjugal Bond in *Amoris Laetitia*", *Scripta Fulgentia* 26 (2016): 83–119.

indissolubility. I focus especially on Aquinas' treatment of marital indissolubility as part of the created order (Mt 19:4–6) and on his analysis of the Matthean exception clause (Mt 5:32; 19:9) and "Pauline
privilege" (1 Cor 7:15). I seek to explain why it makes sense that
indissoluble Christian marriage belongs to the core of the merciful
Gospel of Jesus Christ.

In my conclusion, I set forth some brief considerations regarding the way forward, theologically and pastorally, for the Catholic
doctrine of marital indissolubility. Dominik Cardinal Duka remarks
that we should remember that the Cross of Christ, in which spouses
share, is good for individuals and communities not because it is
"the exaltation of torture" but because it is "the exaltation of faithful love" and "the exaltation of keeping one's word, of the oath
that God gave to mankind".[13] Even in the midst of tragedies such
as the experience of being abandoned by one's spouse, cleaving to
the Cross serves the good of individual persons because of the self-
sacrificial love and the fidelity that the innocent spouse enacts in
union with Christ and his Spirit. Recently, Rainer Beckmann has
written a powerful testimony to the goodness of such fidelity.[14] On
the basis of his personal experience of being abandoned by his spouse
after twenty-five years of marriage, he shows how and why it is that
in Christ, "we rejoice in our sufferings, knowing that suffering produces endurance, and endurance produces character, and character
produces hope, and hope does not disappoint us, because God's love
has been poured into our hearts through the Holy Spirit who has
been given to us" (Rom 5:3–5).

The Contemporary Catholic Debate: A Brief Sketch

It is necessary to give some context for a book like this one, which
touches upon matters that have been debated by Catholics especially over the past fifty years, and that have become particularly

---

[13] Dominik Cardinal Duka, O.P., "Reflections on the Family", in Aymans, *Eleven Cardinals Speak*, 43.

[14] See Rainer Beckmann, *Das Evangelium der ehelichen Treue: Eine Antwort auf Kardinal
Kasper* (Kisslegg: Fe-Medienverlag, 2015).

prominent during Pope Francis' pontificate. In an essay published in 2015, Willem Cardinal Eijk notes that throughout Western Europe most divorced and remarried persons (without annulment) have long been freely receiving the Eucharist.[15] In light of Pope Francis' 2016 letter to the bishops of the Buenos Aires region, many interpreters and bishops have now concluded that *Amoris Laetitia*, as understood by Pope Francis, intends to open Eucharistic Communion to some divorced and (civilly) remarried persons.[16]

Inevitably, the question then becomes, what has happened to the valid and consummated indissoluble marriage and to its obligations, if a person bound by an indissoluble marriage can have sexual relations with a new partner? Have the person's obligations to his or her indissoluble spouse vanished or become morally irrelevant? Julie Hanlon Rubio points out, "Because of God's grace, the ontological reality of a sacramental marriage never fully disappears."[17]

In response to such questions, Walter Cardinal Kasper has remarked that "one ought not to understand this teaching [about the indissoluble bond of marriage] as a kind of metaphysical hypostasis beside or

---

[15] See Willem Jacobus Cardinal Eijk, "Can Divorced and Civilly Remarried Persons Receive Communion?", in Aymans, *Eleven Cardinals Speak*, 45.

[16] See, for representative examples, Bishop Franz-Josef Overbeck, "What Theological Resources Did the German Bishops Mine for Their Reception of *Amoris Laetitia*?", in Gallicho and Keenan, *Amoris Laetitia*, 139–45; Bishop Robert W. McElroy, "Diocesan Topical Synods: A Pathway for Pastoral Consultation in the Local Church", in Gallicho and Keenan, *Amoris Laetitia*, 122–29; Archbishop Wilton D. Gregory, "*Amoris Laetitia*: A New Momentum for Moral Formation and Pastoral Practice", in Gallicho and Keenan, *Amoris Laetitia*, 152–55; Archbishop Charles Jude Scicluna, "The Guidelines of the Maltese Bishops: The Theological Principles We Mined", in *Amoris Laetitia*, 146–51. For the opposite approach, set forth prior to the promulgation of Pope Francis' letter but still a valid (and permitted) interpretation of the words of *Amoris Laetitia*, see Archbishop Charles Chaput, O.F.M. Cap., "Pastoral Guidelines for Implementing *Amoris Laetitia*", *Nova et Vetera* 15 (2017): 1–7. Gerhard Cardinal Müller and Raymond Cardinal Burke have also discussed the implementation at some length, mounting cogent arguments for why divorced and remarried persons (without annulment or stopping sexual relations with the new partner) should not be admitted to Eucharistic Communion.

[17] Julie Hanlon Rubio, "The Newness of *Amoris Laetitia*: Mercy and Truth, Truth and Mercy", in Gallicho and Keenan, *Amoris Laetitia*, 63. Notably, Rubio does not consider this to be an unsurpassable impediment. In her view, God, by his "grace and mercy", may be calling the person to enter into or remain within the life-giving second marriage (ibid., cf. 65). She concludes that "if divorce and second marriage are the best option", such persons should "return to their parishes alongside the other sinning saints gathered around the eucharistic table" (ibid., 66).

over the personal love of the spouses."[18] Yet, indissoluble marriage can only be indissoluble if the sacrament does indeed establish an objectively secure bond between husband and wife. This ensures that even if their feelings fade or if one spouse falls out of love and acts accordingly, the marriage is not destroyed, because it has been established on something more solid than the subjective dispositions of the spouses.[19] In Christian marriage, the man and woman freely give themselves to each other through their vows; and this mutual gift, sacramentally elevated, constitutes an indissoluble bond while the spouses live.[20] Such a marriage sacramentally signifies the union of Christ and the Church. The objective security of this bond is crucial not only for the well-being of children and of communities, but also for the personal flourishing of the spouses themselves, as they learn to embody Christian self-sacrificial love.

The moral philosopher Stephan Kampowski reminds us that "the marital bond cannot be thought of apart from the spouses' personal love."[21] The bond is "the objectification of this love", a form that enables the man and woman to commit to the stable and unconditional relationship that is needed for healthy family life.[22] Kampowski compares it to the relationship of a parent to a child: the relationship,

---

[18] Walter Kasper, *The Gospel of the Family*, trans. William Madges (New York: Paulist Press, 2014), 16. See the response offered by Juan José Pérez-Soba and Stephan Kampowski, *The Gospel of the Family: Going beyond Cardinal Kasper's Proposal in the Debate on Marriage, Civil Re-Marriage, and Communion in the Church*, trans. Michael J. Miller (San Francisco: Ignatius Press, 2014). By contrast, for the argument that Kasper's proposal does not go far enough, see Hermann Häring, *Keine Christen zweiter Klasse!: Wiederverheiratete Geschiedene—Ein theologischer Zwischenruf* (Freiburg: Herder, 2014).

[19] The subjective dispositions of the spouses are shaky soil indeed, as Stephanie Höllinger points out, citing studies in cognitive psychology that show that "goals that the individuals wish to realise in their relationship with their partner" can significantly strain the relationship, since inevitably certain goals go unfulfilled (Stephanie Höllinger, "Do We Expect Too Much? A Reflection on Expectations and Marriage in *Amoris Laetitia*", in Knieps-Port le Roi, *Point of No Return?*, 107; cf. 110–11). Höllinger also points to "the often stressful situation of having to simultaneously manage household chores, go to work, raise children and have an intact and loving relationship with one's spouse" (ibid., 109). Unfortunately, Höllinger seems to associate marital indissolubility with the *ideal* of the perfect marriage, rather than realizing that indissolubility is in fact a bulwark against such perfectionism.

[20] See the discussion of "promising" as an intersubjective reality in Stephan Kampowski, *Embracing Our Finitude: Exercises in a Christian Anthropology between Dependence and Gratitude* (Eugene, OR: Cascade, 2018), 93–104. See also Guy Mansini, O.S.B., *Promising and the Good* (Naples, FL: Sapientia Press, 2005).

[21] Kampowski, *Embracing Our Finitude*, 108.

[22] Ibid.

in order to be one of real love, must be secure, not based upon shifting feelings or behaviors. Just as a father is always the father of his son, so also a husband is always the husband of his wife, while they both live. This analogy is not arbitrary; parenting and marriage go together in providing a secure foundation for human relationships across generations. This secure foundation is what Pope Francis calls the "exclusive and indissoluble union between a man and a woman" that forms the basis of stable family life and of flourishing communities.[23]

It follows that today's debates are not between those who care about Christians who have been divorced and remarried, and those who do not care about such persons—as though the debate were in fact a choice between "truth or mercy".[24] On the contrary, all sides know that Jesus cares for and loves persons precisely in the midst of their troubles. The truth that Jesus wills for the Church is the path of true mercy, namely, the divinizing path of the life of grace.

Today's debates are also fueled in part by the fact that some Catholics conceive of divine revelation primarily as the awakening of the human spirit to divine love through the privileged instrumentality of Jesus, rather than also as including a specific truth-content.[25] In this

---

[23] Pope Francis, post-synodal apostolic exhortation *Amoris Laetitia* (March 19, 2016), no. 52.

[24] Rubio, "Newness of *Amoris Laetitia*", 61. Rubio suggests that mercy and truth must go together: "The newness of *AL* [*Amoris Laetitia*] for the laity—especially those in second marriages—lies not only in mercy but also in truth, in a strong vision of marriage as a deeply personal, lifelong, outward-facing union of two imperfect but committed people" (ibid., 62). Arnauld Join-Lambert contrasts "the rigorists who defend the pure doctrine" with "those who work on the ground level and are confronted with a multitude of painful situations" (Arnauld Join-Lambert, "Accompanying, Discerning and Integrating the Fragility of Couples: Pastors and Theologians at a Crossroads", in Knieps-Port le Roi, *Point of No Return?*, 145). He goes on to say that these "rigorists" use words that are "linked to fear", by contrast to the "hope" of those who wish "to encounter and to accompany in truth those who live in a situation of failure and suffering" (ibid., 145–46).

[25] For the contrary view, see Vatican II's Dogmatic Constitution on Divine Revelation, *Dei Verbum* (November 18, 1965), no. 10, in *Decrees of the Ecumenical Councils*, vol. 2, *Trent to Vatican II*, ed. Norman P. Tanner, S.J. (Washington, D.C.: Georgetown University Press, 1990), 975. Hans Urs von Balthasar comments that for theological liberalism, "dogmas are but crystallized forms of the existential faith-relationship to God, forms of vital religious intuitions and needs, valid as long as they foster the existential reality, but harmful once the life has gone out of them and they have stiffened into dead formulae. This process of stiffening can be posited in this way only because the life that generated the forms is sought for in the religious subject himself, while this life is also thought of as having produced the dogmas" (Hans Urs von Balthasar, *The Glory of the Lord: A Theological Aesthetics*, vol. 1, *Seeing the Form*, trans. Erasmo Leiva-Merikakis, ed. Joseph Fessio, S.J., and John Riches [San Francisco: Ignatius Press, 1982], 177).

vein, the theologian Arnauld Join-Lambert argues that "we shall arrive at the fullness of truth only at the end of time. In the present time, we remain marked by our multiple cultural contexts, which make different interpretations possible. The very reason for the existence of the Church is to make it possible for these cultures to be embodied against a horizon of unity, and hence of hope."[26] For Join-Lambert, the Church is an umbrella structure that unites diverse culturally and historically contextualized pastoral-doctrinal syntheses, which will differ in every epoch and whose unity does not and cannot reside in any kind of doctrinal or propositional permanence or continuity. He argues that the "tension between the doctrinal and the pastoral" rests upon a mistaken understanding of supposedly unchangeable doctrine that fails to recognize doctrine's radical provisionality, given the ever-changing cultural and historical contexts in which humans experience the divine love.[27]

Indeed, the history of papal teaching shows that popes have felt free to reverse course on various pastoral matters and on nondefinitive doctrinal matters.[28] For example, Pope John Paul II's *Ut Unum Sint* (1995) and the Second Vatican Council's *Unitatis Redintegratio* (1964) differ rather sharply from the antiecumenical encyclicals of Pope Leo XIII and Pope Pius XI, *Satis Cognitum* (1896) and *Mortalium Animos* (1928), respectively. Even so, however, the idea that a pan-Christian federation should be the foundation for a new ecumenically unified

---

[26] Join-Lambert, "Accompanying, Discerning and Integrating the Fragility of Couples", 147–48. Join-Lambert approvingly cites François Bousquet, "Principe dogmatique et théologie contemporaine?", *Recherches de science religieuse* 95 (2007): 545–58. Join-Lambert argues that Pope Francis attempts to avoid the word "doctrine" in *Amoris Laetitia.*

[27] Join-Lambert, "Accompanying, Discerning and Integrating the Fragility of Couples", 148, 154, 160. Join-Lambert sums up his point: "The recurring antitheses between the doctrinal and the pastoral are obsolete" (ibid., 160). For the term "pastorality", quoted by Join-Lambert, see Christoph Theobald, S.J., "Postface", in *Exhortation apostolique Post-Synodale du pape François La Joie de l'Amour: Édition présentée et annotée sous la direction du Service national Famille et Société—Conférence des évêques de France—et de la Faculté de théologie du Centre Sèvres* (Paris: Éditions Jésuites, 2016), 322. See also Theobald's *Urgences pastorales du moment présent: Pour une pédagogie de la réform* (Paris: Bayard, 2017), chap. 5, " 'Hiérarchie des vérités' et pastoralité".

[28] See, for example, the important insights of the following: Yves Congar, O.P., *True and False Reform in the Church*, trans. Paul Philibert, O.P. (Collegeville, MN: Liturgical Press, 2011); the Congregation for the Doctrine of the Faith, Instruction on the Ecclesial Vocation of the Theologian *Donum Veritatis* (May 24, 1990), no. 24.

Church, an idea opposed by popes Leo and Pius, still remains firmly outside the Catholic conception of the Church's unity as dogmatically taught in the Second Vatican Council's *Lumen Gentium* (1964). The fact that not everything in a particular pope's teaching is binding for all time does not mean that nothing is. There is a core of received doctrine to which all Catholics are accountable in Christ.[29] I argue in this book that included in such definitive doctrine is the Church's teaching on marital indissolubility, expressive of Christ's own teaching. *Amoris Laetitia* affirms this teaching about the indissolubility of marriage.

In *Amoris Laetitia*, Pope Francis rightly insists that divorced and (without annulment) remarried persons must be integrated in every appropriate way into the Church's life, with respect for the suffering that they have gone through and in light of the complex subjective factors at work in their personal situations. If, as Pope Francis has suggested in response to the bishops of the Buenos Aires pastoral region, this integration into the Church's life may include full participation in the Eucharist, which is a communion of charity,[30] then the question arises about what has happened to the objective obligations owed in charity to one's indissolubly married spouse.

To sum up the pressure point in the contemporary debate: Is it not the task of the Church to call persons to live in accord with their status before God, and therefore to call every indissolubly married person to live out the obligation of sexual exclusivity?[31] The theologian

---

[29] On this point see my *An Introduction to Vatican II as an Ongoing Theological Event* (Washington, D.C.: Catholic University of America Press, 2017), as well as Eduardo J. Echeverria, "The Essentialist versus Historicist Debate about the Truth Status of Dogmatic Formulations: A Critique of the Cimorelli-Minch Proposal", *Louvain Studies* 38 (2014): 356–69. Echeverria is responding to Christopher Cimorelli and Daniel Minch, "Views of Doctrine: Historical Consciousness, Asymptotic Notional Clarity, and the Challenge of Hermeneutics as Theology", *Louvain Studies* 37 (2013): 327–63.

[30] See John Corbett, O.P., et al., "Recent Proposals for the Pastoral Care of the Divorced and Remarried: A Theological Assessment", *Nova et Vetera* 12, no. 3 (2014): 619.

[31] While granting that Jesus "clearly treats a man's divorce and remarriage as akin to adultery, and from the earliest times in the Christian community, that judgment has been extended to a woman's divorce and remarriage", Cathleen Kaveny holds that the second wedding ceremony constitutes the sole sinful act and that what follows (including the sexual acts of the civilly married couple) are simply effects from a completed sin (Cathleen Kaveny, "How Is *Amoris Laetitia* Being Received? Mercy and *Amoris Laetitia*: Insights from Secular Law", in Gallicho and Keenan, *Amoris Laetitia*, 38). On this view, the "adultery" named by

Branislav Kuljovsky raises this concern in relation to *Amoris Laetitia*: "*Amoris laetitia* seems to suggest that now pastors should assess subjective culpability in order to direct prospective action without either seeking to remove the factors by appropriate instruction (in case of ignorance) or encouraging the penitents to overcome them (in case of psychological or sociological factors affecting one's freedom of choice)."[32]

The Church today needs theological reflection on this matter that takes as its starting point, in accord with *Amoris Laetitia*, the indissolubility of marriage and asks why Jesus included this teaching so prominently within the good news of the Gospel. Kuljovsky is correct that "choosing to do moral evil, whether culpably or inculpably, always involves harm to the good of the person, regardless of the circumstances and further noble motivations", and also that "knowingly and willfully to engage in non-marital sexual action

---

Jesus could be repented of simply by repenting of the second wedding ceremony, and the remarried (and forgiven) person could then allow the effects—i.e., the second marriage—to proceed. In my view, however, the ongoing choice not to live in accord with one's obligation of sexual exclusivity toward one's indissoluble spouse is a state of sin. *Pace* Kaveny, this state of sin causes moral harm so long as it persists, and to repent of it requires the firm intention to return to one's obligation of sexual exclusivity to one's indissoluble spouse. As a state of sin, it does not require the confessor or moral theologian to count up discrete acts of adultery committed within the second marriage. See also Cathleen Kaveny, "Mercy, Justice, and Law: Can Legal Concepts Help Foster New Life?", in *Marriage and Family: Relics of the Past or Promise of the Future?*, ed. George Augustin (Mahwah, NJ: Paulist Press, 2015), 75–106.

[32] Branislav Kuljovsky, "The Law of Gradualness or the Gradualness of Law? A Critical Analysis of *Amoris Laetitia*", in Knieps-Port le Roi, *Point of No Return?*, 61. Kuljovsky raises additional concerns: "Instead of demanding that pastors encourage the penitents to break with morally evil actions (a purpose of amendment), *Amoris laetitia* names 'sincere search for God's will' and 'more perfect response to it' (AL 300) as the conditions for the right execution of the pastors' discernment of the penitent's degree of responsibility. Referring to the avoidance of evil action (i.e. adultery) as merely a 'more perfect response' implies that failing to avoid this evil, is just a 'less perfect action' but no evil. Such a language undermines the church's teaching on moral absolutes and leads to the gradualness of law. Moreover, with such statements as 'search for God's will', *Amoris laetitia* gives the impression that God's will is something unknown to the individual person, something different from the revealed moral order taught by the Catholic Church.... Since *Amoris laetitia* speaks here about people living in extra-marital sexual unions, it is clear that the 'search for God's will', the 'special discernment' and the 'conscience's recognition of God's will' involves here a process of deliberating whether, due to the existing difficult circumstances (mitigating factors), the penitent may legitimately continue to violate the norm against adultery" (ibid., 62–63). See also Corbett et al., "Recent Proposals", 620–21.

is always morally evil regardless of one's circumstances or moti-vations."[33] Pastorally, Christine Galea, who has endured her own broken marriage, has suggested that the doctrine of marital indis-solubility aids couples in growing "throughout their lifetimes in a faithful, committed, loving union.... As Pope Francis points out, today, it is becoming more and more commonplace for spouses to reason that, if things do not turn out as they wish, there are sufficient grounds for their marriage to end. If this were the case, no marriage would last."[34]

In this debate, all can agree that the doctrinal and pastoral aspects of marital indissolubility should not be sharply separated. Paul Josef Cardinal Cordes directs attention to an interview given in 2015 by Bishop Franz-Josef Hermann Bode, the head of the Pastoral Com-mission of the German Bishops' Conference. Bishop Bode argues that the pastoral care for the divorced and remarried needs to change because the Church's approach no longer resonates in any way with the Catholic faithful. Along lines that Cordes rightly calls into ques-tion, Bishop Bode asks rhetorically, "What relationship does the doctrine of the Church still have today to people's everyday lives? In our doctrine do we take sufficiently into account the concrete experience of people?"[35] The bishop drives home his point that the Church's teaching on marriage has no purchase upon the Catholic

[33] Kuljovsky, "Law of Gradualness or Gradualness of Law?", 62 (including note 45).

[34] Christine Galea, "Reflections on Commitment and the Indissolubility of Christian Mar-riage", in Knieps-Port le Roi, *Point of No Return?*, 180, citing paragraph 237 of *Amoris Laetitia*. Galea recognizes that "the way in which the trend is going in our contemporary society, shows clearly that the ideal of commitment to an indissoluble marriage is being severely challenged from every corner, even within the church itself" (ibid., 174). She also discusses Margaret A. Farley's *Personal Commitments: Beginning, Keeping, Changing*, rev. ed. (New York: Orbis, 2013), as well as Farley's "The Meaning of Commitment", anthologized in *Perspec-tives on Marriage: A Reader*, ed. Kieran Scott and Michael Warren (Oxford: Oxford Uni-versity Press, 2007), 344–56. For Farley, loss of love—as expressed in a feeling of constraint or repulsion—justifies the end of a marital commitment, but Galea (having gone through a divorce herself) is doubtful about this. For Galea, "The [marital] bond is indissoluble from the moment of consent, but commitment should increase as the marital relationship matures" (Galea, "Reflections on Commitment and Indissolubility", 176n18; and see also her point at 179–80: "I still hold strongly that marriage is indissoluble, and that in the event of marriage breakdown, legal separation or a declaration of nullity are the only viable options for a prac-tising Catholic").

[35] Quoted (without citation of source) by Paul Josef Cardinal Cordes, "Without Rupture or Discontinuity", in Aymans, *Eleven Cardinals Speak*, 21.

faithful by concluding, "Doctrine and life must not be completely separate from each other."[36]

From the opposite side of the spectrum, Angelo Cardinal Scola has recognized "the intrinsically pastoral character of Christian doctrine".[37] Pastorally, the paradox of Christian faith is that bearing one's cross in love is the path of human flourishing, not only in terms of the attainment of eternal life, but also in the graced fulfillment here and now of our created ordering toward communion with God and neighbor. The philosopher D. C. Schindler puts this point eloquently: "Instead of freedom as the power to choose, we need to understand freedom as the gift of self.... When we think of it in this way, marriage comes to present itself not as the free cancellation of freedom—the 'liberty to sell one's liberty,' as Chesterton put it—but the *free perfection* of freedom: the liberty to *be* free, the self-gift that enables one to make a gift of oneself."[38]

Catholics should therefore receive *Amoris Laetitia* with eagerness to heed Pope Francis' warning that "our teaching on marriage and the family cannot fail to be inspired and transformed by this [Gospel] message of love and tenderness; otherwise, it becomes nothing more than the defence of a dry and lifeless doctrine. The mystery of the Christian family can be fully understood only in the light of the

---

[36] Ibid. See also, on this point, Maurice Blondel's *Action (1893): Essay on a Critique of Life and a Science of Practice*, trans. Oliva Blanchette (Notre Dame: University of Notre Dame Press, 1984). As Blondel was aware—through his debates with Catholic modernists such as Albert Loisy—this principle can be misapplied.

[37] Angelo Cardinal Scola, "Marriage and the Family between Anthropology and the Eucharist: Comments in View of the Extraordinary Assembly of the Synod of Bishops on the Family", trans. Michael J. Miller, *Communio* 41 (2014): 209. Notably, Scola directs attention to the witness of elderly couples whom he meets in the parishes he visits, "who, after forty, fifty, or even sixty years, speak with tender joy about their marriage and witness to how, with the help of the Lord and with the practical support of the Christian community, so many trials and sufferings can be confronted and overcome"; and Scola also pays tribute to the "testimony of those who have suffered abandonment by their spouse and have chosen to remain faithful to the marriage bond" (ibid., 224).

[38] D. C. Schindler, "The Crisis of Marriage as a Crisis of Meaning: On the Sterility of the Modern Will", *Communio* 41 (2014): 370; emphasis in original. Such a self-gift is not an "obliteration of self", let alone a willingness to be used or abused (since a true lover would separate from an abuser in order to stop the abuser's self- and other-destructive acts), but rather is an act of definitive love for and commitment toward another person, in a mutual exchange of vows.

Father's infinite love revealed in Christ."[39] Taking up Pope Francis'
call, we must strive to ensure that, as he insists must be the case, the
pastoral approaches of the present and of the future do not "pre-
scind from the Gospel demands of truth and charity, as proposed by
the Church",[40] and that these pastoral approaches do not undermine
"what Jesus offers to the human being", which is "the exclusive and indissoluble union between a man and a woman" now elevated and
sealed by sacramental grace.[41] In the midst of the "pain, evil and violence that break up families and their communion of life and love",[42]
Catholics should seek the deeper reasons why Jesus' insistence upon
the indissolubility of marriage belongs to the merciful and costly grace
of God. If, as the canon lawyer Cormac Burke says, "indissolubility
is good news",[43] we must ask more persistently how it is that in the
very midst of our trials, Jesus promises that we will discover his joy
and "be consecrated in truth" (Jn 17:19).

---

[39] Pope Francis, *Amoris Laetitia*, no. 59.

[40] Ibid., no. 300. Note the cogent concerns raised by Branislav Kuljovsky regarding the
use of the term "discernment" in chapter 8 of *Amoris Laetitia*. With regard to paragraph 300,
Kuljovsky observes, "The pope teaches us that the 'responsible personal and pastoral discernment of particular cases' is the only possible approach if we consider 'the immense variety
of concrete situations' of the divorced and remarried couples. No 'new set of rules' can be
provided. So what are the pastors supposed to discern? The pope states that this discernment
should recognize that 'since "the degree of responsibility is not equal in all cases" [*Relatio
Finalis*, 51], the consequences or effects of a rule need not necessarily always be the same' (AL
300). This statement ... exhibits a certain ambiguity. For example, it is unclear whether 'the
degree of responsibility' refers to the responsibility for the failure of the first marriage or to
the responsibility for engaging in a new non-marital relationship that includes sexual intimacy;
these are two different things. The fact that one is not responsible for the failure of his or
her previous marriage does not justify his or her free engagement in other evil action, i.e. a
sexual relationship with someone else than a legitimately married spouse" (Kuljovsky, "Law
of Gradualness or Gradualness of Law?", 60).

[41] Pope Francis, *Amoris Laetitia*, nos. 307, 52.

[42] Ibid., no. 19.

[43] Cormac Burke, *Covenanted Happiness: Love and Commitment in Marriage* (San Francisco:
Ignatius Press, 1990), 43; emphasis in original. Burke emphasizes that "these 'bona' [the three
'goods' of marriage] are good things, they are *desirable*; and *it is natural to want them*. It is natural, because it corresponds to the nature of human love. Man finds something deeply good in
the idea of a love: (i) of which he is the privileged and singular object; (ii) which will be his
for as long as life lasts; (iii) and through which, by becoming a co-creator, he can perpetuate
himself (and, as we shall see, more than himself)" (ibid.).

Chapter 1

Eastern Orthodox, Patristic, Protestant, and Historical-Critical Perspectives on Marital Indissolubility

In 1929, the philosopher Dietrich von Hildebrand, a convert to the Catholic Church, admitted: "There are few things in our Holy Church which cause as many conflicts, as many desertions and apostasies, as does the dogma of the indissolubility of marriage."[1] People feel trapped in unhappy marriages, and when they get a divorce, the Catholic Church tells them that they cannot remarry unless their first marriage can be shown to have been canonically invalid. Susan Aranoff and Rivka Haut remark plaintively in their *The Wed-Locked Agunot: Orthodox Jewish Women Chained to Dead Marriages* that Orthodox Jewish women are sometimes "chained to dead marriages because their husbands refuse to give them a *gett*", namely, a religious divorce.[2] This concept of a religious divorce—in the sense of a divorce permitted or, in certain cases, even approved by the religious

---

[1] Dietrich von Hildebrand, *Marriage: The Mystery of Faithful Love*, trans. Emmanuel Chapman and Daniel Sullivan (Manchester, NH: Sophia Institute Press, 1991), 57. Von Hildebrand adds, "Certainly this decision [to bestow oneself irrevocably upon another person] involves a great risk; and when the choice of spouse happens to be based on an illusion, the indissolubility of marriage may prove a great cross for one or both consorts. But it lies in the nature of conjugal love to be bold, heroic, not to shrink back from taking a risk.... Marriage is not a bourgeois affair, a kind of insurance for happiness, providing a way of escape from every eventual cross. Does not every love as such carry with it a great risk of suffering? In attaching our hearts to a person, do we not run the risk of enduring terrible sufferings, through misfortunes that may happen to our beloved or separation from her when she dies? ... He whose life is dominated by the intention of avoiding any possible cross excludes everything that gives human life grandeur and depth" (ibid., 60–61). I agree with von Hildebrand's point, although his language here is colored by romanticism.

[2] Susan Aranoff and Rivka Haut, *The Wed-Locked Agunot: Orthodox Jewish Women Chained to Dead Marriages* (Jefferson, NC: McFarland, 2015), 1.

community—has some parallels in Eastern Orthodox and Protestant Christianity. In this chapter, therefore, I examine Orthodox and Protestant perspectives on divorce and remarriage, and I place these discussions within the context of the teachings of the Church Fathers and of contemporary exegesis of the disputed biblical passages.

Eastern Orthodox Perspectives

Most contemporary Eastern Orthodox Christians theologians hold that it is possible for a valid and consummated sacramental marriage, in certain circumstances, to cease to exist. Thus, the theologian Oliver Clément points out that "the Orthodox Church, in its love as mother, does not exclude the divorced from communion and, in certain cases, determines that a marriage does not exist, going so far as to bless subsequent marriages, when they are entered into a spirit of repentance."[3] Here the Orthodox Church seeks to exemplify God's *oikonomia*, the mercy by which God governs his household in Jesus Christ.[4] Clément warns that it would be "legalism" to suppose that Jesus' teaching about divorce and remarriage applies to all cases in a hard and unbending way.[5]

Along the same lines, the theologian Paul Evdokimov states that "according to the Gospel, adultery destroys the very reality, the mystical essence, of marriage. If love is the matter of the sacrament—and

[3] Oliver Clément, foreword to *The Sacrament of Love: The Nuptial Mystery in the Light of the Orthodox Tradition*, by Paul Evdokimov, trans. Anthony P. Gythiel and Victoria Steadman (Crestwood, NY: St. Vladimir's Seminary Press, 1985), 12.

[4] See Angelo Altan, "Indissolubilitá ed oikonomia nella teologia e nella disciplina orientale del matrimonio", *Sacra Doctrina* 49 (1968): 87–112. For further analysis by Catholic authors who seek to encourage the Catholic Church to change her position, see Ladislas Örsy, S.J., "In Search of the Meaning of Oikonomia: Report on a Convention", *Theological Studies* 43 (1982): 312–19; Kevin Schembri, "The Orthodox Tradition on Divorced and Remarried Faithful: What Can the Catholic Church Learn?", *Melita Theologica* 65 (2015): 121–41; Paul M. Zulehner, *Vom Gesetz zum Gesicht: Ein neuer Ton in der Kirche: Papst Franziskus zu Ehe und Familie: Amoris Laetitia* (Ostfildern: Patmos, 2016), 91ff.; Basilio Petrà, *Divorzio e seconde nozze nella tradizione greca: Un altra via* (Assisi: Cittadella Editrice, 2014). See also, for background to the last-noted monograph, Basilio Petrà, *Il matrimonio può morire? Studi sulla pastorale dei divorziati risposati* (Bologna: EDB, 1995); Basilio Petrà, *Divorziati e risposati e seconde nozze nella Chiesa: Una via di soluzione?* (Assisi: Cittadella Editrice, 2012); and, in response to Petrà's early work, Angel Rodríguez Luño, "L'estinzione del matrimonio a causa della morte: Obiezioni alla tesi di B. Petrà", *Rivista di teologia morale* 130 (2001): 237–48.

[5] Clément, foreword to *Sacrament of Love*, 13.

Justinian declares that matrimony becomes real only through love (*Novella* 74)—the exchange of promises is only a telling sign of the real presence of love."[6] It follows that adultery makes clear that in fact "nothing is left of the matter of the sacrament."[7] Since "nothing is left" of the sacramental marriage, remarriage is fully possible. Orthodox theologians deny that this necessarily means rejecting marital indissolubility. The theologian Alexander Schmemann, for example, teaches that a marriage can be indissoluble in God's eyes while being, at the same time, fully dissoluble in its human reality.[8]

Orthodox theologians find patristic support most importantly in Basil the Great's Letter 188, "To Amphilochius, Concerning the Canons".[9] Here Basil addresses the teaching of Christ in the Gospel of

[6] Evdokimov, *Sacrament of Love*, 189; see also Paul Evdokimov, "La grace du sacrement de mariage selon la tradition orthodoxe", *Parole et Pain* 35–36 (1969): 382–94. For background to this view, see Nikodim Milaš, *Das Kirchenrecht der morgenländischen Kirche* (Mostar: Verlag der Verlagsbuchhandlung von Parcher & Kisić, 1905), 629–41; Hamicar S. Alivisatos, *Marriage and Divorce in Accordance with the Canon Law of the Orthodox Church* (London: Faith Press, 1948), 12. For further discussion see Archbishop Cyril Vasil', S.J., "Separation, Divorce, Dissolution of the Bond, and Remarriage: Theological and Practical Approaches of the Orthodox Churches", in *Remaining in the Truth of Christ: Marriage and Communion in the Catholic Church*, ed. Robert Dodaro, O.S.A. (San Francisco: Ignatius Press, 2014), 124–25.

[7] Evdokimov, *Sacrament of Love*, 189.

[8] See Alexander Schmemann, "The Indissolubility of Marriage: The Theological Tradition of the East", in *The Bond of Marriage: An Ecumenical and Interdisciplinary Study*, ed. William W. Bassett (Notre Dame: University of Notre Dame Press, 1968), 97–112; Pierre L'Huillier, "L'indissolubilité du mariage dans la droit et la pratique orthodoxes", *Studia Canonica* 21 (1987): 239–60; Theodore Stylianopoulos, "The Indissolubility of Marriage in the New Testament: Principle and Practice", *Greek Orthodox Theological Review* 34 (1989): 335–45.

[9] John M. Rist concludes that "Basil's name must be added to that of Ambrosiaster as a man prepared, less willingly though more fatefully, at least to tolerate a second marriage after divorce in limited circumstances" (John M. Rist, "Divorce and Remarriage in the Early Church: Some Historical and Cultural Reflections", in Dodaro, *Remaining in the Truth of Christ*, 64–92, at 90–91). For his part, Archbishop Cyril Vasil', S.J., deems that in Matthew 5:32 and 19:9, *porneia* means "fornication [i.e., adultery], concubinage, and illegitimate union", and he maintains that among the early Christians "it is an open question whether a separation caused by adultery opened the way for both parties, or at least the innocent party, to a new marriage or not" (Vasil', "Separation, Divorce, Dissolution of the Bond, and Remarriage", 96–97). For the opposite view, see the assessment of Corbett and others with regard to Basil's Canon 77, found in Basil's Letter 217: "There are some ambiguous fourth-century texts dealing with divorce and an adulterous second relationship. They speak of admitting one who has entered such an adulterous relationship to Communion only after a lengthy period of penance (*e.g.*, seven years). It is implausible, however, that they permitted that second relationship—which they condemned as adulterous—to continue. The more natural reading is that repenting of adultery formed a part of the penance necessary for Communion" (John Corbett, O.P., et al., "Recent Proposals for the Pastoral Care of the Divorced and Remarried: A Theological Assessment", *Nova et Vetera* 12, no. 3 [2014]: 611).

Matthew (5:32; 19:9) that "it is unlawful to withdraw from wedlock, save on account of fornication."[10] Basil asks whether women can validly divorce their husbands. He concludes that when a woman divorces her husband, this may be a case of marital desertion on the wife's part, even if the reason is the husband's fornication. As a general rule, then, he suggests that "the man who has been abandoned is pardonable, and the woman who lives with such a man is not condemned [as an adulteress]."[11] By contrast, "the wife, if she leaves her husband and goes to another, is an adulteress", and likewise, "if the man who has deserted his wife goes to another, he is himself an adulterer because he makes her commit adultery; and the woman who lives with him is an adulteress, because she has caused another woman's husband to come over to her."[12] Basil's meaning in saying that an abandoned man is pardonable and that a woman (presumably not the woman who has abandoned him) can live with him without being an adulteress has been debated, in part because in his *On Christian Ethics*, the relevant portion of which appears to have been written late in his career, he judges not only that "it is necessary for a husband not to be divorced from his wife nor a wife from her husband unless one of them should fall into sexual immorality or be a hindrance to godly piety", but also—crucially for present purposes—that "neither is the one who has divorced himself from his wife permitted to marry another nor the one divorced from her husband to marry someone else".[13]

Another witness sometimes adduced from the patristic period in support of the possibility of divorce and remarriage is Justinian, the sixth-century Christian emperor who reigned at Constantinople. Emperor Justinian published his *Novella* 117 on marriage in the year 542.[14] In this *Novella*, Justinian sets forth ten legitimate grounds for divorce. In each case, the innocent spouse has permission to remarry,

[10] Basil the Great, Letter 188, "To Amphilochius, concerning the Canons", in *Nicene and Post-Nicene Fathers*, 2nd series, ed. Philip Schaff and Henry Wace, vol. 8, *Basil: Letters and Select Works*, trans. Blomfield Jackson (Peabody, MA: Hendrickson, 1995), 227.

[11] Ibid.

[12] Ibid.

[13] Basil the Great, *On Christian Ethics* 73.1–2, trans. Jacob N. Van Sickle (Yonkers, NY: St. Vladimir's Seminary Press, 2014), 299, 301.

[14] A few years prior to this, in 536, Justinian had published his *Novella* 22 on marriage, which is even less strict than *Novella* 117 and which advances the principle of the dissolubility of marriage; see John T. Noonan, Jr., "Novel 22", in *The Bond of Marriage: An Ecumenical and Interdisciplinary Study*, ed. William W. Bassett (Notre Dame: University of Notre Dame

and in general both spouses can remarry. Although the earliest extant Greek collection of canon law does not contain excerpts from *Novella* 117, by the mid-seventh century ecclesiastical and civil law had been combined into one in the Eastern Church. The result was that soon "the imperial ecclesiastical laws" were considered to be "as authoritative for the Church as the canons issued by church councils".[15]

Recognizing that divorce and remarriage often involves injustices, the theologian John Meyendorff notes that for the Eastern Churches in the late patristic period, remarrying after divorce—in cases where the person remarrying is guilty of adultery and therefore makes the remarriage adulterous—carried seven years of penance prior to the person's being restored to the Sacrament of the Eucharist.[16]

Press, 1968), 41–96. As Noonan points out, Justinian's lawmaking frequently sought to legislate Christian beliefs and practice, including by purging non-Christians from legal practice, and bishops played a prominent role in the judicial system. Noonan seeks to demonstrate that Justinian's stance on marriage, reflective of traditional Roman marriage law, "establishes ... that for a substantial period of time marriages were viewed by many Christians as dissoluble" (ibid., 85). Prior to Augustine, Noonan notes, "The most important bishop to teach the indissolubility of marriage was Ambrose.... Yet there is no record of his protesting to the emperor on the laws on divorce in force in his day. Christians in good faith could believe that marriage was dissoluble or indissoluble without anyone's calling his opponent a heretic. The calm acceptance of dissolubility by the law shows that at this time, between 331 and 566, no definitive Christian position had been established on remarriage and divorce" (ibid., 87). Noonan also observes that Justinian's law code supported slavery. See also Gregory of Nazianzus' Letter 144, where Gregory argued that a proposed divorce "is entirely contrary to our [Christian] law, though the Roman law may determine otherwise" (in *Nicene and Post-Nicene Fathers*, 2nd series, ed. Philip Schaff and Henry Wace, vol. 7, *Cyril of Jerusalem, Gregory Nazianzen*, ed. and trans. Charles Gordon Browne and James Edward Swallow [Peabody, MA: Hendrickson, 1994], 480).

[15] Clarence Gallagher, *Church Law and Church Order in Rome and Byzantium: A Comparative Study* (Cornwall: Ashgate, 2002), 40.

[16] See John Meyendorff, *Marriage: An Orthodox Perspective*, 3rd rev. ed. (Yonkers, NY: St. Vladimir's Seminary Press, 1975), 106–7. Earlier Meyendorff remarks that "the Christian empire continued to admit divorce and remarriage as a regular social institution. The laws of the Christian emperors, especially Constantine, Theodosius and Justinian, defined the various legal grounds and conditions on which divorce and remarriage were permissible. It is impossible for us here to enumerate them all. It will be sufficient to say that they were relatively lenient.... No Father of the Church ever denounced these imperial laws as contrary to Christianity. There was an evident consensus of opinion that considered them as inevitable.... Pastoral exhortations on the evil of divorce are of course innumerable; but the toleration of existing state laws, as well as of the 'facts of life,' as they occurred, is equally evident on the part of all, in both East and West. Was this simple lenience or a capitulation? Certainly not. During this entire period, without a single known exception, the Church remained faithful to the *norm* set by the New Testament revelation: *only the first and unique marriage was blessed in the Church during the Eucharist*" (ibid., 56–57).

Meyendorff maintains that the Eastern Church of this period "neither 'recognized' divorce, nor 'gave' it. Divorce was considered as a grave sin; but the Church never failed in giving to sinners a 'new chance,' and was ready to readmit them after they repented."[17] Meyendorff defends the acceptability of remarriage after divorce on the grounds that it was explicitly taught by a canon that he associates with the Sixth Ecumenical Council, namely, Canon 87 of the Council of Trullo (692). As he knows, the authority of this canon has been a long-standing controversy between East and West.[18] Although the Orthodox East accepted the canons of the Council of Trullo as authoritative addenda to the Fifth and Sixth Ecumenical Councils, Pope Sergius I rejected the canons (for which he was persecuted by Emperor Justinian II) and the Catholic Church never accepted the canons. The theologian Christian Brugger goes further and suggests that Canon 87 actually may not even approve divorce and remarriage, since the canon, in addressing the status of the innocent party in a divorce, does not clearly address the issue of remarriage. Brugger argues that the first "unambiguous evidence" for Eastern canonical acceptance of divorce dates to 883, and "Alexius I, patriarch of Constantinople 1025–43, seems to be the first patriarch explicitly to grant approval to divorce and remarriage in the form of synodical decrees."[19]

Whether or not Brugger's arguments are persuasive, all scholars agree that by the second millennium the Orthodox Church had taken full control of granting divorces. Brugger remarks that "by the middle of the fifteenth century Greek canon law admitted divorce and remarriage for at least eighteen 'just causes,' including

---

[17] Ibid., 58. For broader background, see Alexis Torrance, *Repentance in Late Antiquity: Eastern Asceticism and the Framing of the Christian Life, ca. 400–650* (Oxford: Oxford University Press, 2013).

[18] Norman Tanner comments, "Matters of church discipline, which the councils of Constantinople II and III did not touch, were taken up by the council of Trullo (sometimes called 'Quinisext' or 'Fifth-Sixth') which was summoned by Emperor Justinian [II] in 692. This council issued 102 canons, which have been regarded as decrees of an ecumenical council in eastern canon law." See Norman P. Tanner, S.J., introduction to the text of the Third Council of Constantinople (680–681), no page number, fn 2; in *Decrees of the Ecumenical Councils*, vol. 1, *Nicaea I to Lateran V* (Washington, D.C.: Georgetown University Press, 1990).

[19] E. Christian Brugger, *The Indissolubility of Marriage and the Council of Trent* (Washington, D.C.: Catholic University of America Press, 2017), 44.

adultery, a spouse conspiring against the emperor or plotting to kill the other spouse; a wife dining or bathing or residing at another's house against her husband's consent; [and] her attending a circus, theater, or arena without his knowledge."[20] The Orthodox Church itself, and not merely the state, granted divorces on these grounds. In Meyendorff's view, contemporary Orthodox Churches in countries where the Church still has governance over marriage should stop granting divorces and instead should recognize simply that once a civil divorce has occurred, the marriage no longer exists. In such cases Orthodox Churches can then "issue 'permissions to remarry'" that "should entail at least some forms of penance (in conformity with each individual case) and give the right to a Church blessing according to the rite of 'second marriage'".[21] At present, Orthodox Churches around the world vary in penitential practice associated with divorce and remarriage, but strict penances are a thing of the past. Orthodox Churches celebrate second and third marriages liturgically, though with a different (more penitential) rite than is used for first marriages.[22]

[20] Ibid., 45.

[21] Meyendorff, *Marriage*, 58. Note that, as Vasil' says, "Among Orthodox authors and bishops, opponents to divorce are not lacking. Some of these authorities uphold the complete observance of the indissolubility of marriage and the impossibility of divorce for any reason. For example, the Russian Archbishop Ignatius (in the Russian Orthodox Church, Saint Ignatius Brianchaninov [1807–1867]) did not permit divorce for any reason, not even for adultery. More moderate, but nevertheless appreciable opposition to divorce has also been evidenced both by Archbishop Iakovos (Coucouzis) (1911–2005), the Orthodox Metropolitan of North and South America (1959–1996), who insisted already in 1966 that concessions of divorce should be limited, and by the Coptic Patriarch Shenouda III (1923–2012), who following his enthronement in 1971 reduced the many reasons considered valid for granting divorce in the Coptic Church to one—adultery" (Vasil', "Separation, Divorce, Dissolution of the Bond, and Remarriage", 122). For further background on the development of divorce law in Russia and Greece, see ibid., 105–20, indebted to Jiří Dvořáček, "Il divorzio del vincolo matrimoniale nelle Chiese ortodosse e le sue conseguenze giuridiche per la Chiesa cattolica", in *Rodina, konflikt a možnosti mediace*, ed. Slávka Michančová and Lenka Pavlová (Křtiny: Evropský smírčí institut, 2011), 25–67.

[22] With regard to the Catholic Church, John Corbett and others point out that "present proposals advocate what even the Eastern Orthodox would not accept: Communion for those in unblessed *civil* (adulterous) unions. The Eastern Orthodox admit the divorced and remarried to Communion only if their subsequent union has been blessed in an Eastern Orthodox rite. In other words, admitting the divorced and remarried to Communion would inevitably require the Catholic Church to recognize and bless second marriages after divorce" (Corbett et al., "Recent Proposals", 612–13).

Mention should also be made here of Archbishop Elias Zoghby's intervention, as the leader of the Melkite Church in Egypt, in the discussion of Schema XIII (which was to become *Gaudium et Spes*) on the floor of the Second Vatican Council on September 29, 1965. Addressing the place of "indissolubility" in the Schema's treatment of marriage, Zoghby raised a concern about the innocent spouse in a divorce who thereby is condemned to lifelong sexual abstinence, despite not possessing a celibate vocation. As Zoghby points out, such persons often end up contracting a civil marriage. Zoghby argues that the Catholic Church might here be able to learn from the Eastern Orthodox Churches' practice in favor of the innocent spouse, whom they understand the exception clause of the Gospel of Matthew (5:32; 19:9) to protect. It should be noted, however, that in response to Archbishop Zoghby's comments, the Melkite Patriarch Maximos IV felt the need to present his own qualifying remarks regarding the official position of the Melkite Catholic Church on this matter.[23]

[23] For Archbishop Zoghby's speech, see the *Acta synodalia Sacrosancti Concilii Oecumenici Vaticani II*, vol. 4, pt. 3 (Vatican City: Typis polyglottis Vaticanis, 1980), 45–47. For further background, see Maximos IV Sayegh, *L'Eglise Grecque Melkite au Councile: Discours et notes du patriarche Maximos IV et des prélats de son Église au Concile oecuménique Vatican II* (Beirut: Dar al-Kalima, 1967), as well as Gerasimos Murphy, *Maximos IV at Vatican II: A Quest for Autonomy* (Boston: Sophia Press, 2011). A full translation of the first text can be found at the website of the Melkite Greek Catholic Eparchy of Newton at https://melkite.org /faith/faith-worship/introduction; an English translation of the chapter of this text dealing with the debates surrounding marriage can be found at https://melkite.org/wp-content /uploads/2012/02/CouncilChapter15.pdf. This chapter contains not only Archbishop Zoghby's speech, but also his further precisions, as well as the responses made by Patriarch Maximos IV. Of particular interest is the latter's official memorandum issued in November 1966. In this text, the patriarch of Antioch affirms quite clearly that the Council of Trent solemnly defined the doctrine of indissolubility. However, he also makes some statements regarding what he calls the "safety valve" of *oikonomia* that edge him closer toward the Orthodox outlook. He sees this as being an equivalent to the Petrine and Pauline privileges, as well as the pope's ability to dissolve unconsummated marriages. For discussion of the response to Archbishop Zoghby that Charles Cardinal Journet made on the floor of the council at the request of Pope Paul VI, see Roger W. Nutt, "*Gaudium et Spes* and the Indissolubility of the Sacrament of Matrimony: The Contribution of Charles Cardinal Journet", *Nova et Vetera* 11 (2013): 619–26. Journet argues that Matthew 5:32 and 19:9 should be read in accord with Mark 10:11–12 and 1 Corinthians 7:10–11, rather than being read in opposition to those clear texts against the practice of divorce and remarriage. Journet also points out that, in fact, the Eastern Orthodox Churches allow divorce and remarriage in cases other than an innocent party whose spouse has committed adultery. See also Charles Journet, *Le mariage indissoluble* (St-Maurice: Editions St-Augustin, 1968).

The Church Fathers on Divorce and Remarriage

After the Second Vatican Council, an energetic debate among Catholic scholars arose concerning the views of the Fathers of the Church regarding remarriage after divorce. The Origen scholar Henri Crouzel argued in a series of publications that the Fathers were nearly unanimous in forbidding remarriage after divorce.[24] More recently, the patristics scholar John Rist has concluded that "although among ancient Christians second marriages during the lifetime of a spouse were normally forbidden and those who were engaged in them were denied Communion, there were a very small but noticeable number of exceptions to the rule that, however, were almost invariably condemned."[25] Other scholars such as Philip Reynolds, Pierre Nautin, Charles Munier, Giovanni Cereti, Riccardo Bof, Conrad Leyser, Miguel Garijo-Guembe, and David Hunter have suggested on the contrary that even in the West, no normative position existed prior to the second half of the ninth century.[26]

---

[24] See Henri Crouzel, *L'Église primitive face au divorce: Du premier au cinquième siècle* (Paris: Beauchesne, 1971). See also the extensive studies by Crouzel, written in preparation for his book and after his book, including (among others) Henri Crouzel, "Séparation et remariage selon les Pères anciens", *Gregorianum* 47 (1966): 472–94; Henri Crouzel, "Les Pères de l'Église ont-ils permis le remariage après séparation?", *Bulletin de Littérature ecclésiastique* 70 (1969): 3–43; Henri Crouzel, "Remarriage after Divorce in the Primitive Church? A Propos of a Recent Book", *Irish Theological Quarterly* 28 (1971): 21–41; Henri Crouzel, "Le texte patristique de Matthieu V, 32 et XIX, 9", *New Testament Studies* 19 (1972–1973): 98–119; Henri Crouzel, "Le marriage des chrétiens aux premiers siècles de l'Église", *Esprit et Vie* 83, no. 6 (1973): 3–13; Henri Crouzel, "A propos du Concile d'Arles: Faut-il mettre *non* devant *prohibentur nubere* dans le canon 10 (ou 11) du Concile d'Arles de 314 sur le remariage après divorce?", *Bulletin de Littérature ecclésiastique* 75 (1974): 25–40; Henri Crouzel, "Le remariage après séparation pour adultère selon les Pères latins", *Bulletin de Littérature ecclésiastique* 75 (1974): 189–204. Crouzel sums up his research in his "Divorce et remariage dans l'Église primitive", *Nouvelle revue théologique* 98 (1976): 891–917; for an English translation see Henri Crouzel, "Divorce and Remarriage in the Early Church: Some Reflections on Historical Methodology", trans. Michelle K. Borras, *Communio* 41 (2014): 472–503.

[25] Rist, "Divorce and Remarriage in the Early Church", 92.

[26] See Philip Lyndon Reynolds, *Marriage in the Western Church: The Christianization of Marriage during the Patristic and Early Medieval Periods* (Leiden: Brill, 1994); Pierre Nautin, "Divorce et remariage dans la tradition de l'Église latine", *Recherches de science religieuse* 62 (1974): 7–54; Charles Munier, "L'échec du mariage dans l'église ancienne", *Revue de droit canonique* 38 (1988): 26–40; Giovanni Cereti, *Matrimonio e indissolubilità*, 2nd ed. (Bologna: Edizioni Dehoniane, 2014), 137–71; Giovanni Cereti, *Divorzio, nuove nozze e penitenza nella chiesa primitiva*, 3rd ed. (Rome: Aracne Editrice, 2013); Riccardo Bof and Conrad Leyser, "Divorce and Remarriage between Late Antiquity and the Early Middle Ages: Canon Law and Conflict

Some early Christian teachings on divorce and remarriage have been taken as support by advocates of both sides. For example, the 314 Council of Arles promulgated a decree that when young Christian men divorce their wives for committing adultery, these men "as far as possible should be counseled not to marry again as long as their wives are alive, even though the latter are adulteresses".[27] It is possible to read this decree as supporting the Catholic Church's later understanding of divorce and remarriage, but it is also possible to find the contrary by noting that the counsel given here is not an absolute prohibition. Similarly, in the third century Origen commented that "some leaders of the Church recently permitted a certain woman to remarry while her husband was still living. By so doing they acted in a way that was not in accordance with the Scriptures."[28] Despite his view that this remarriage cannot really be a marriage at all, Origen grants that what the leaders "did was not entirely unreasonable", since the leaders' concession was made "in view of worse things that might happen".[29] Pope Leo the Great's 458 letter *Regressus ad nos* to Bishop Nicetas of Aquileia has also proven difficult to interpret with surety. On the one hand, Pope Leo insists that a husband who had been thought dead or forever lost must be able to reclaim marital rights if and when he returns, thereby showing any later marriage to be null. But Pope Leo also seems to indicate that this reclamation of marital rights may not be automatic but may require instead the persevering desire of the once-lost husband.[30] I have already discussed Basil the Great's various comments on divorce and remarriage, which leave his final viewpoint ambiguous.

Resolution", in *Making Early Medieval Societies: Conflict and Belonging in the Latin West, 300–1200*, ed. Kate Cooper and Conrad Leyser (Cambridge: Cambridge University Press, 2016), 155–80; Miguel M. Garijo-Guembe, "Unauflöslichkeit der Ehe und die gescheiterten Ehen in der Patristik", in *Geschieden Wiederverheiratet Abgewiesen? Antworten der Theologie*, ed. T. Schneider (Freiburg: Herder, 1995), 68–83; and David G. Hunter, "Augustine's Doubts on Divorce: Reconsiderations on Remarriage", *Augustinian Studies* 48 (2017): 161–82. I note that these scholars, of course, are not monolithic but represent diverse areas of specialization and perspectives. See also Marie-François Berrouard, O.P., "Saint Augustin et l'indissolubilité du mariage. Évolution de sa pensée", *Recherches Augustiniennes et patristique* 5 (1968): 139–55.

[27] See *Concilium Arelatense*, c. 11 (10) (CCSL 148:11), translated in Reynolds, *Marriage in the Western Church*, 181.

[28] Origen, *Comment. In Mattheum* 14.23 (PG 13:1245A–B), translated in Reynolds, *Marriage in the Western Church*, 179.

[29] Ibid.

[30] See Pope Leo the Great, Letter *Regressus ad Nos* to Bishop Nicetas of Aquileia, March 21, 458, in *Compendium of Creeds, Definitions, and Declarations on Matters of Faith and Morals*, 43rd

There are numerous early Christian theologians who clearly take the position that eventually became formalized as the Catholic Church's. For example, commenting on Matthew 5:32, the Antiochian exegete Theodore of Mopsuestia states that Christ "does not allow the divorced woman to remarry. The man she lives with must pay the penalties of an adulterer. For even if, to all appearances, she is separated from her husband, in spiritual reality she remains his body."[31] Earlier, the second-century philosopher-apologist Justin Martyr quotes Christ's words as authoritative in his discussion of Christian chastity: "Whosoever shall marry her that is divorced from another husband, commits adultery."[32] Another second-century philosopher-apologist, Athenagoras, in his *A Plea for the Christians*, says that in accordance with Jesus' teaching in Matthew 19:9, "a person should either remain as he was born, or be content with one marriage; for a second marriage is only a specious adultery."[33] The early third-century theologian Tertullian, in his *On Monogamy*, emphasizes that Christ prohibits divorce "first because 'from the beginning it was not so,' like plurality of marriage; secondly, because 'What God has conjoined, man shall not separate' [see Mt 19:3–8]."[34] Tertullian adds that although Christ permits divorce for the sole reason of adultery,

---

ed., by Heinrich Denzinger, rev. and ed. Peter Hünermann with Helmut Hoping. English edition ed. and trans. Robert Fastiggi and Anne Englund Nash (San Francisco: Ignatius Press, 2012), nos. 311–14.

[31] Quoted in *Matthew 1–13*, ed. Manlio Simonetti, vol. 1a of the Ancient Christian Commentary on Scripture Series, ed. Thomas C. Oden (Downers Grove, IL: InterVarsity Press, 2001), 113.

[32] Justin Martyr, *First Apology of Justin Martyr* 15, in *Ante-Nicene Fathers*, vol. 1, *The Apostolic Fathers, Justin Martyr, Irenaeus*, ed. and trans. Alexander Roberts and James Donaldson, rev. A. Cleveland Coxe (Peabody, MA: Hendrickson, 1994), 167 (translation slightly altered). See also the mid-second-century Christian work *The Shepherd of Hermas*, which teaches that a husband may divorce his wife if she is engaged in unrepentant and ongoing adultery, but which adds that if he divorces his wife and marries another woman, then he too commits adultery; see *The Pastor of Hermas* 2.4, trans. F. Crombie, in *Ante-Nicene Fathers*, vol. 2, *Fathers of the Second Century: Hermas, Tatian, Athenagoras, Theophilus, and Clement of Alexandria*, ed. Alexander Roberts and James Donaldson, rev. A. Cleveland Coxe (Peabody, MA: Hendrickson, 1994), 21. *The Shepherd of Hermas* continues: "In case, therefore, that the divorced wife may repent, the husband ought not to marry another, when his wife has been put away. In this matter man and woman are to be treated exactly in the same way" (ibid.).

[33] Athenagoras, *A Plea for the Christians* 33, trans. B. P. Pratten, in *Ante-Nicene Fathers*, 2:146.

[34] Tertullian, *On Monogamy* 9, trans. S. Thelwall, in *Ante-Nicene Fathers*, vol. 4, *Fathers of the Third Century: Tertullian, Part Fourth; Minicius Felix; Commodian; Origen, Parts First and Second*, ed. Alexander Roberts and James Donaldson, rev. A. Cleveland Coxe (Peabody, MA: Hendrickson, 1994), 66 (translation slightly altered).

nonetheless the divorced spouse cannot remarry: "(he) who shall have married a (woman) dismissed by her husband, of course commits adultery. A divorced woman cannot even marry legitimately.... The admission of a second man (to intercourse) is pronounced adultery by Him."[35] Another early third-century theologian, Clement of Alexandria, surveys the viewpoints of various pagan philosophers about marriage, and then concludes on the basis of Matthew 19:9 that "Scripture counsels marriage, and allows no release from the union."[36] Clement states expressly that Scripture "regards as fornication, the marriage of those separated while the other is alive".[37] In fact, it is commonly recognized that no Church Father from the first three centuries thought that Jesus allowed remarriage after divorce, while both spouses were alive.

In the late fourth- and early fifth-century West, Jerome and Augustine teach that although Christ permitted divorce in the case of adultery, Christ prohibited remarriage while one's divorced spouse is still alive.[38] Jerome states that the exception clause means that "whenever there is fornication and suspicion of fornication, a wife is freely divorced", but he adds that "it is commanded [by Christ] to divorce the first wife in such a way that he has no second wife while the first one is living", on pain of adultery.[39] For his part, Augustine argues that a husband does not "have freedom to marry another after he leaves an adulteress", just as "a woman does not have freedom to marry another if she leaves an adulterer."[40] In *On Marriage and Concupiscence*, Augustine identifies the third and final good of marriage as "a

---

[35] Ibid. For similar texts, see Tertullian's *Of Patience* 12 and *Against Marcion* 4.34. See *Of Patience*, trans. S. Thelwall, in *Ante-Nicene Fathers*, vol. 3, *Latin Christianity: Its Founder*, ed. Alexander Roberts and James Donaldson, rev. A. Cleveland Coxe (Peabody, MA: Hendrickson, 1994), 715; *Against Marcion*, trans. Peter Holmes, in *Ante-Nicene Fathers*, 3:405.

[36] Clement of Alexandria, *The Stromata, or Miscellanies*, bk. 2, chap. 23, in *Ante-Nicene Fathers*, 2: 379.

[37] Ibid.

[38] See Reynolds, *Marriage in the Western Church*, 200–12.

[39] Saint Jerome, *Commentary on Matthew*, trans. Thomas P. Scheck (Washington, D.C.: Catholic University of America Press, 2008), 216.

[40] *St. Augustine on Marriage and Sexuality*, ed. Elizabeth A. Clark (Washington, D.C.: Catholic University of America Press, 1996), 49; the quotations are taken from Augustine's *The Good of Marriage* (written around 410). Note that in *On Faith and Works*, written in 413, Augustine wobbles on whether the man can remarry: "The man who leaves his wife because of adultery and marries another is not, it seems, as blameworthy as the man who for no reason leaves his wife and marries another. Nor is it clear from Scripture whether a man who has left

certain sacramental bond", and he explains the "sacrament" or "mystery" (Eph 5:32) as marriage's indissolubility.[41] He affirms that "in the City [that is, Church] of our God, where also from the first union of two human beings marriage bears a kind of sacred bond, it can be dissolved in no way except by the death of one of the parties."[42]

Pope Innocent I taught formally along these same lines in 405, in a letter that decrees that "any man who hastens to marry again while his wife is alive, even though his marriage seems to have been broken up [*quamvis dissociatum videatur esse coniugium*], cannot but be considered an adulterer, to the extent even that the person to whom he has become joined will also be considered to have committed adultery."[43] The Council of Carthage in 407 took this position as well. Admittedly, later fifth- and sixth-century councils (at Vannes and Agde, respectively), according to the historian Philip Reynolds, "suggest that men who could prove that their wives were guilty of adultery could remarry without being excommunicated".[44] Of course, the truth of the teaching of the Catholic Church does not

---

his wife because of adultery, which he is certainly permitted to do, is himself an adulterer if he marries again. And if he should, I do not think that he would commit a grave sin" (Augustine, *On Faith and Works* 19.35, trans. Gregory J. Lombardo, C.S.C. [New York: Paulist Press, 1988], p. 43). In an endnote, the translator comments on this passage: "Augustine expresses a doubt here regarding the indissolubility of marriage. However, he gives his definitive doctrine in *De conjugiis adulterinis*, which he wrote six years later in 419. There he says that only death can break the bond.... The husband as well as the wife commits adultery in contracting another marriage" (ibid., 98n198). In his "Augustine's Doubts on Divorce", David Hunter notes that in his *Retractions*, Augustine allows that he may not have fully understood the meaning of "fornicatio" (the Latin translation of *porneia*), and thus that he may not have precisely identified the range of cases in which a divorce (though not a remarriage) could be permitted.

[41] Augustine, *On Marriage and Concupiscence* 1.11, trans. Peter Holmes, in *Nicene and Post-Nicene Fathers*, 1st series, ed. Philip Schaff, vol. 5, *Augustine: Anti-Pelagian Writings* (Peabody, MA: Hendrickson, 1995), 268. Augustine wrote *On Marriage and Concupiscence* around 418.

[42] *St. Augustine on Marriage and Sexuality*, 55 (a quotation from *The Good of Marriage*). See also John Chrysostom, Homily 62, in *Nicene and Post-Nicene Fathers*, 1st series, ed. Philip Schaff, vol. 10, *Chrysostom: Homilies on the Gospel of Saint Matthew*, trans. George Prevost, rev. M.B. Riddle (Peabody, MA: Hendrickson, 1995), 381–86. In view of Matthew 19:5–6, Chrysostom states that "both by the manner of the creation, and by the manner of lawgiving, He [Jesus] showed that one man must dwell with one woman continually, and never break off from her" (ibid., 382). Chrysostom does not explain the meaning of the exception clause of Matthew 19:9.

[43] Pope Innocent I, *Epist.* 6.6.12 (*PL* 20:500–501); translated in Reynolds, *Marriage in the Western Church*, 214.

[44] Reynolds, *Marriage in the Western Church*, 215.

depend upon patristic unanimity, any more than the truth of Trinitarian doctrine does.

Paying insufficient attention to the testimony of the first three centuries, Reynolds blames the Western Church's rejection of remarriage
after divorce upon Augustine's allegedly baleful influence. Augustine's position "became a cornerstone of the Carolingian reforms,
and by the twelfth century it had triumphed throughout the Western
Church."[45] Reynolds recognizes that for the past millennium, the
Catholic Church has frequently reiterated and reaffirmed its teaching
on marital indissolubility in the solemnest possible ways.

Protestant Viewpoints

The Protestant Reformers adopted the view put forward by the
sixteenth-century Catholic scholar Desiderius Erasmus, who argued
that the Matthean exception clause (Mt 5:32; 19:9) shows that Jesus
allowed for remarriage after divorce in cases of *porneia*. In the words
of Luther, "In the case of adultery, Christ permits divorce of husband
and wife so that the innocent person may remarry."[46] The Reformers
rejected the notion that Christ, in speaking of a permissible divorce,
had in view merely a legal separation rather than dissolution of the
marriage.[47] The historian John Witte comments, "Because they

---

[45] Ibid.

[46] Martin Luther, *Luther's Works*, vol. 45, *Christian in Society II*, ed. Walther I. Brandt (Philadelphia: Fortress Press, 1962), 30–31. Distinguishing between the moral law that Christians
follow and the civil law binding all citizens, Luther elsewhere proposes that "it might be
advisable nowadays that certain queer, stubborn, and obstinate people, who have no capacity
for toleration and are not suited for married life at all, should be permitted to get a divorce,
since people are as evil as they are, any other way of governing is impossible. Frequently
something must be tolerated, even though it is not a good thing to do, to prevent something
even worse from happening" (*Luther's Works*, vol. 21, *Sermon on the Mount and the Magnificat*,
ed. Helmut T. Lehmann [Philadelphia: Fortress, 1956], 94). Both of these passages are quoted
by John Witte, Jr., in his *From Sacrament to Contract: Marriage, Religion, and Law in the Western
Tradition*, 2nd ed. (Louisville, KY: Westminster John Knox, 2012), 150–52. Witte observes
that Luther accepted divorce (and remarriage for the innocent party) on the grounds of adultery, desertion, and quasi-desertion (or "unjustifiable abstention from sexual intercourse");
see ibid., 153–54.

[47] Witte sums up the Catholic Church's understanding of divorce-as-separation in medieval canon law: "Since the twelfth century, the Catholic Church had consistently taught that
(1) divorce meant only separation of the couple from bed and board; (2) such separation had

rejected the sacramental nature of marriage, the Reformers allowed
... for divorce on grounds of adultery, desertion, and other serious
fault, and remarriage at least for the innocent party".[48] Led by Martin Bucer and Ulrich Zwingli, some early Reformation communities allowed divorce—understood as dissolution of the marriage—on
grounds such as "grave incompatibility, sexually incapacitating ill-
nesses, felonies, deception, and one spouse's serious threats against
the life of the other spouse", as well as (by the 1550s) "confessional
differences between the couple, defamation of a spouse's moral character, abuse and maltreatment, conspiracies or plots against a spouse,
acts of incest and bigamy, delinquent frequenting of 'public games' or
places of ill repute, and acts of treason or sacrilege".[49]

---

to be ordered by a church court on proof of adultery, desertion, or cruelty; divorce cannot be
undertaken voluntarily; and (3) despite the divorce, the sacramental bond between the parties
remained intact, and thus neither party was free to remarry until the death of the estranged
spouse. Once properly established, the marriage bond could not be severed, even if the parties
became bitter enemies" (Witte, *From Sacrament to Contract*, 149–50). See also Reynolds, *Marriage in the Western Church*. More broadly, indicating the problems of patriarchy, see Charles J.
Reid, Jr., *Power over the Body, Equality in the Family: Rights and Domestic Relations in Medieval
Canon Law* (Grand Rapids, MI: Eerdmans, 2004).

[48] Witte, *From Sacrament to Contract*, 7; he later explains that "the Lutheran Reformers
replaced the sacramental model of marriage with a new social model. Marriage, they taught,
was part of the earthly kingdom, not the heavenly kingdom. Though a holy institution of
God, marriage required no prerequisite faith or purity and conferred no sanctifying grace,
as did true sacraments.... As an estate of the earthly kingdom, marriage was subject to the
prince, not the pope. Civil law, not canon law, was to govern marriage. Marital disputes
were to be brought before civil courts, not church courts. Marriage was still subject to God's
law, but this law was now to be administered by the civil authorities, who had been called
as God's vice-regents to govern the earthly kingdom" (ibid., 155–56). Witte notes that John
Calvin, while allowing for divorce and remarriage for the innocent party in cases of adultery,
protested against the Catholic acceptance of divorce (understood as separation) in situations
other than adultery. By contrast, Calvin's successor Theodore Beza held that desertion (either
physical desertion or spiritual desertion through religious difference) counted as adultery, and
therefore justified divorce and remarriage for the innocent party. See ibid., 198–99. See also
V. Norskov Olsen, *The New Testament on Divorce: A Study of Their Interpretation from Erasmus
to Milton* (Tübingen: Mohr, 1971), and Steven E. Ozment, *When Fathers Ruled: Family Life in
Reformation Europe* (Cambridge, MA: Harvard University Press, 1983).

[49] Witte, *From Sacrament to Contract*, 154–55. Even so, as Witte says, "Couples who publi-
cized their intent to divorce invited not only the counsel and comfort of friends and pastors
but frequently also the derision of the community and the discipline of the church. Furthermore, judges had great discretion to deny or delay petitions for divorce and to grant interim
remedies short of this irreversible remedy. Particularly in conservative courts, the petitioner
had a heavy burden of proof to show that the divorce was mandated by statute, that all
efforts at reconciliation had proved fruitless, and that no alternative remedy was available"

Almost all Protestant Christians today would agree that even when a person sins in divorcing and remarrying, "the divorces are real, the new marriages are real, and the old marriages no longer exist."[50] This is so even among Protestants who hold a high view of marriage. For example, although the Reformed pastor Timothy Keller holds that divorce dissolves a marriage, he also states, "Sex is God's appointed way for two people to say to one another reciprocally, 'I belong completely, permanently, and exclusively to you.' You must not use sex to say anything less."[51] For Keller, marital sex must always bespeak a *permanent and exclusive* bond, but he nonetheless holds that a valid and consummated Christian marriage can be dissolved—and

---

(ibid., 155). See also Joel F. Harrington, *Reordering Marriage and Society in Reformation Germany* (Cambridge: Cambridge University Press, 1995), which takes a somewhat different line from that of Witte, by emphasizing that "all Protestant authorities displayed obvious apprehension about making divorce and remarriage too accessible.... Reformed Zweibrücken and Neuchâtel, for instance, both only had annual divorce rates of .02 per 1,000 of general population, and even the most active sixteenth-century court—Basel—averaged only .57 (cf. the 1980 US rate of 5.2). On an individual basis, of course, there was at least the possibility of legal remarriage where there had not been before—a confessional distinction painfully apparent to Veronica Sulz after the Catholic Privy Council's rejection of her husband's thirteen-year absence as sufficient basis for her new marriage to Georg Degen.... What is clear, however, is that differences between Protestant and Catholic legal treatment of marital offenses during this time were minimal" (268–69). Sadly, as Harrington records, "few authorities, Protestant or Catholic, ever considered physical abuse in itself—except in life-threatening situations—as worthy of serious punishment" (ibid., 266).

[50] Jim Newheiser, *Marriage, Divorce, and Remarriage: Critical Questions and Answers* (Phillipsburg, NJ: P&R Publishing, 2017), 231; emphasis in original. Newheiser goes further than most Protestants when he nonetheless grants that "Jesus teaches the general rule that remarriage after divorce is adulterous, and Paul teaches the general rule that a spouse who has wrongfully divorced should either remain unmarried or else be reconciled to his or her former spouse" (ibid., 232). He explains that when marriages are dissolved due to reasons that are biblically unwarranted (i.e., by falling outside the exception for *porneia* or other highly serious reasons), "the parties *are* divorced and should not consider themselves still to be married. What both Paul and Jesus are teaching is that after a sinful divorce, the parties shouldn't consider themselves free from obligation to seek reconciliation. Nor should they consider themselves free to remarry" (ibid., 233). This interpretation does not seem to me to accord with what Jesus and Paul say in the relevant biblical passages.

[51] Timothy Keller with Kathy Keller, *The Meaning of Marriage: Facing the Complexities of Commitment with the Wisdom of God* (New York: Riverhead Books, 2011), 257. Even when a person obtains a divorce on nonbiblical grounds, Keller assumes that time and repentance dissolve the marriage; see ibid., 299, drawing upon Jay E. Adams, *Marriage, Divorce, and Remarriage in the Bible* (Grand Rapids, MI: Zondervan, 1980), 92. See also Peter J. Leithart, *The Gospel of Matthew through New Eyes*, vol. 1, *Jesus as Israel* (Monroe, LA: Athanasius Press, 2017), 134–39.

thus, even while both spouses are still alive, their marriage is never intrinsically permanent or exclusive.

A few contemporary evangelical theologians consider that Jesus forbade remarriage after divorce. The most prominent example is the prolific author and Reformed pastor John Piper. Piper advocates two simultaneous ways of caring for divorced persons: first, we must "come alongside divorced persons and stand by them as they grieve and repent of any sinful part of their own"; second, we must "lovingly and caringly ... articulate a hatred of divorce, and why it is against the will of God, and do all we can biblically to keep it from happening".[52] The latter may seem judgmental, but it is actually an act of mercy. Piper points out, "Compromises on the sacredness and lifelong permanence of marriage—positions that weaken the solidity of the covenant-union—may feel loving in the short run but wreak havoc for thousands over the decades."[53]

For Piper, Christian marriage has its ultimate meaning in representing *"the covenant-keeping love between Christ and his church"*.[54] He argues that this meaning, drawn from Ephesians 5:21–33, is the primary reason that God instituted marriage in the first place. Although marriage is important as a natural and social institution for the flourishing of families, the primary purpose of marriage—revealed in Christian marriage—is to signify God's plan for uniting his people to himself in Christ. Just as Christ's bond with the Church is unbreakable, so also Christian marriage must be unbreakable. In Christ, God himself unites the Christian couple who pledge marital vows to each other (see Mk 10:8). Once God has joined the couple, only God can separate them; and God does not will to do so, except by death. Piper draws the conclusion that Christian "marriage is sacred beyond what most people imagine. It is a unique creation of God, a dramatic portrayal of God's relation to his people, and a display of the glory of God's covenant-keeping love."[55]

---

[52] John Piper, *This Momentary Marriage: A Parable of Permanence* (Wheaton, IL: Crossway, 2009), 158–59. Piper advances the same viewpoint in *What Jesus Demands from the World* (Wheaton, IL: Crossway, 2006), 301–22; and John Piper, "Divorce and Remarriage: A Position Paper", DesiringGod.org, July 21, 1986, http://www.desiringgod.org/articles/divorce -remarriage-a-position-paper.

[53] Piper, *This Momentary Marriage*, 159.

[54] Ibid.; emphasis in original.

[55] Ibid.

Piper is aware that many Christians think that biblical texts such as Ephesians 5:21–33 and Mark 10:8 are portraying an eschatological ideal. On this view, Christians still suffer from "hardness of heart" (Mk 10:5), and Jesus permits divorce (in the sense of the dissolution of a marriage, freeing a person to marry again) for his still hard-hearted followers. As Piper observes, the question for exegesis of Mark 10:2–12 is "will the emphasis fall on the fact that in the church there is still hardness of heart, or will the emphasis fall on the fact that the old has passed away and the new has come (2 Cor 5:17)?"[56] Piper answers that Jesus came to give his followers, through the outpouring of the Spirit, the ability to live according to the will of God. By fulfilling the Mosaic Law on his Cross, Jesus draws "his ransomed and forgiven and justified followers into the higher standards that were really intended when *all* of Moses is properly understood".[57] These higher standards belong to the Gospel of mercy by which Jesus, in the Spirit, saves us.

But what about the allowance for divorce on the ground of *porneia*, given in Matthew 5:32 and 19:9? Piper thinks that it is significant that *porneia* is not the normal Greek word for "adultery". Directing attention to Matthew 15:19 and John 8:41, he suggests that the proper translation of *porneia* is "fornication"—which would necessarily mean that it must have occurred prior to the wedding. Piper remarks in this regard, "Matthew is the one Gospel that tells about Joseph's intention to 'divorce' his betrothed Mary because he thought she had committed fornication."[58] Such a "divorce" would have indeed been justified (prior to actual marriage) had the Virgin Mary actually committed fornication. I consider that stronger arguments can be given with regard to the interpretation of Matthew 5:32 and 19:9, as I will discuss below. But the key point that Piper makes is that "the coming of Jesus into the world, and the beginning of the last days, and the outpouring of the Holy Spirit, and the inauguration of the kingdom of God, and the promised presence of the living Christ, and the radical nature of his commands point toward an elevation of expectation for his new-covenant people in this crooked and passing world."[59]

---

[56] Ibid., 161.

[57] Ibid., 162; emphasis in original.

[58] Ibid., 174.

[59] Ibid., 174. Note that Piper rejects the "Pauline privilege", arguing that even if a divorce (understood as separation) is possible in the marriage of a Christian and an unbeliever, no remarriage is possible—given that Paul does not explicitly approve remarriage. See ibid., 171–73.

Piper adds that Christians who have already remarried after divorce should not break their new bond. He comments, "The marriage should not have been done, but now that it is done, it should not be undone by man. It is a real marriage. Real covenant vows have been made. And that real covenant of marriage may be purified by the blood of Jesus and set apart for God."[60] In other words, Jesus can forgive the sin of the second marriage, and the repentant couple can flourish in the Lord. Piper does not inquire into what has happened to the obligations intrinsic to the original, still existent indissoluble marriage.

The evangelical biblical scholar Gordon Wenham devoted much of his career to arguing against the validity of remarriage after divorce (for Christians). Like Piper, Wenham maintains that the first Christians, in obedience to Jesus' commandment, "sometimes tolerated divorce for *porneia* (Matt. 5:32) or desertion (1 Cor. 7:15)", but "never tolerated, let alone approved of, marriage after divorce".[61] Wenham finds it significant that "in the first three centuries of the Christian era, not a single writer supposes that the New Testament allows remarriage after divorce."[62] He also observes that 1 Corinthians 7:10–11, Romans 7:2–3, Mark 10:11, and Luke 16:18 do not support remarriage after divorce.[63] Thus, the case for the notion that

---

[60] Ibid., 170. Jay Adams acknowledges the impact (in 1980) of the rapid rise in divorce and remarriage: "Divorced persons are flooding into our congregations. Remarriages are taking place everywhere" (Adams, *Marriage, Divorce, and Remarriage in the Bible*, xiv). In Adams' view, adultery is an acceptable ground for divorce. Adams also considers that in cases where one spouse sins by pushing a divorce upon the other spouse—and where the sinful spouse refuses all efforts of reconciliation—the sinful spouse is excommunicated and becomes like an unbeliever. In such a case, Adams argues, Paul's words in 1 Corinthians 7 show that the innocent spouse has a right to remarry.

[61] Gordon J. Wenham, "No Remarriage after Divorce", in *Remarriage after Divorce in Today's Church: Three Views*, ed. Mark L. Strauss (Grand Rapids, MI: Zondervan, 2006), 19–42, at 41.

[62] Ibid., 21.

[63] For a more typical Protestant perspective, arguing that Scripture itself allows for various viewpoints on divorce and remarriage, see the remarks of Mary Foskett at the outset of her chapter on marriage in her *Moral Teachings of Jesus* (Nashville, TN: Abingdon Press, 2004), 61–62: "New Testament writing concerning these matters shows that there was some variation in early Christian regard for marriage and divorce. It seems that, much like today, communities of believers acting faithfully and out of goodwill came to somewhat different conclusions about the value of marriage and the appropriateness of divorce. Whereas Mark's Gospel holds an absolutist, negative view of divorce (Mark 10:2–12), Paul and Matthew allow for separation in certain circumstances (1 Corinthians 7:15; Matthew 5:32). Moreover,

the New Testament allows for remarriage after divorce relies largely upon Matthew 5:32 and 19:9. But in these verses, Jesus states firmly that "whoever marries a divorced woman commits adultery." Jesus does not qualify this point; rather, Jesus apodictically condemns anyone who marries "a divorced woman". For this reason, Wenham considers that the exception clause means solely to describe a situation in which divorce itself is permissible, rather than to describe a situation in which divorce actually dissolves a marriage so that remarriage is permissible. Wenham cites the biblical scholar Hans Dieter Betz's conclusion regarding Matthew 5:32 and 19:9 that "Matthew seems to be affirming ... that any remarriage after divorce is adulterous but that divorce alone is not."[64]

In addition, Wenham observes that Matthew 19:9's context is the debate between Pharisaic schools concerning the grounds for divorce. Jesus shocks his own disciples, as well as the Pharisees, by permitting divorce (understood as separation) on only one ground, and by not permitting remarriage at all. Wenham emphasizes the disciples' response: "If such is the case of a man with his wife, it is not expedient to marry" (Mt 19:10). If the Erasmian interpretation were correct, Jesus would have merely been agreeing with "the Shammaite Pharisees, who allowed divorce and remarriage in a few

---

while Matthew and Mark view divorce as a divine concession, Paul views marriage itself as a concession and a kind of prophylactic against sexual misconduct (1 Corinthians 7:9). In short, even in earliest Christianity, people of faith pondered the meaning and moral complexity of marriage and divorce and sometimes drew different conclusions. It should come as no surprise, then, to find Christians today in a similar position. With that said, it is worth mentioning that adultery is viewed in a decidedly negative light by the New Testament writings that comment on it. Although there is no uniform view of divorce and remarriage (whether after the death of a spouse or divorce), it is also fair to say that divorce is seen as something less than ideal." Foskett adds that even if there were a "uniform view" of marriage and divorce in the New Testament, we would still need to correct it in applying it today, due to the patriarchal culture of Jesus' day. But she argues that we can take three key principles or "foundational blocks" for Christian marital ethics from the New Testament's teachings: "(1) Jesus' vision for marriage is rooted in his vision of the very humanity we were created to embody from the very beginning of creation. (2) Divorce is a divine concession, not an ideal. (3) A marriage is not easily dissolved" (ibid., 70). Foskett finds in Jesus' teachings about marital indissolubility "descriptive, rather than prescriptive, language that pertains to the everyday realities that continue well beyond the legal termination of a marriage. It is not so much the 'if you divorce you will be committing adultery' but the more pastoral, 'marriage is not so easily given to dissolution' that can also speak to us today" (ibid., 73).

[64] Hans Dieter Betz, *The Sermon on the Mount* (Minneapolis, MN: Fortress Press, 1995), 257; cited in Wenham, "No Remarriage after Divorce", 30.

cases"[65]—and this position would not have shocked his disciples. On this basis Wenham concludes, "There is no need to suppose different gospels disagree on what Jesus taught about marriage or to suppose that he backed down when challenged by the Pharisees or his disciples."[66] At the same time, recognizing that contemporary evangelicals who argue in favor of remarriage after divorce are often "strongly motivated by pastoral concern for divorced persons who remarry",[67]

[65] Wenham, "No Remarriage after Divorce", 31.

[66] Ibid., 32. For further discussion, see William A. Heth and Gordon J. Wenham, *Jesus and Divorce*, 3rd ed. (Carlisle: Paternoster, 2002); Gordon J. Wenham, "Does the NT Approve Remarriage after Divorce?", *Southern Baptist Journal of Theology* 6 (2002): 30–45; Gordon J. Wenham, "Matthew and Divorce: An Old Crux Revisited", *Journal for the Study of the New Testament* 22 (1984): 95–107; Gordon J. Wenham, "The Syntax of Matthew 19:9", *Journal for the Study of the New Testament* 24 (1986): 17–23. Wenham critically engages David Atkinson's *To Have and to Hold: The Marriage Covenant and the Discipline of Divorce* (Grand Rapids, MI: Eerdmans, 1979). Wenham draws positive attention to Jacques Dupont, *Mariage et divorce dans l'évangile* (Bruges: Desclée de Brouwer, 1959), and John Murray's *Divorce* (Philadelphia: Presbyterian and Reformed, 1961). In response to Craig S. Keener's point that Second Temple Jews assumed that *any* divorce, if valid, allowed for remarriage (see Craig S. Keener,... *And Marries Another* [Peabody, MA: Hendrickson, 1991], 44), Wenham emphasizes that Jesus' position greatly surprised his fellow Jews (including the Pharisees) rather than remaining within their expectations. In addition, Wenham points out that even those who hold to the Erasmian interpretation accept that in Matthew 5:32 and 19:9, Jesus clearly employs the (Greek) word used for divorce, in order to describe not marital dissolution but marital *separation* (namely, when the divorce is not based upon *porneia*). This demonstrates that Jesus is using the word "divorce" in a manner that already differs from almost all of his contemporaries. For the same position as Keener's, see David Instone-Brewer, *Divorce and Remarriage in the 1st and 21st Century* (Cambridge: Grove, 2001), and David Instone-Brewer, *Divorce and Remarriage in the Bible: The Social and Literary Context* (Grand Rapids, MI: Eerdmans, 2002). For a critique of Dupont's position, see Frans Neirynck, "Huwelijk en Echtscheiding in het Evangelie", *Collationes Brugenses et Gandavenses* 6 (1960): 123–30, mentioned in Raymond F. Collins, *Divorce in the New Testament* (Collegeville, MN: Liturgical Press, 1992), 317.

[67] Gordon J. Wenham, "A Response to Craig S. Keener", in *Remarriage after Divorce in Today's Church*, 121. See the position of William A. Heth, who co-authored *Jesus and Divorce* with Wenham, but who changed his position after 1997: William A. Heth, "A Response to Gordon J. Wenham", in *Remarriage and Divorce in Today's Church*, 43–47. Heth points to various reasons for his change of views, and one important reason is experiential: "I could not come up with a satisfactory biblical answer for the practical dilemmas caused by a blanket no-remarriage conclusion. Upon hearing about my no-remarriage position, a fellow seminary student blurted out, 'Do you mean to tell me that my friend, whose wife left him and his four kids for a lesbian, has to remain single for the rest of his life?' To 'suffer for what is right' (1 Pet. 3:14) may well cover such cases, given the assumption that marriage is indissoluble. However, I struggled with why Jesus would impose such remarriage restrictions on an offended innocent party" (ibid., 44). For Heth's earlier viewpoint, see William A. Heth, "Divorce, but No Remarriage", in *Divorce and Remarriage: Four Christian Views*, ed. H. Wayne House (Downers Grove, IL: IVP Academic, 1990), 73–129.

Wenham cautions against being uncaring with respect to the plight of many divorced Christians who have remarried.

Geoffrey Bromiley, who with T. F. Torrance was the general editor of the English translation of Karl Barth's *Church Dogmatics*, provides a final example of evangelical scholarship in favor of Christian marriage's indissolubility. Commenting on the Synoptic Gospels' accounts of Jesus' teachings about divorce and remarriage, Bromiley states that "for Jesus and those who follow him, whose stony hearts have been replaced by hearts of flesh (Ezek. 36:26) [due to the Messianic inauguration of the kingdom and sending of the Spirit], the Old Covenant law is withdrawn and the created order of marriage comes back into full force."[68] If so, the question immediately arises, what then of the exception due to *porneia* (Matthew 5:32; 19:9)? In response, Bromiley notes that the meaning of *porneia* is unclear, and furthermore the Synoptics' "story of the encounter with Pharisees seems to make no final sense if Jesus finishes up by endorsing the Mosaic law which at first he so bravely describes as a concession and replaces with the original creation principle."[69]

What about the exception opened up in 1 Corinthians 7:15? Bromiley suggests that it applies to the case of a believer married to an unbeliever, but not to extensions of this case. After all, as he says, "Once one considers the position that the permission of 1 Corinthians 7 might be a kind of blank check to be filled out as individual situations suggest, there is hardly any end to the extension of possibilities," opening the door to divorcing a spouse who acts in unbelieving and unchristian ways.[70] This is precisely what has happened among Christian communities that have relaxed Jesus' teaching (and

---

[68] Geoffrey W. Bromiley, *God and Marriage* (Grand Rapids, MI: Eerdmans, 1980), 44.

[69] Ibid., 45.

[70] Ibid., 68. For an example of an evangelical biblical scholar attempting—unpersuasively in my view—to limit such grounds by construing Christian marriage as an indissoluble covenant so long as both spouses continue to meet a set of "covenant stipulations", see Yordan Kalev Zhekov, *Defining the New Testament Logia on Divorce and Remarriage in a Pluralistic Context* (Eugene, OR: Pickwick, 2009). Nobly, Zhekov is concerned to care for persons who might otherwise be locked into abusive marriages. In the case of abusive marriages, however, divorce understood as legal separation from bed and board suffices to assure (insofar as humanly possible) that the abuse will not continue; and it also needs to be remarked that the ability of an abuser to make a valid marital vow in the first place is doubtful, which means that annulment could also resolve the difficulty.

Paul's teaching in 1 Corinthians 7:10–11 and Romans 7:2–3). Bromiley grants solely that in certain cases it can be shown that the marital consent was null from the outset, which makes divorce and remarriage acceptable in such cases.

Of course, the great majority of Protestant theologians and exegetes find remarriage after divorce to be acceptable. Intriguingly, Karl Barth insists that this Protestant perspective does not undermine the indissolubility of Christian marriage. Agreeing up to a certain point with the Catholic position, Barth observes that if marriage were *not* permanent and indissoluble, "Love would ... be replaced by what is essentially a constant playing at love, and the full and exclusive life-partnership of marriage by a flabby and non-binding experimentation which dispenses with all real discipline".[71] Indeed, Barth affirms that a marriage that "God has joined together" (Mt 19:6; cf. Gen 2:24) cannot be dissolved under any circumstances by human authority. But he denies that every marital union of Christians has been joined together by God and bears the *divine command* of indissolubility.[72]

---

[71] Karl Barth, *Church Dogmatics*, vol. 3, *The Doctrine of Creation*, pt. 4, trans. A. T. Mackay et al., ed. G. W. Bromiley and T. F. Torrance (Edinburgh: T&T Clark, 1961), 206. Barth's long-term adulterous relationship with his assistant, Charlotte von Kirschbaum, is surely in the background of his treatment of adultery in ibid., 235–41, which should be read as an attempt to justify continuing in his actions. For example, he states of the adulterous woman of John 8 that "the summons ['Go, and do not sin again' (Jn 8:11)] is that from now on she may and must live as a transgressor who even in her condition as a sinner stands under the powerful impulsion of her translation in Jesus into the condition of eternal righteousness, innocence and blessedness, who even in the irreparable disorder of her life is already orientated towards the order of the divine kingdom" (ibid., 236). For the details of Barth's long-standing open adultery, see Christiane Tietz, "Karl Barth and Charlotte von Kirschbaum", *Theology Today* 74 (2017): 86–111.

[72] Barth takes a broad view of the impediments to human freedom in contracting a marriage. He comments, "It is flagrant disobedience to the command of God to enter marriage merely for the satisfaction of general or specific physical desire, or for the sake of security or enrichment, or out of regard for the concerns or wishes of one's parents or family, or in the expectation of social or professional advantage. When this is done, marriage is only approached and not entered" (Barth, *Church Dogmatics* 3.4, 219). He adds somewhat later, "The equation of marriage with the wedding ceremony is a dreadful and deep-rooted error. Two people may be formally married and fail to live a life which can seriously be regarded as married life. And it may happen that two people are not married and yet in their precarious way live under the law of marriage. A wedding is only the regulative confirmation and legitimation of a marriage before and by society. It does not constitute marriage" (ibid., 225). Barth does not deny, of course, that the marriage couple should "be prepared for a public confession of their marriage and desire public confirmation of it" through "the domestic, legal and ecclesiastical institution of marriage" (ibid., 226).

Given that some marriages were never joined by God's command, God may reveal to a Christian spouse a "Word of judgment which tells him that the marriage has no divine basis [and never had one] and is thus dissoluble".[73]

Even in such a case, Barth observes, it is only in the most extraordinary situation that a divorce should be pursued. In such extraordinary situations, however, marriage—though indissoluble when God has in fact joined the couple—may for Barth rightly end in divorce: namely, when in his or her conscience a married man or woman hears the definitive judgment that the "marriage is condemned by God".[74]

Historical-Critical Perspectives

Can we clarify matters by appeal to historical-critical biblical scholars? It may seem that where Catholic, Orthodox, and Protestant theologians could not agree, historical-critical biblical scholars may be able to do better. This hope appears, for example, in "A Pastoral Statement on Orthodox/Roman Catholic Marriages", published in 1990 by the Joint Committee of Orthodox and Catholic Bishops under the sponsorship of the Standing Conference of Canonical Orthodox Bishops in America and the National Conference of Catholic Bishops.[75] They observe, "A number of scholars of

---

[73] Ibid., 211. Barth goes on to explain, "Legal divorce is no part of the divine command concerning marriage; for this proclaims and requires its indissolubility. It [legal divorce] belongs only to the institution of marriage. The human institution takes into account the possibility of marriages which have no divine foundation and constitution, which are not contracted and lived out in obedience to God's command, and which can therefore be dissolved. The whole weakness of marriage as an institution [i.e., a human institution] is revealed at this point. It thinks in terms of the situation prior to the dawn of the new age, the coming of the kingdom and the fulfilment of the covenant. It presupposes that the Word of God concerning marriage, His promise and His command, cannot be heard and taken to heart. It reckons with the old hardness of heart. It thus deduces that there are marriages which are not made by God and are not therefore permanent. But the possibility of divorce, which on these grounds is an essential part of the institution, coincides with the insight which can force itself upon even a believer that his marriage is condemned by God.... In the decree of divorce pronounced by the human judge he will hear again the divine judgment to which he fell victim in His marriage" (ibid., 212).

[74] Ibid., 213.

[75] The statement can be found on the USCCB's website at http://www.usccb.org/beliefs -and-teachings/ecumenical-and-interreligious/ecumenical/orthodox/pastoral-orthodox -catholic-marriage.cfm.

Sacred Scripture in our churches consider it likely that Jesus' teaching about the indissolubility of marriage may have already been interpreted and adjusted by New Testament writers, moved by the Holy Spirit, to respond to new circumstances and pastoral problems (cf. Mt 5:32 and 1 Cor 7:15)."[76] On this basis, they suggest that the traditional Catholic view can be changed to allow for exceptions in which remarriage after divorce is permissible in the Church. Along these lines, they ask rhetorically, "If Matthew, under the inspiration of the Holy Spirit, could have been moved to add an exceptive phrase to Jesus' saying about divorce, or if Paul, similarly inspired, could have introduced an exception on his own authority, then would it be possible for those exercising authoritative pastoral decision-making in today's Church to explore the examination of exceptions?"[77] In fact, their question comes almost verbatim from a book by the historical-critical biblical scholar Joseph Fitzmyer that I will discuss below.

On historical-critical grounds, the Catholic theologian Eberhard Schockenhoff argues that the hard teachings of Jesus on divorce and remarriage were never accepted in their full difficulty by anyone. It is evident that "the biblical authors recorded Jesus' word on the indissolubility of marriage and his calling for unconditional marital faithfulness."[78] But in the Gospel of Matthew and the letters of Paul, it becomes clear that "the communities of the New Testament felt authorized to adjust Jesus' instructions on marriage on the grounds of his word on binding and loosening (cf. Mt 16,19; 18,18)."[79] On this view, Jesus gave to the Church the power to overrule him, or at least the Church immediately claimed that power.

This reading of Matthew 16:19, however, is eccentric. The historical-critical exegete Rudolf Schnackenburg argues that Matthew 16:19 means that "through preaching the will of God, a preaching that obliges its hearers and includes a judgment as to the fulfillment or nonfulfillment of that divine will ... the authorized

---

[76] Ibid.

[77] Ibid.

[78] Eberhard Schockenhoff, "Our Understanding of Moral Sin: The Competence of Conscience of Divorced Remarried Persons", *INTAMS Review* 20 (2014): 252.

[79] Ibid.

agent opens the door to the Reign of God."[80] For Schnackenburg, rather than granting itself justification for overruling Christ's will, the Matthean community stands under "the will of God". The evangelist Matthew gives no indication that what Jesus teaches as God's will can be rejected or modified by the Church. Another historical-critical biblical scholar, Robert Gundry, observes that "in rabbinic literature, binding and loosing usually signify interpretative decisions of prohibition and permission; but they also signify condemnation and acquittal in disciplining members of the synagogue who disobey the interpretative decisions", and he adds that in Matthew 18:18, "binding and loosing will be associated with church discipline and forgiveness."[81] This differs from giving the Church free rein to reject or change Jesus' will. Gundry interprets Matthew 16:19 to be confirming the authority of "Jesus' teaching".[82]

---

[80] Rudolf Schnackenburg, *The Gospel of Matthew*, trans. Robert R. Barr (Grand Rapids, MI: Eerdmans, 2002), 160. For Schnackenburg on the Matthean "exception" clause (Mt 5:32; 19:9), see ibid., 57–58. Schnackenburg considers that Jesus in Matthew 5:32 (and 19:9) forbids divorce entirely except for in the case of *porneia*, which here may mean either union with a near relative or adultery. Schnackenburg leaves open the question of whether, even if one receives a permissible divorce, one can remarry (according to Jesus in Matthew 5:32; 19:9). He concludes that Jesus has issued a hard teaching indeed: "At all events, the Matthean unchastity clause along with Jesus' unqualified prohibition of divorce threw primitive Christian (here Jewish Christian) communities into great difficulties (for Gentile communities, see 1 Cor. 7:10–16). Jesus had made his determination solely in accordance with the holy will of God, without regard for its practical realization in this world—the basic problem of the Sermon on the Mount!" (Schnackenburg, *Gospel of Matthew*, 58). See also the conclusion of W.D. Davies and Dale C. Allison, Jr., on the basis of their sifting of various interpretations: "We should like to suggest that consideration be given to the possibility that vv. 19a and 19b–c ... belonged together from the first and that both had to do with Peter's evangelistic mission. If certain Jewish teachers shut the door of the kingdom to others by what they said and did (Mt 23:13 par.), Peter was to open that door by his missionary activity. The apostle had the keys of the kingdom insofar as he proclaimed the good news. By his preaching did he not in effect open the kingdom for those who accepted the gospel, and by the same preaching did he not close the kingdom to those who rejected him and his message?" (W.D. Davies and Dale C. Allison, Jr., *A Critical and Exegetical Commentary on the Gospel According to Saint Matthew*, vol. 2, *Commentary on Matthew VIII–XVIII* [London: T&T Clark International, 2004], 641). Again, it is the authority of the Gospel that is in play here, not a supposed ecclesial authority to overrule the Gospel. *Pace* Schockenhoff's view that the author of the Gospel of Matthew (or the Matthean community) overruled and changed Jesus' words, Matthew 16:19 offers no support for such an action—nor is such an action exegetically necessary in the case of Matthew 5:32; 19:9.

[81] Robert H. Gundry, *Matthew: A Commentary on His Handbook for a Mixed Church under Persecution*, 2nd ed. (Grand Rapids, MI: Eerdmans, 1994), 336.

[82] Ibid., 335.

In his massive historical-critical study of the Gospel of Matthew, the Protestant biblical scholar Ulrich Luz concludes that the traditional Catholic understanding of Matthew 5:32 and 19:9 is the exegetically correct one, at least in its essentials. Luz states, "In my judgment, in practice the *Catholic position*, which provides the possibility of a separation of table, bed, and dwelling with a continuing *vinculum* of the marriage, comes especially close to the Matthean position."[83] He knows that this will be surprising to many contemporary Catholic biblical scholars. But in his view, "Matthew and Catholic practice converge... in the prohibition against marrying a divorced woman. Corresponding to it is the denial of the possibility of a second marriage."[84] Although Matthew 5:32 is directed only to the man, Luz interprets it to mean that "neither divorced men nor divorced women" can marry again: the marital bond continues despite the divorce.[85] What then is the purpose of the exception clause? It means that adultery *must* be followed by divorce. This is so because "for Judaism divorce is mandatory when adultery happens. Thus according to the Jewish Christian Matthew, a marriage *must* be terminated in the case of πορνεία, because according to Jewish conviction continuing it would contradict God's commandment."[86]

Nonetheless, Luz does not endorse the Catholic position *for today*. He observes, "Marriage is no longer what it was in Jesus' day; people's experiences in marriage, not least of all the experiences of women, are different; and above all the church itself is different from Matthew's community."[87] He supposes that the Matthean community's

---

[83] Ulrich Luz, *Matthew 1–7: A Commentary*, trans. James E. Crouch, ed. Helmut Koester (Minneapolis, MN: Fortress Press, 2007), 256; emphasis in original.

[84] Ibid. Well aware of the diversity of patristic voices, Luz adds that "the church fathers generally maintained" the prohibition of second marriage "with great decisiveness", at least until the fourth century (ibid., 256n46). He cites the *Shepherd of Hermas* as well as Justin, Athenagoras, Clement, Tertullian, Theodoret of Cyrus, Euthymius Zigaabenus, Hilary of Poitiers, Augustine, and Jerome, in addition to the councils of Elvira and Arles and the twelfth-century *Decretum Gratiani*. As counterwitnesses, he cites Origen, Pollentius, Basil, Epiphanius, and Ambrosiaster.

[85] Ibid., 257.

[86] Ibid., 255. Luz rejects the view that "πορνεία" means "incest" (in the sense prohibited in Leviticus 18), but he grants that it is not possible to define "πορνεία" with precision, and he knows that its translation as "adultery" has to deal with the counterargument that the normal Greek word for adultery is μοιχεία.

[87] Ibid., 258.

freedom in bringing Jesus' teaching into line with Jewish views of adultery should allow the Church today to be "flexible ... even in adapting laws given by the Lord".[88] At the same time, he grants that "Jesus' categorical prohibition of divorce, formulated as a sentence of law, was more than a guideline."[89] It was a legal command, binding upon his followers. But today Christians should not obey Jesus' precept in this regard. Luz thinks that "modern experiences" have shown Jesus' "unconditional requirement of the indissolubility of marriage" to be wrong.[90]

In their historical-critical work on the Gospel of Matthew (published before Luz's study appeared), the Protestant exegetes W. D. Davies and Dale Allison provide a detailed analysis of Matthew 5:32 and 19:9. What they say about Matthew 5:32 can be summarized as follows. First, they note one of the differences between Mark 10:11–12 and Matthew 5:32, and they tentatively attribute this difference to the hypothetical "Q" source. They state, "We thus appear to have two slightly different traditions. In Mark the husband commits adultery (because he remarries) while in Q (= Matthew) the husband causes the woman to commit adultery (because she, it is assumed, will remarry)."[91] Then they turn to the "except on the ground of unchastity [παρεκτὸς λόγου πορνείας]" clause.

Their first remark regarding this clause is that "we have here in all probability an editorial addition."[92] In their view, even if Matthew did not add the qualifying phrase, we can be sure that it did not come from Jesus. If Jesus' own position had originally included such a qualifier, then earlier texts (such as Mark 10 or 1 Corinthians 7) would have been sure to report the qualifier, given the unusual stringency of what the earlier texts reported. Davies and Allison argue further that the qualifying phrase is likely "based on the 'erwat dābār of Deut 24.1'", which reads as follows: "because he has found some indecency

[88] Ibid.

[89] Ibid., 259.

[90] Ibid.

[91] W. D. Davies and Dale C. Allison, Jr., *A Critical and Exegetical Commentary on the Gospel According to Saint Matthew*, vol. 1, *Introduction and Commentary on Matthew I–VII* (London: T&T Clark, 1988), 528.

[92] Ibid.

in her".[93] They go on to describe the traditional interpretations of the exception clause: "According to Erasmus and most Protestant scholars since his time, Matthew allows the innocent party to divorce and remarry in the event of adultery. According to the almost universal patristic as well as Roman Catholic opinion, Matthew permits only separation for adultery, not remarriage (cf. 1 Cor 7)."[94]

Against the hope that the controversy can be settled on the basis of historical-critical evidence, Davies and Allison argue that it cannot be settled on such grounds. They hold that "Matthew's words are simply too cryptic to admit of a definitive interpretation."[95] They are almost equally reticent in determining what the intended meaning of πορνεία is. In their view, πορνεία could mean either "fornication", "incest", or "adultery". They think that "fornication" is unlikely because it is not strong enough. In advancing their own preferred translation, they remark, "Choosing between the two remaining alternatives—'incest' or 'adultery'—is nearly impossible, and if we favour the translation, 'adultery', it is only with great hesitation."[96]

[93] Ibid. See also Stephen Westerholm, *Law and Ethics in Early Judaism and the New Testament* (Tübingen: Mohr Siebeck, 2017), 116: "In the discussion of divorce (19:3–9), any suggestion that Jesus opposes Moses is ruled out by Matthew: what Jesus actually sets aside is a mere concession that Moses 'allowed,' not a procedure that Moses 'commanded' (19:8; contrast Mark 10:3, 5); and when Jesus allows that a man who divorces his wife because of her 'unchastity' is himself guiltless (Matt 5:32; 19:9), the exception may itself represent an interpretation of the words 'something objectionable [or "indecent"]' in Deuteronomy 24:1." Westerholm is clear that Jesus' followers (as distinct from society as a whole) are required to live according to Jesus' teachings in the Sermon on the Mount: "Jesus' disciples must be 'doers,' not mere 'hearers,' of Jesus' words if they are to enter the kingdom…. In spelling out what God requires of those who would enter his kingdom, Jesus speaks with the same authority as the law itself: an authority that demands recognition" (ibid., 5–6). In an earlier study, Westerholm affirms that in Jesus' teaching on divorce (Mark 10:11–12 and parallels), Jesus states "God's will in casuistic form" (Stephen Westerholm, *Jesus and Scribal Authority* [Lund, Sweden: CWK Gleerup, 1978], 124). Westerholm adds, however, that "Jesus' prohibition of divorce is not to be understood as a statute demanding submission for its own sake, but as the definition of an area of potential human activity impossible for the one who rightly understands God's will and obeys it radically" (ibid., 125). According to Westerholm in *Jesus and Scribal Authority*, Jesus differs from the practitioners of halakhah because he is able to go entirely behind the law (such as the Mosaic Law on divorce) in order to identify God's will.

[94] Davies and Allison, *Commentary on the Gospel according to Saint Matthew*, 1:529. They cite Crouzel, *L'Église primitive face au divorce*.

[95] Davies and Allison, *Commentary on the Gospel according to Saint Matthew*, 1:529.

[96] Ibid. Mankowski defends the translation "incest"; see Paul Mankowski, S.J., "Dominical Teaching on Divorce and Remarriage: The Biblical Data", in Dodaro, *Remaining in the Truth of Christ*, 57–62. By contrast, in their Anchor Bible commentary, W. F. Albright and C. S. Mann

Before defending their preferred translation, they give four grounds why one might favor the translation "incest". The first is that this is the meaning of πορνεία in 1 Corinthians 5:1 (which the RSV translates as "immorality"). The second is that the evangelist Matthew already has a word that he uses consistently for "adultery"—μοιχεύω—and he does not use that word here. The third is that in Acts 15:29 and 21:25, we find the Council of Jerusalem ruling that Gentiles must abstain from πορνεία, and it is likely that the council's list of four proscribed things (including πορνεία) comes from Leviticus 17–18's holiness code, which proscribes sexual intercourse with near relatives (see Lev 18:6–18). Fourth and most significantly, "If Matthew's Christian community was, as seems most likely, a mixed body of Jews and Gentiles, the evangelist could easily have faced a situation in which Gentiles entering the community were found to be, because of marriages made before their conversions, in violation of the Levitical incest laws (cf. 1 Cor 5). (Incest was much more common among Gentiles than among Jews.)"[97] If the fourth reason were the real issue, then the marriages would be invalid from the outset.

In favoring the translation "adultery", Davies and Allison admit that the Shammaite Pharisees interpreted the *erwat dābār* of Deuteronomy 24:1 "as unchastity on the part of the woman within marriage", which would make Matthew 5:32 and 19:9 merely "a Christian statement of the Shammaite position".[98] Since they think that Matthew

---

argue, "The Greek word *porneia* quite certainly means adultery here, and generally is used of illicit sexual relations, which the school of Shammai held to be the only ground of divorce.... Mark (x 11) and Luke (xvi 18) both represent Jesus as giving a simple prohibition of divorce. Paul's understanding of the matter (I Cor vii 10–11) reinforces this: divorce implies that the woman may well marry again, and in Paul's view (implicitly, too, in Jesus' view) this leads her to adultery.... What Jesus is emphasizing is the principle, the foundation, of marriage. In principle, the divorced woman is still the wife of her husband, and the man who divorces his wife makes her an adulteress, on the presumption that she will marry again. The man who marries the divorced woman both shares in her adultery and also commits that offense himself, because in principle—though not legally—the divorced woman is still married to her first husband" (W. F. Albright and C. S. Mann, *Matthew: Introduction, Translation, and Notes* [Garden City, NY: Doubleday, 1971], 65). Albright and Mann hold nonetheless that in Matthew 5:32 and Matthew 19:9, Jesus adopts the position of the Pharisaic school of Shammai. In my view, this is unlikely, because this would not have provoked his disciples to complain: "If such is the case of a man with his wife, it is not expedient to marry" (Mt 19:10).

[97] Davies and Allison, *Commentary on the Gospel according to Saint Matthew*, 1:530.
[98] Ibid.

5:32 does not state clearly whether remarriage is permitted after a legitimate divorce, they hold that a simple "reassertion of Shammai's position on divorce would perhaps have been sufficiently isolated as to be considered much more strict than general Jewish opinion (cf. Mt 19.11)".[99] In my view, however, the disciples' stunned reaction in Matthew 19:11 could only make sense if Jesus has ruled out remarriage; they would not have been stunned by the Shammaite view.

In a recent article, Markus Bockmuehl turns to the Dead Sea Scrolls and other late Second Temple texts for evidence. As we might expect, he finds that "1QapGen 20.15, seconded by references like Philo, *Abr.* 98; Matt 1.19; etc., clearly establishes a pre-rabbinic exegetical tradition (based on Deut 24.4 and Lev 18.20; Num 5.13–14, 20) to the effect that adultery (and rape) requires divorce."[100] He argues that Matthew 5:32 and 19:9 fits within this tradition, and he suggests that the exception clause in these verses therefore may be in support of divorce but without allowing remarriage. Thus, Bockmuehl favors the position adopted by Luz.

What about other New Testament passages about divorce and remarriage? Joseph Fitzmyer, who thinks that Matthew 5:32 and 19:9 offer an exception that contradicts the Catholic position, has the following to say about 1 Corinthians 7:10–11: "The prohibition of divorce, as formulated by Paul, is absolute, with no exceptions envisaged, as it appears also in Mark 10:9–12 and Luke 16:18."[101] Fitzmyer adds that "the prohibition is attributed to 'the Lord.' Thus Paul invests the prohibition with the authority of *ho Kyrios*, meaning not only that the teaching does not originate with himself, in contrast to 7:12, 25, but also that, even though it stems from the earthly Jesus, it now bears the authority of the risen Christ."[102] Fitzmyer mentions that some Pauline scholars consider that the phrase in 7:11, "but if she does, let her remain single, or else be reconciled to her husband", is an interpolation by Paul into the commandment of Jesus. It is for this reason that it is marked in parentheses in the RSV. But in his

---

[99] Ibid.

[100] Markus Bockmuehl, *Jewish Law in Gentile Churches: Halakhah and the Beginning of Christian Public Ethics* (Grand Rapids, MI: Baker Academic, 2000), 21.

[101] Joseph A. Fitzmyer, S.J., *First Corinthians: A New Translation with Introduction and Commentary* (New Haven, CT: Yale University Press, 2008), 288.

[102] Ibid., 290.

own translation, Fitzmyer excludes the parentheses, on the grounds that the whole of 1 Corinthians 7:10–11 is Paul's paraphrase of Jesus' authoritative teaching.

Fitzmyer quotes another prominent Catholic exegete, Jerome Murphy-O'Connor, to the effect that 1 Corinthians 7:10–11 is not a binding precept of Jesus but, for Paul, merely a directive meeting the needs of a specific pastoral situation. In response, Fitzmyer firmly rejects such a view: "That v. 10c is an afterthought and not a binding precept is highly speculative and ultimately to be rejected."[103] For Fitzmyer, it is clear that on the authority of Jesus Christ, Paul considers himself to be asserting "a general prohibition of another marriage after divorce".[104]

At the same time, Fitzmyer denies that this is the same position as the Catholic Church's, because Fitzmyer does not think that Paul knows of a distinction between "separation" and "divorce". Fitzmyer points out that the word translated as "separate" in 1 Corinthians 7:10 (RSV) means the same thing as "divorce". He concludes, "The whole point in vv. 10–11 is that Christians must not divorce."[105] The Catholic Church has traditionally accepted divorce understood as separation, whereas in Fitzmyer's view, Paul means to say that the Lord utterly rejects divorce of any kind.

According to Fitzmyer, however, Paul in verse 15 goes ahead and changes Jesus' own command. Fitzmyer sees this as a parallel to the exception clause of Matthew 5:32 and 19:9, which he assumes should be read as allowing for divorce and remarriage in the case of adultery. Fitzmyer expresses himself along the very same lines that we found in the later document of the Joint Committee:

> If Matthew under inspiration could have been moved to add an exceptive phrase to the saying of Jesus about divorce that he found in an absolute form in either his Marcan source or in "Q," or if Paul likewise under inspiration could introduce into this writings an exception on his own authority, then why cannot the Spirit-guided institutional

---

[103] Ibid., 291. See Jerome Murphy-O'Connor, "The Divorced Woman in 1 Cor 7:10–11", *Journal of Biblical Literature* 100 (1981): 606.

[104] Fitzmyer, *First Corinthians*, 294.

[105] Ibid., 295.

church of a later generation make a similar exception in view of problems confronting Christian married life of its day or so-called broken marriages (not really envisaged in the NT)—as it has done in some situations?[106]

In fact, as shown by Luz and Bockmuehl, Matthew's "exceptive phrase" is almost surely not exceptive. In 1 Corinthians 7:12 and 15, furthermore, Paul is speaking of the marriage of a Christian and an unbeliever. He clearly does not think that such marriages, contracted under Roman marriage law (for which marriage was fully dissoluble), carry the status of indissolubility. Fitzmyer recognizes that in such cases "a married Christian person is freed from the marital bond, not by divorce (vv. 10–11), not by adultery, but by desertion of the unbelieving spouse."[107]

Fitzmyer briefly comments on the Catholic Church's later development of the "Pauline privilege", which he considers to go "beyond the limits of the case envisaged by Paul".[108] It seems to me that the case for the Pauline privilege is much more plausible than Fitzmyer grants, because Paul differentiates between Christian marriage and the marriage of unbelievers, that is, Roman or Jewish understandings of marriage. But the key point for my purposes is that there is no need to read 1 Corinthians 7:12–15 as though Paul were contradicting the Lord's command (right after Paul himself described that command as binding). As the Catholic biblical scholar George Montague says, Paul holds that "for Christian couples the word of the Lord is authoritative: Neither husband nor wife may initiate divorce, for divorce itself [in the sense that dissolves the marital bond and therefore permits remarriage] is forbidden."[109]

Two final examples from historical-critical biblical scholarship may be helpful. In *The Gospel According to Saint Mark*, Morna Hooker proposes with regard to Mark 10:9: "In affirming the principle set out at the creation, Jesus is perhaps proclaiming that the time for the

---

[106] Joseph A. Fitzmyer, S.J., *To Advance the Gospel: New Testament Studies* (New York: Paulist Press, 1981), 100; quoted in Fitzmyer, *First Corinthians*, 298.

[107] Fitzmyer, *First Corinthians*, 301.

[108] Ibid., 302–3.

[109] George T. Montague, S.M., *First Corinthians* (Grand Rapids, MI: Baker Academic, 2011), 117–18.

eschatological ideal (or new creation) has arrived."[110] She emphasizes that "the teaching in Mark is seen as directed to disciples, and
in 1 Corinthians Paul is addressing the Christian community: there
is no question at this stage of applying them to others who are not
committed to Christian discipleship."[111] In her view, this focus on
the community of the inaugurated eschatological kingdom is what
makes the words understandable and acceptable. As an eschatological
prophet, Jesus wished to set his hearers "an eschatological challenge
which calls for perfection" and thereby "to shock men out of com-
placency".[112] But she concludes that whatever Jesus intended, the fact
is that "hardness of heart" (Mk 10:5) continues among Christians,
and therefore, as in the Torah, the permission of divorce must continue. In her view, Jesus' inauguration of the kingdom and sending
of his Spirit are insufficient to enable his followers to live in accord
with his eschatological announcement.[113] This strikes me as unduly

---

[110] Morna D. Hooker, *The Gospel According to Saint Mark* (London: A. & C. Black, 1991),
236.

[111] Ibid., 237.

[112] Ibid.

[113] For another example, noteworthy for its taking book-length form, see the reconstruc-
tion offered by the Catholic exegete Raymond F. Collins in his *Divorce in the New Testament*.
Collins asks such questions as "What might have been the *situation in Jesus' life* which war-
ranted such a prophetic statement [as Matthew 5:31–32]? Or is the utterance merely a literary
creation of Matthew, the evangelist?" (ibid., 170). Collins argues on narrative grounds that
"focusing on 'the exception' treats the logion of Matt 5:32 as if it were really a law, which it
is not. It may have the form, but it does not have the force of law" (ibid., 169–70). He attributes Matthew 5:32 to "the Q-source", which in his view was "based on Aramaic traditions"
and "was written in Greek, sometime before 60 A.D." (ibid., 173). In his view, the original
Q-form of the verse read "anyone who divorces his wife involves her in adultery, and whoever marries a divorced woman commits adultery" (ibid., 183). He briefly reviews the various
exegetical opinions from the Fathers onward, remarking upon the near-unanimity of the
Fathers and the retrieval of their view in the works of Jacques Dupont and Wenham, as well
as Joseph Bonsirven's 1948 proposal (influential especially upon the preconciliar generation of
Catholic scholars) that "the term *porneia* was used in the New Testament to indicate marriages
that were contracted in violation of the prescriptions in Leviticus 18 relating to the degrees
of kinship within which marriage was not permitted" (ibid., 202; see Joseph Bonsirven's *Le
divorce dans le Nouveau Testament* [Paris: Desclée, 1948]). In Collins' view, the exception clause
"may well allow remarriage", but "the appendage of the eunuch saying to the Matthean version of the discussion with the Pharisees would seem to reinforce the idea that divorce with
remarriage—apart from that limited case to which the *porneia*-clause referred—was excluded
for Christians of Matthew's community by the time of the redaction of his gospel" (Collins,
Divorce in the New Testament, 230).

pessimistic about the life of grace, and also forgetful of Jesus' command that we follow him by carrying our crosses.

Somewhat similarly, the Catholic biblical scholar Anne-Marie Pelletier has argued that Jesus' appeal to the origins of marriage cannot be a reference to anything that actually had historical existence: "We know clearly today that the origin is by nature an inaccessible reality."[114] For Pelletier, therefore, when Jesus answers the Pharisees by appeal to the will of "he who made them from the beginning" (Mt 19:4), his appeal to "the beginning" (or to Genesis 1–2) can only be referring to a "root anterior to time", not to a temporal beginning.[115] The same is true for Ephesians 5:31's appeal to Genesis 2:24 ("they become one flesh"). Pelletier concludes that "to argue today in terms of a 'primitive marriage' between Adam and Eve is to posit as the foundation of theological reflection what can only appear as a historical phantasm, with the risk of accrediting a simplistic and unrealizable vision of marriage."[116] Pelletier thereby sets to the side Jesus' teaching about marriage, on the grounds that he was not historically sophisticated. She adds that we do not need to follow Jesus' strict command about marriage, because Scripture shows that God works out his covenantal will not through ideal marriages but through "highly contestable paths of conjugality", such as polygamy.[117] Pelletier's solution amounts to perceiving Jesus as a misguided sage whose strict teaching on marriage should be rejected in favor of modern marital practices.

---

[114] Anne-Marie Pelletier, "Réponse d'Anne-Marie Pelletier [II]", in *"La vocation et la mission de la famille dans l'Église et dans le monde contemporain"*: *26 théologiens répondent* (Paris: Bayard, 2015), 72. Pelletier, the 2014 winner of the Ratzinger Prize, is responding to the following questions: "Si l'histoire est le lieu théologique de la Révélation, doit-on 'retrouver le projet original de Dieu'? Peut-on parler du 'mariage primordial' entre Adam et Ève? Le mariage est-il paradis perdu ou vocation?" (If history is the theological place of Revelation, ought one "to recover the original project of God"? Can one speak of the "primordial marriage" between Adam and Eve? Is marriage a lost paradise or a vocation?) The internal quotations in these rather leading questions come from the 2014 *Relatio Synodi*, nos. 14–15.

[115] Pelletier, "Réponse d'Anne-Marie Pelletier [II]", 73.

[116] Ibid., 74.

[117] Anne-Marie Pelletier, "Réponse d'Anne-Marie Pelletier [I]", in *"La vocation et la mission de la famille dans l'Église et dans le monde contemporain"*, 58. Here Pelletier is responding to the following question (again a strikingly leading question): "L'enseignement de l'Église sur la famille et le mariage honorent-ils la richesse et la complexité de la parole de Dieu?" (Does the teaching of the Church about the family and about marriage honor the richness and complexity of the word of God?)

It is clear that Jesus Christ intended for his followers to uphold absolute marital indissolubility. The only way to get around this is to argue that he intended for his followers to reject his teaching in their concrete practice, or to argue that he was either proclaiming an eschatological ideal (impossible for his followers to observe) or invoking an idealized past that never existed. The former argument is unpersuasive exegetically, while the latter is unpersuasive theologically. As the Creator and Lord, Jesus taught that marriage must be absolutely indissoluble among his followers, because this is the true path of human flourishing in families; and he makes this possible through the grace of his Spirit, which also enables believers in difficult or broken marriages to live their vocation.

In sum: Given Jesus' authoritative teaching and Paul's confirmation of the Lord's teaching, and given the strong patristic witness, it is no wonder that the Council of Trent and Vatican II, as well as many popes, have solemnly affirmed the doctrine of marital indissolubility. To explore this further, let me turn to the teaching of the Catholic Magisterium, beginning with the Council of Trent.

Chapter 2

Marital Indissolubility from Trent through Pope Benedict XVI

For Catholic theologians, in order to understand the authoritative scriptural teaching, attention to the living apostolic tradition of the Church is needed. We need to understand how Jesus' and Paul's words have been (in the words of Gerhard Cardinal Müller) "expounded in the Church's Tradition and interpreted by the Magisterium in a binding way".[1] Admittedly, influenced by the prevailing culture, Catholic clergy and laity today often conceive of marriage in a manner that lacks essential elements such as indissolubility and openness to children.[2] On this basis, Cardinal Müller reasons that

---

[1] Gerhard Ludwig Cardinal Müller, "Testimony to the Power of Grace: On the Indissolubility of Marriage and the Debate concerning the Civilly Remarried and the Sacraments", in *Remaining in the Truth of Christ: Marriage and Communion in the Catholic Church*, ed. Robert Dodaro, O.S.A. (San Francisco: Ignatius Press, 2014), 149. See also the cognate point of Robert Cardinal Sarah: "Very often young people influenced by secularism no longer know at all what conjugal life is. For them, human love is disconnected from ideas of commitment, fidelity, and even more so from indissolubility and fertility.... In order for the natural reality of love to open the hearts of the engaged couple to faith, hope, and charity, a *sanatio*, a healing of their view and their practice of human love is necessary" (Robert Cardinal Sarah, "Marriage Preparation in a Secularized World", in *Eleven Cardinals Speak on Marriage and the Family: Essays from a Pastoral Viewpoint*, ed. Winfried Aymans, trans. Michael J. Miller et al. [San Francisco: Ignatius Press, 2015], 90).

[2] With regard to openness to children, the Eastern Orthodox thinker Alexander F. C. Webster points out that when a Christian couple refuses "even to allow the possibility of having children", then their wedding cannot be celebrated in an Orthodox marriage liturgy; see Alexander F. C. Webster, "Icons of the 'Nuclear' Family", in *Glory and Honor: Orthodox Christian Resources on Marriage*, ed. David C. Ford, Mary S. Ford, and Alfred Kentigern Siewers (Yonkers, NY: St. Vladimir's Seminary Press, 2016), 175. See also John Meyendorff, *Marriage: An Orthodox Perspective*, 3rd rev. ed. (Yonkers, NY: St. Vladimir's Seminary Press, 1975), 59: "There can be no Christian marriage without an immediate and impatient desire of both parents to receive and share this joy [of children]."

"marriages nowadays are probably invalid more often than they were previously, because there is a lack of desire for marriage in accordance with Catholic teaching."[3] In cases of an invalid marriage, of course, annulment is appropriate, and so its growing frequency would make sense.[4] The fundamental issue, however, is more complicated. Namely, if many Catholics today no longer understand marriage as indissoluble, then this situation inevitably leads to questions about the truth of the Church's *doctrine* of marital indissolubility, questions that arise frequently in pastoral practice.

Thus, it is necessary to investigate the Catholic Church's teaching about the indissolubility of marriage. Has the Church solemnly defined the meaning of the apostolic deposit of faith with respect to the nature of marriage, grounded in the explicit teaching of the Lord Jesus? As we will see, the most notable magisterial landmark in this regard remains the Council of Trent, but the solemn teachings of

---

[3] Müller, "Testimony to the Power of Grace", 157.

[4] There are numerous possible grounds for annulment. Citing *The Order of Celebrating Matrimony* (Washington, D.C.: Catholic University of America Press, 2014), the *Catechism of the Catholic Church*, 2nd ed. (Vatican City: Libreria Editrice Vaticana, 1997), and the *Code of Canon Law: Latin-English Edition*, New English Tradition (*Codex Iuris Canonici [CIC]*) (Washington, D.C.: Canon Law Society of America, 1998), Perry J. Cahall explains that for a marriage to be valid (and thus indissoluble), the couple must give a free and wholehearted consent, must have no natural or ecclesiastical impediments to marriage, must "evidence the commitment to permanently bind themselves to each other", and must be willing "to 'accept children lovingly from God,/ and to bring them up/ according to the law of Christ and his Church' (OCM, 60)" (Perry J. Cahall, *The Mystery of Marriage: A Theology of the Body and the Sacrament* [Chicago: Hillenbrand Books, 2016], 303). Cahall adds further explanation of grounds for annulment: "First, potential spouses must have the capacity to exhange consent freely and unconditionally, otherwise there is a defect of form. This means that both potential spouses must be mentally and psychologically capable of understanding the commitment of marriage and what it entails (CIC, c. 1095 1°, 2°, 3°). Free consent also implies that one cannot be in serious error regarding the person one is marrying (CIC, c. 1097 §1) and that there can be no deceit or fraud that would have affected a spouse's consent to the union (CIC, c. 1098). In addition, exchanging free consent means that the consent is unconditional, free from some future condition being placed upon the marriage, such as a prenuptial agreement (CIC, c. 1102 §1). Next, for a couple to exchange consent validly, free of defect, they must consent to do what the Church does in the celebration of the sacrament. 'If, however, either or both of the parties by a positive act of the will exclude marriage itself, some essential act of marriage, or some essential property of marriage, the party contracts invalidly' (CIC, c. 1101, §2). To validly exchange consent and administer the Sacrament of Marriage, which is an ecclesial act, baptized Catholics must also follow the proper celebration of the sacrament, or liturgical form, as it is specified by the Church (CIC, c. 1108, 1118, 1119)" (ibid., 307).

later popes and of the Second Vatican Council also have confirmed and clarified what Christ wills for the Sacrament of Matrimony.

The Council of Trent and Marital Indissolubility

The Council of Trent offers a number of teachings on marriage in its authoritative doctrinal canons, in response to concerns raised by the Reformers and discussed above in my first chapter. In *The Indissolubility of Marriage and the Council of Trent*, the theologian Christian Brugger sets the scene: "On November 11, 1563, at the start of session 24, Trent published twelve canons on marriage preceded by a doctrinal introduction. The canons were published as solemn anathemas."[5] In its doctrinal introduction to the canons, Trent quotes Matthew 19 and Ephesians 5 in favor of the "lasting nature" and "unbreakable unity" of the marriage bond according to the will of Jesus Christ.[6] With Matthew 19:5 in view, the doctrinal introduction to the canons defines the nature of marriage as follows: "Inspired by the Holy Spirit, the forefather of the human race pronounced marriage to be a perpetual and indissoluble bond when he said: *This at least is bone of my bone and flesh of my flesh.... Therefore a man will leave his father and mother and cleave to his wife, and the two will become one flesh.*"[7] In the same place, the doctrinal introduction quotes the words of Jesus, who confirms "the lasting nature of the same bond" by teaching that "they are no longer two but one. What therefore God has joined together, let no man put asunder" (Mt 19:6).[8] With regard to the Christian

---

[5] E. Christian Brugger, *The Indissolubility of Marriage and the Council of Trent* (Washington, D.C.: Catholic University of America Press, 2017), 7. For the diversity of views among sixteenth-century theologians with regard to marriage's indissolubility, prior to the promulgation of these canons, see Luigi Bressan, *Il Canone Tridentino sul Divorzio per Adulterio e L'interpretazione degli Autori* (Rome Università Gregoriana Editrice, 1973). Notably, Thomas Cardinal de Vio Cajetan agreed with Erasmus' position; see Michael O'Connor, *Cajetan's Biblical Commentaries: Motive and Method* (Leiden: Brill, 2017), 212–16, and André-François von Gunten, "La doctrine de Cajétan sur l'indissolubilité du mariage", *Angelicum* 43 (1966): 62–72.

[6] Council of Trent, Session 24 (Nov 11, 1563), "Teaching on the Sacrament of Marriage", in *Decrees of the Ecumenical Councils*, vol. 2, *Trent to Vatican II*, ed. Norman P. Tanner, S.J. (Washington, D.C.: Georgetown University Press, 1990), 753–54.

[7] Ibid., 753; emphasis in original.

[8] Ibid., 754.

Sacrament of Matrimony, the doctrinal introduction observes that by the grace flowing through the sacrament, Christ wills to "strengthen the unbreakable unity and sanctify the spouses".[9]

In light of the doctrinal introduction, Canon 5 states that "if anyone says that the bond of marriage can be dissolved by a spouse on the grounds of heresy, or irksome cohabitation, or continued absence: let him be anathema."[10] Building upon Canon 5, Canon 7 teaches:

> If anyone says that the church erroneously taught and teaches, according to the evangelical and apostolic doctrine, that the bond of marriage cannot be dissolved by the adultery of one of the spouses; and that neither party, even the innocent one who gave no grounds for the adultery, can contract another marriage while their spouse is still living; and that the husband commits adultery who dismisses an adulterous wife and takes another woman, as does the wife dismissing an adulterous husband and marrying another man: let him be anathema.[11]

In these canons, while affirming the possibility of annulment due to impediments at the time of the contracting of the marriage— impediments that are named and discussed at length in its "Canons on the Reform of Marriage"[12]—Trent rejects the possibility of divorce in the sense of the dissolution of a validly contracted and consummated sacramental marriage. Canon 8 indicates what legal separation or divorce may *licitly* involve: "If anyone says the church is in error in deciding that for a variety of reasons a separation between spouses from bed or from cohabitation may take place for a stated or an indefinite time: let him be anathema."[13]

---

[9] Ibid.

[10] Canon 5, in *Decrees of the Ecumenical Councils*, 2:754. Brugger comments, "A century before the Council began, Greek canon law had already noted more than fifteen legitimating causes for divorce. Those Council fathers who were more familiar with the beliefs of the Greeks would have known that apostasy, enmity between spouses, and prolonged absence were among those 'exceptions.' When, in November 1563, the Council published canon 5 ... addressing the dissolution of marriages in cases of heresy, enmity between spouses, and the willful desertion of a spouse, the canon condemned *anyone*, not just Calvin or Protestants, who held the errors. The *ritus* of the Greeks was clearly not spared under this formulation" (*Indissolubility of Marriage and the Council of Trent*, 46–47).

[11] Canon 7, in *Decrees of the Ecumenical Councils*, 2:754–55.

[12] See "Canons on the Reform of Marriage", in *Decrees of the Ecumenical Councils*, 2:755–59.

[13] Canon 8, in *Decrees of the Ecumenical Councils*, 2:755.

To understand the final form of these canons, it needs to be recognized that during the sixteeenth century, the Catholic Republic of Venice exercised rule over the Christian populations on certain islands in the Mediterranean (e.g., Crete, Cyprus, Corfu), where a majority of the inhabitants were Greek (Orthodox) Christians. The Venetian government permitted the Greeks to celebrate their own liturgies and exercise limited self-rule under Greek bishops in exchange for the Greek Christians' periodic acknowledgment of the authority of Rome and loose submission to Rome-appointed bishops. Late into the council's discussion of indissolubility, a delegation of diplomats from the Republic of Venice requested that the language of Canon 7 cause as little consternation to these Greek Christians as possible. In response, the Council Fathers changed the formulation of Canon 7 from directly condemning anyone who denies marital indissolubility in cases of adultery, to directly condemning anyone who says that the Church erroneously teaches that marriage is indissoluble in cases of adultery. Since the Greek Orthodox Christians in question had no interest in publicizing their long-standing practice of divorce or in speaking against the Catholic Church for its stricter position, the new formulation spared them direct condemnation.

The conciliar discussions preserved in the Vatican archives demonstrate that the Council Fathers' willingness to spare the feelings of the Greeks in no way implied a lack of resolve to teach the absolute indissolubility of marriage solemnly. Their strategy was to reject the position of the Greeks without directly condemning their persons. Trent condemns anyone who says that the Church errs when she teaches the following three propositions: (1) that the bond of marriage cannot be dissolved in cases of adultery, (2) that second marriages cannot be contracted, and (3) that spouses who thus attempt remarriage commit adultery. In defining that the Church does not err in asserting these propositions, the council was teaching that the Church is certainly correct in teaching them (i.e., that the propositions asserted are true). The effect of the reformulation is the same: to define the indissolubility of marriage in cases of adultery. Therefore, Brugger concludes, "Because of the logical relationship between the canons and the doctrinal introduction, the definitive teaching that the church is not in error in its teaching on adultery logically entails that the church is not in error in teaching that consummated sacramental marriages are absolutely indissoluble."[14]

The argument of Piet Fransen, Walter Kasper, Victor Pospishil, and others is that Trent aimed to condemn certain Protestant errors without settling "the question of the status of the doctrine of indissolubility in Catholic teaching" vis-à-vis the position of the Orthodox.[15] In 1978, the International Theological Commission similarly argued that Canon 7 does not aim at "solemnly defining marriage's indissolubility as a truth of faith".[16] The mid-twentieth-century work of Fransen provided a key impetus for this line of thinking. He maintained that in its canons on marriage, Trent intended narrowly to condemn Luther's opinion that the Church exceeds her competence whenever she exercises her authority over Christian marriages, a charge Luther indeed made in his early work, *On the Babylonian Captivity of the Church* (1520).[17] On this view, what really occupied the minds of the Council Fathers was Luther's denial of

---

[14] Brugger, *Indissolubility of Marriage and the Council of Trent*, 145. The doctrinal introduction to the canons teaches the "unbreakable unity [*indissolubilem unitatem*]" of a sacramental marriage. In the same vein, see Andreas Wollbold, *Pastoral mit widerverheirateten Geschiedenen: Gordischer Knoten oder ungeahnte Möglichkeiten?* (Regensburg: Pustet, 2015), 107–18. Wollbold shows that Jesus intends his teaching on marriage as a "genuine command [echtes Gebot] and not merely as a so-called ideal [Zielgebot]" (ibid., 44).

[15] Brugger, *Indissolubility of Marriage and the Council of Trent*, 13. See Victor J. Pospishil, *Divorce and Remarriage* (New York: Herder and Herder, 1967); Walter Kasper, *Theology of Christian Marriage*, trans. David Smith (New York: Seabury Press, 1980); Piet F. Fransen, S.J., *Hermeneutics of the Councils and Other Studies*, ed. H.E. Mertens and F. de Graeve (Leuven: Leuven University Press, 1985), chaps. 1–7; Piet F. Fransen, S.J., "Divorce on the Ground of Adultery—The Council of Trent (1563)", in *The Future of Marriage as an Institution*, ed. Franz Böckle (New York: Herder and Herder, 1970), 89–100; Karl Lehmann, *Gegenwart des Glaubens* (Mainz: Matthias-Grünewald-Verlag, 1974); Francis A. Sullivan, S.J., *Creative Fidelity: Weighing and Interpreting Documents of the Magisterium* (New York: Paulist Press, 1996), 131–34. Brugger also treats earlier advocates of the same thesis, beginning with Paolo Sarpi's antipapal *Istoria del Concilio Tridentino* (London: 1619) and including Johannes Launoy's *Regia in Matrimonium Potestas* (Paris: Edmundi Martini, 1674), vol. 1, pt. 2, and Pierre François Le Courayer, *Histoire du Concile de Trente* (Amsterdam: 1750), vol. 3, as well as various nineteenth-century examples.

[16] International Theological Commission, "Propositions on the Doctrine of Christian Marriage", *Origins* 8 (1978): 238. See also Gustave Martelet, S.J., "Christological Theses on the Sacrament of Marriage", *Origins* 8 (September 4, 1978): 200–204. Martelet significantly influenced the International Theological Commission's document.

[17] See Martin Luther, *On the Babylonian Captivity of the Church*, in *Luther's Works*, vol. 36, Word and Sacrament II, ed. Helmut T. Lehmann and Abdel R. Wentz (Philadelphia: Fortress Press, 1959), 105–6; Fransen, "Divorce on the Ground of Adultery", 92.

Roman authority, not the question of the substantive nature of the marriage bond.

In his *Theology of Christian Marriage*, Kasper accepts that "the Council of Trent taught unambiguously the indissolubility of marriage", but he denies that Trent intended "to provide an all-embracing doctrine of the indissolubility of marriage".[18] For this reason, Kasper contends that it is possible for the Catholic Church to continue fully to affirm marital indissolubility, in accord with Trent's definitive teaching against the Reformers, while at the same time opening Eucharistic Communion to repentant divorced and civilly remarried Catholics. Writing in 1977, Kasper accepts that the Church "cannot simply pay lip-service to its confession of the indissolubility of marriage and undermine it in practice"; but he adds that nonetheless "whenever faith is present in the second, civilly contracted marriage, and is expressed in love and made effective in penance for the guilt incurred by the breaking of the first marriage, then the second marriage also participates in the spiritual life of the Church."[19] Kasper fully affirms, as he continues to do today, "the lasting reality of the first marriage and therefore the continued existence of the Christian bond of marriage".[20] But he holds that Trent allows for the solution of the Orthodox, which he construes to be a combination of insistence upon the indissolubility of marriage with a merciful allowance for repentant divorced and (civilly) remarried persons, "in cases where people are prepared for conversion and reconciliation and do what is humanly possible in their situation", to return to Eucharistic Communion.[21]

---

[18] Kasper, *Theology of Christian Marriage*, 62.

[19] Ibid., 64, 67.

[20] Ibid., 68. Going beyond this position, the Joint Committee of Orthodox and Catholic Bishops argues, "While it is true that the Roman Catholic Church does not grant dissolution of the bond of a consummated sacramental marriage, it remains a question among theologians whether this is founded on a prudential judgment or on the Church's perception that it lacks the power to dissolve such a bond" ("A Pastoral Statement on Orthodox/Roman Catholic Marriages", October 5, 1990, http://www.usccb.org/beliefs-and-teachings/ecumenical-and -interreligious/ecumenical/orthodox/pastoral-orthodox-catholic-marriage.cfm). I hold that the teachings of Trent and the consistent teachings of multiple popes, in a solemn fashion and rooted in the words of Jesus (and Paul), make clear that the answer must be "the Church's perception that it lacks the power to dissolve such a bond".

[21] Kasper, *Theology of Christian Marriage*, 68.

Brugger shows appreciation for the determination of the Council Fathers not to wound the "fragile relations between Greek and Latin Christians living in Venetian territories".[22] But his research demonstrates that, as a matter of historical fact, Trent's solution never intended to exempt "the divorce practices of the Greeks" from the authoritative teaching of the canons.[23] As he remarks, "*When discussing indissolubility*, the Council, from its first considerations in 1547 to its final discussions in Fall 1563, expresses almost no interest at all in Luther's denial of Roman authority and great and sustained interest in the nature of the marriage bond and implications of that nature for the questions of marital dissolubility, divorce, and remarriage."[24]

---

[22] Brugger, *Indissolubility of Marriage and the Council of Trent*, 140.

[23] Ibid., 34. Brugger's additional remarks regarding the Council of Florence are worth quoting: "The Council fathers did know of the negotiations for reunion between the Roman Church and Armenian Orthodox Christians at the Council of Florence (1439). And they knew that the Council's *Bulla unionis Armenorum* (Decree of Union with the Armenians) taught that the bond of a Christian marriage is absolutely indissoluble. It is true that there was no anathema to back up that teaching. But 'this was no wonder,' as the bishop of Corosopitanus stated at Trent, since Florence did not use anathemas. So we cannot infer from the absence of an anathema at Florence that the Council fathers (at Florence) were opposed to a formal definition of the doctrine. Greeks and Latins were equally represented at Florence seeking ecclesial union in the face of increasing threats from the Turks. Mackin argues that because the Council did not address the issue of divorce and remarriage in its negotiations for union with the Greeks, this suggests both Latins and Greeks 'were quietly willing to allow the other to its position.' Mackin's vague statement should not be taken to mean that Florence judged the Greek practice to be acceptable. Joyce recounts how after the union was effected, Pope Eugenius IV 'summoned the Greek bishops, who were still in the city and informed them that divorce was one of the points in Greek practice which must be corrected.' This makes evident that the pope believed the practice was wrongful. The fact that Florence did not require conformity with the Roman position as a condition for reunion should be taken to mean no more than that the church of Rome was willing to tolerate a practice it believed to be contrary to the teaching of divine revelation in order to realize what unity was possible with the Greeks in hopes that through it a more perfect communion with the Greeks might later be realized" (ibid., 36–37). See Theodore Mackin, S.J., *Divorce and Remarriage* (New York: Paulist Press, 1984), 376, and George Hayward Joyce, S.J., *Christian Marriage: An Historical and Doctrinal Study* (London: Sheed and Ward, 1933), 387.

[24] Brugger, *Indissolubility of Marriage and the Council of Trent*, 33; emphasis in original. Brugger adds the point that "by the middle of the 1530s, Luther had already defended multiple times divorce and remarriage in the case of adultery. He believed his conclusion was consistent with Christ's teaching in the Gospel of Matthew. Attempting to maintain some continuity with the ancient Christian view that only death dissolves a marriage, he drew an analogy between adultery (as well as spousal conflict and denial of conjugal right) and death, concluding that in God's eyes adultery (etc.) was a kind of death; and just as bodily death dissolves a marriage, so too the spiritual death caused by adultery (etc.) dissolves a marriage.

As a truth of faith pertaining to the nature of the marriage bond and not merely aimed at condemning the Reformers' denial of Roman authority over Christian marriages, Trent intended to teach that a valid and consummated marriage of two Christians is absolutely indissoluble and therefore that no additional marriage is possible while both spouses are alive, on pain of the sin of adultery. As the theologian Andreas Wollbold concludes his own brief but expert treatment of this topic, Trent's teaching on divorce and remarriage "represents a watershed, behind which the Catholic Church can no longer go back" without supposing that the dogmatic teachings of a council, solemnly interpreting the words of Christ, have erred.[25]

From Pope Clement VII through Pope Benedict XVI

In 1595, Pope Clement VIII firmly condemned divorce, with the Eastern practice in view, as did Pope Urban VIII (1623–1644) and Pope Benedict XIV (1740–1758). In 1803, Pope Pius VII warned the German bishops against celebrating second (civil) marriages— indicating that pressures bubbling up today in Germany were felt then too.[26] In 1880, Pope Leo XIII published an encyclical on Christian marriage, *Arcanum Divinae*.

In this encyclical, Leo XIII observes first that Jesus abolished the permission for divorce given to the people of Israel, and renewed God's original intention (in creation) for marriage, "by commanding most strictly that no one should dare to dissolve that union which

---

Consequently, the innocent party at least ... should be free to remarry. In addition to Luther's arguments, we see that Calvin published denials of the Catholic doctrine of indissolubility between 1536 and 1561, and we know these were evident to the Council fathers by their final discussions on marriage in summer 1563. To suggest that the only clear threat from Luther's teaching against Catholic doctrine known at Trent was his denial of church authority over Christian marriage is erroneous" (ibid., 32).

[25] Wollbold, *Pastoral mit wiederverheirateten Geschiedenen*, 118; cf. 243. Notably, John W. O'Malley, S.J., does not contest this point in his *Trent: What Happened at the Council* (Cambridge, MA: Harvard University Press, 2013). His discussion of Trent's teachings on marriage focuses instead on the reversal of the Church's position on clandestine marriages in Trent's decree *Tametsi*; see *Trent*, 223–28.

[26] See John Corbett, O.P., et al., "Recent Proposals for the Pastoral Care of the Divorced and Remarried: A Theological Assessment", *Nova et Vetera* 12, no. 3 (2014): 606–7.

God had sanctioned by a bond perpetual".[27] Citing Ephesians 5 and
1 Corinthians 7:10–11, 39, Pope Leo adds that "from the teaching
of the apostles we learn that the unity of marriage and its perpetual
indissolubility" must "be holy and inviolable without exception".[28]
He also responds to the view according to which the state has authority over the marriage contract and the Church over the sacrament.
His point is that in Christian marriage, the two (contract and sacrament) are intrinsically joined, rather than the sacrament being an
extrinsic addition. He notes that especially where marriage is not
viewed as being sealed by God, it easily happens that "the mutual
services and duties of marriage seem almost unbearable; and thus very
many yearn for the loosening of the tie which they believe to be
woven by human law and of their own will, whenever incompatibility of temper, or quarrels, or the violation of the marriage vow, or
mutual consent, or other reasons induce them to think that it would
be well to be set free."[29]

Although he understands the reasons why some couples want to
divorce, Leo XIII points out that divorce causes a number of evils
that work sharply against human flourishing, not only for the couple
and for children, but also for society.[30] He concludes by reiterat-
ing the teaching of Trent and of earlier popes, in accord with Jesus'
commandment. Although the Church permits legal separation for
just cause, "no power can dissolve the bond of Christian marriage
whenever this has been ratified and consummated", and therefore,
"husbands and wives are guilty of a manifest crime who plan, for
whatever reason, to be united in a second marriage before the first
one has been ended by death."[31]

In his 1930 encyclical *Casti Connubii*, Pope Pius XI is responding
to the Anglican Communion's decision to permit contraception, a
decision that ensured that the Catholic Church would face increasing

[27] Pope Leo XIII, *Arcanum Divinae*, in *The Great Encyclical Letters of Pope Leo XIII* (Rockford, IL: TAN Books, 1995), 62. For recent discussion of this encyclical, see Anthony Esolen,
*Reclaiming Catholic Social Teaching: A Defense of the Church's True Teachings on Marriage, Family,
and the State* (Manchester, NH: Sophia Institute Press, 2014), 63–67.

[28] Pope Leo XIII, *Arcanum Divinae*, 63.

[29] Ibid., 73–74.

[30] He predicts that the liberalizing of divorce laws, even if at first the legislators put in place
restraints, will soon lead to widespread divorce.

[31] Pope Leo XIII, *Arcanum Divinae*, 80.

pressure to permit contraception. For my purposes here, however, what is notable is the terms with which he affirms the indissolubility of sacramental marriage and the impossibility of validly marrying again so long as one's sacramental marriage is in force. According to Pope Pius XI, not even the power of the Church "can ever affect for any cause whatsoever a Christian marriage which is valid and has been consummated, for as it is plain that here the marriage contract has its full completion, so, by the will of God, there is also the greatest firmness and indissolubility which may not be destroyed by any human authority."[32]

Vatican II's Pastoral Constitution on the Church and the Modern World, *Gaudium et Spes* (1965), highlights the "covenant, or irrevocable personal consent" that establishes a marriage.[33] It emphasizes that the stability of the bond derives not from the couple's own resources but from God, who seals the bond. Attending to the personal flourishing that arises from a holy marriage, *Gaudium et Spes* observes that in sacramental marriage, the supernatural charity of the husband and wife leads them "to a free and mutual self-giving shown in tender feelings and actions, and permeates the whole of their lives".[34] Such a love "is indissolubly faithful" and "is therefore far removed from all adultery and divorce".[35] *Gaudium et Spes* is aware, of course, that its description of marital love does not describe the existential situation of all married couples. But the point is that the "unbreakable covenant [*foederis indissolubilis*]" between the husband and wife will be served by the maturation of their interpersonal love through the grace of the sacrament.[36] The mutual

---

[32] Pope Pius XI, *Christian Marriage: Casti Connubii Encyclical Letter of Pius XI* (Boston: St. Paul Books & Media, n.d.), p. 19.

[33] *Gaudium et Spes*, no. 48, in *Decrees of the Ecumenical Councils*, 2:1100. For discussion of *Gaudium et Spes*'s teaching on marriage, see José Granados, *Una Sola Carne en un Solo Espíritu: Teología del Matrimonio* (Madrid: Ediciones Palabra, 2014), 33–57; Theodore Mackin, S.J., *What Is Marriage?* (New York: Paulist Press, 1982); and Nicholas J. Healy, Jr., "Christian Personalism and the Debate Over the Nature and Ends of Marriage", *Communio* 39 (2012): 186–200.

[34] *Gaudium et Spes*, no. 49, in *Decrees of the Ecumenical Councils*, 2:1102.

[35] Ibid.

[36] Ibid., no. 50, in *Decrees of the Ecumenical Councils*, 2:1103. Perry Cahall offers a helpful clarification in this regard: "It should be noted that it is possible for a married couple in a state of mortal sin to thwart the ability for Christ to enliven and empower their love with his grace. However, their state of sinfulness does not extinguish the Sacrament of Marriage, nor does it

self-giving of the spouses and the good of the children both "call for their union being indissoluble".[37]

Two further magisterial texts, each of which is an apostolic exhortation, deserve mention here: Pope John Paul II's 1981 *Familiaris Consortio* and Pope Benedict XVI's 2007 *Sacramentum Caritatis*. In *Familiaris Consortio*, Pope John Paul II begins with an emphasis on love and communion: the husband and wife "are called to grow continually in their communion through day-to-day fidelity to their marriage promise of total mutual self-giving".[38] He then turns to indissolubility, arguing that indissolubility is required by the couple's vow of "total mutual self-giving" and that it becomes possible in

---

extinguish the grace that Christ offers them. In fact, a couple can even get married in a state of mortal sin and administer the Sacrament of Marriage validly to each other, even though the grace of the sacrament will be rendered unfruitful in its effects upon them as individuals. The reason that a couple finding themselves in this situation can still validly administer the sacrament is that by virtue of the indelible character of their Baptism, they are united to each other by Christ *ex opere operato*. Thus, even though one or the other spouse may be in a state of serious sin, an indissoluble bond (*res et sacramentum*) is still forged between them that has a real effect on the life of the Church. Additionally, should the couple repent of their sin and receive Christ's healing in the Sacrament of Penance, the grace of the Sacrament of Marriage will 'revive' in them due to the abiding bond that was effected between them by Christ. Thus, even though through sin a couple can at any time in their married life render unfruitful this special share in Jesus' love, this love can be reenlivened throughout the course of the couple's life together" (Cahall, *Mystery of Marriage*, 314–15).

[37] *Gaudium et Spes*, no. 48, in *Decrees of the Ecumenical Councils*, 2:1101.

[38] *Apostolic Exhortation of John Paul II, The Role of the Christian Family in the Modern World* (Familiaris Consortio), Vatican trans. (Boston: St. Paul Books & Media, 1981), no. 19. For a reading of *Familiaris Consortio* in light of Pope Francis' *Amoris Laetitia*, seeking to demonstrate that *Amoris Laetitia* rightly corrects *Familiaris Consortio*, see E.-M. Faber and Martin M. Lintner, "Theologische Entwicklungen in *Amoris laetitia* hinsichtlich der Frage der geschiedenen Wiederverheirateten", in *Amoris laetitia—Wendepunkt für die Moraltheologie?* ed. S. Goertz and C. Witting (Freiburg: Herder, 2016), 279–320. For analysis of *Familiaris Consortio*, connecting it with Pope John Paul II's theology of the body, see Richard M. Hogan and John M. LeVoir, *Covenant of Love: Pope John Paul II on Sexuality, Marriage, and Family in the Modern World: With a Commentary on* Familiaris Consortio, 2nd ed. (San Francisco: Ignatius Press, 1992), 177–305. See also Pope John Paul II's *Letter to Families* (February 2, 1994). Commenting on paragraph 17 of the *Letter to Families*, Angelo Scola notes that Pope John Paul II "attributes a 'sovereign power' to the family founded on an indissoluble marriage. This sovereignty rests ultimately on the indissolubility of the marriage bond before God and men. Being *forever* belongs in fact to matrimonial consent. A 'yes' that is not forever would be hardly credible; it would not seem completely true. If the *consent* of the spouses includes a temporal limit (even as a hypothetical possibility), a *dissent* is inevitably introduced which eventually corrupts the very nature of the marriage" (Angelo Cardinal Scola, *The Nuptial Mystery*, trans. Michelle K. Borras [Grand Rapids, MI: Eerdmans, 2005], 155).

Christ, contrary to those who urge that indissoluble marriage is an often impossible ideal. As a sacrament, indissoluble marriage symbolizes the unbreakable love of Christ for the Church. Pope John Paul II states that "Christian couples are called to participate truly in the irrevocable indissolubility that binds Christ to the Church His bride", and that this participation is not only a commandment of Christ, but also a vocation for the married couple's growth (through trials) in love and communion.[39] John Paul II praises "those numerous couples who, though encountering no small difficulty, preserve and develop the value of indissolubility", and who thereby stand in the world as a sign of God's unbreakable love for mankind.[40]

Toward the end of *Familiaris Consortio*, Pope John Paul II gives particular attention to the situation of persons who have suffered "the often irreparable breakdown of valid marriages", and who are now enduring loneliness and sorrow.[41] He urges that such persons be given support and encouragement by the whole Christian community. He gives special recognition to the divorced spouse who is "well aware that the valid marriage bond is indissoluble" and who refuses to contract another union; such persons offer a powerful witness to "fidelity and Christian consistency".[42] As he says, however, "Daily experience unfortunately shows that people who have obtained a divorce usually intend to enter into a new union, obviously not with a Catholic religious ceremony."[43] In such cases, John Paul II first makes a pastoral distinction between the innocent party who has been abandoned and the spouse who has acted against the valid sacramental marriage. He also appreciates the motives for entering into a second union, including the need to have one's children cared for, as well as also in some cases the subjective certainty that the "previous and irreparably destroyed marriage had never been valid".[44] He urges that pastors not shun the divorced and remarried or make them feel cut off from the Church.

At the same time, he reaffirms the pastoral practice of "not admitting to Eucharistic Communion divorced persons who have

---

[39] Pope John Paul II, *Familiaris Consortio*, no. 20.
[40] Ibid.
[41] Ibid., no. 83.
[42] Ibid.
[43] Ibid., no. 84.
[44] Ibid.

remarried".[45] He gives two reasons for this practice. First and most importantly, "their state and condition of life objectively contradict that union of love between Christ and the Church which is signified and effected by the Eucharist."[46] Second, were they admitted to the Eucharistic Communion, "the faithful would be led into error and confusion regarding the Church's teaching about the indissolubility of marriage."[47] He adds that in order for divorced and remarried persons (whose original marriage has not been annulled) to partake in the Sacrament of Penance as a path of returning to Eucharistic Communion, the persons must be willing henceforth to live according to the obligations of the prior indissoluble marriage. As long as the original sacramental marriage exists, they must live continently, abstaining from sexual intercourse with their new partner.[48]

These teachings appear again in Pope Benedict XVI's *Sacramentum Caritatis*. Beginning with the point that the Eucharist is a nuptial mystery, celebrating the union of Christ and his Bride the Church, Benedict XVI observes that "the Eucharist inexhaustibly strengthens the indissoluble unity and love of every Christian marriage" and ensures that the marriage bond is "intrinsically linked to the eucharistic unity of Christ the Bridegroom and his Bride, the Church".[49] He then deepens this exposition of the Eucharist's relationship to marital indissolubility. Just as the Eucharist is an expression of Christ's unbreakable love for the Church, so is marriage. Even in the order of creation, God intended marriage to be indissoluble: one man united with one woman until parted by death. Now that Christ has come, the meaning of the Eucharist finds expression in the meaning of sacramental marriage, possessed of "that indissolubility to which all true love necessarily aspires".[50]

---

[45] Ibid.

[46] Ibid.

[47] Ibid.

[48] See also, for the same emphases, Pope John Paul II's Address to the Pontifical Council for the Family, January 24, 1997. For additional background, see Francis G. Morrisey, O.M.I., "Some Themes to Be Found in the Annual Addresses of Pope John Paul II to the Roman Rota", *Studia Canonica* 38 (2004): 301–28.

[49] *Post-Synodal Apostolic Exhortation of Benedict XVI, Sacrament of Charity* (Sacramentum Caritatis), Vatican trans. (Boston: Pauline Books & Media, 2007), no. 27.

[50] Ibid., no. 29.

However, says Pope Benedict, this truth runs up more and more frequently against "the painful situations experienced by some of the faithful who, having celebrated the sacrament of Matrimony, then divorced and remarried".[51] In accord with the Church's consistent practice—which he emphasizes is not a *mere* practice of the Church but one based upon Jesus' own words—he reaffirms that, assuming that there is an existing sacramental marriage that has not been annulled, the divorced and remarried cannot be admitted to the Sacrament of the Eucharist because "their state and their condition of life objectively contradict the loving union of Christ and the Church signified and made present in the Eucharist."[52]

Benedict XVI adds that pastors should encourage the participation of the divorced and remarried in the community in all possible ways, and, just as importantly, bishops should ensure that there are competent and easily accessible marriage tribunals to review any "doubts ... about the validity of the prior sacramental marriage".[53] He underlines that there is no true division between canonical matrimonial jurisprudence and pastoral care: canonical jurisprudence serves the truth about marriage in Christ, a truth that is deeply pastoral. If there has indeed been a prior, still binding valid and consummated marriage, but the

[51] Ibid. Pope Benedict directs attention here to *Familiaris Consortio*, as well as to the Congregation for the Doctrine of the Faith (CDF), "Letter to the Bishops of the Catholic Church concerning the Reception of Holy Communion by Divorced and Remarried Members of the Faithful (September 14, 1994)", *Acta Apostolicae Sedis* 86 (1994): 974–79. This letter was a response to the argument of bishops Walter Kasper, Oscar Saier, and Karl Lehmann that after sacramental Penance the divorced and remarried could return to full communion in the Eucharist (Die Bischöfe der Oberrheinischen Kirchenprovinz, "Zur seelsorgerlichen Begleitung von Menschen aus zerbrochenen Ehen, Geschiedenen und Wiederverheirateten Geschiedenen: Einführung, Hirtenwort und Grudsätze", http://www.weinzweb.de/Texte HJ/OberrhBischWdvgeschiedeneHirtenwort.pdf). See J. A. Schmeiser, "Reception of the Eucharist by Divorced and Remarried Catholics: Three German Bishops and the Congregation for the Doctrine of the Faith", *Liturgical Ministry* 5 (1996): 10–21. With regard to the CDF's letter, see also the ensuing canon-law debate between Patrick Travers and (advocating what in my view is the correct position) John J. Myers: Patrick Travers, "Reception of the Holy Eucharist by Catholics Attempting Remarriage after Divorce and the 1983 Code of Canon Law", *Jurist* 55 (1995): 187–217; John J. Myers, "Divorce, Remarriage, and Reception of the Holy Eucharist", *Studia Canonica* 57 (1997): 485–516; Patrick Travers, "Holy Communion and Catholics Who Have Attempted Remarriage after Divorce: A Revisitation", *Jurist* 57 (1997): 517–40.

[52] Pope Benedict XVI, *Sacramentum Caritatis*, no. 29.

[53] Ibid.

divorced and remarried couple cannot (for reasons such as the care of children) cease cohabiting, they should live "as brother and sister", and in so doing they will be welcomed back to the Eucharistic table.[54] Benedict XVI notes that given the seriousness of the marriage commitment, there also needs to be extensive marriage preparation prior to a celebration of a marriage, so that pastors can ascertain the couple's "convictions regarding the obligations required for the validity of the sacrament".[55] This will help to ensure that the couple is truly willing and able to live out the sacrament that they are about to receive.

Given this consistent teaching of the Catholic Church about what her divinely given Sacrament of Matrimony accomplishes for the couple—a teaching rooted in Jesus' own words and in the letters of Paul, as well as in the great majority of the Church Fathers, the solemn canons of the Council of Trent, the teaching of Vatican II, and the encyclicals and apostolic exhortations of numerous popes—it is no wonder that the historian Richard Rex can say: "If, however, the Catholic Church were indeed to abandon or reverse the almost total opposition to divorce that it has maintained across two millennia, then its claim to be the privileged vehicle of divine revelation on moral issues would be quite simply, shattered."[56] As a Reformation historian, Rex

---

[54] Ibid.

[55] Ibid.

[56] Richard Rex, "A Church in Doubt", *First Things* 282 (April 2018): 50. Rex's essay is a review of Ross Douthat's *To Change the Church: Pope Francis and the Future of Catholicism* (New York: Simon & Schuster, 2018). Charles E. Curran, a proponent of the reception of the sacraments by divorced and civilly remarried persons (whose sacramental marriage has not been annulled), grants that "there would be strong negative effects if the hierarchical magisterium were willing to admit that some of its teachings had been erroneous or that it had claimed too great a certitude for them. Many people would be deeply hurt. Think, for example, of those who struggled in their marriage to be faithful to the teachings that condemn artificial contraception or divorce and remarriage. Those people obviously suffered and endured many difficulties in order to be faithful to the Church's teaching. I am sure that a good number of Catholics would be very angry with the Church if it were to admit error in some of these significant, specific moral issues. Such a change might easily be the occasion for many leaving the Church. To admit that papal teaching has been wrong on a number of issues also raises grave problems about the credibility of papal teaching on other issues" (Charles E. Curran, *The Development of Moral Theology: Five Strands* [Washington, D.C.: Georgetown University Press, 2013], 279). Curran supposes that after the first shock, the admission "might help the credibility of the hierarchical magisterium in the long run since it would show that the teaching office tries to listen to the Holy Spirit wherever she speaks and is willing to adopt a teaching role that is more open and transparent" (ibid., 280). To my mind, however, it is clear that the Magisterium would not henceforth be able to teach credibly on marriage and sexuality, unless by "credibility" Curran means an ongoing admission that the Church cannot

recalls that Thomas More accepted martyrdom in defense of the truth of the Church's teaching on divorce and remarriage. The Church's teaching on marriage is unusual in the cultural history of marriage, where divorce and polygamy have always been commonplace.[57]

Rex puts his point in strong terms: "If, after all, marriage is not a divine union of male and female in one flesh, dissolved only by the inevitable dissolution of that flesh in death, then the Catholic Church has, in the name of Christ, needlessly tormented the consciences of untold numbers of the faithful for twenty centuries."[58]

---

be expected to know the truth about sacramental and moral matters. For Curran, the morality of divorce and remarriage (without annulment) and other hot-button issues does not rise to the level of "core aspects of Catholic faith" (ibid., 284), but it seems clear to me that indissoluble marriage does indeed rise to such a level. See also ibid., 230–31, on "classicism" versus "historical consciousness".

[57] See the observations regarding Henry VIII in D. L. D'Avray, *Papacy, Monarchy and Marriage, 860–1600* (Cambridge: Cambridge University Press, 2015), 1–2: "First, Henry could not just take Anne Boleyn as a secondary wife. In most non-Western cultures secondary wives, if not full polygamy, were perfectly normal before Westernisation. In Africa and the Islamic world polygamy remains normal. Second, Henry could not in the modern sense divorce his wife: his efforts were directed toward proving that he had never been truly married to Catherine. This is even more remarkable in a broad historical context. Classical Greece and Rome were atypical in being monogamous, but they did allow easy divorce, which made monogamy easier for the restless patriarchal male. Third, again by contrast with ancient Rome, the stakes were high in terms of succession to high office: it was normal for Roman emperors to ensure succession by adoption, while in the medieval and early modern world biological inheritance was the norm, so that marriage was politically crucial, especially since women could take land and political power from one family's control to another—something hard to find in other civilisations. Fourth, to solve his problem he had to go to a power outside his lands and try to play by alien rules—rules that he ended by repudiating. The system Henry ultimately rejected subjected the personal life of powerful patriarchal men to an independent religious government with its own law." See also the legal documents collected in D'Avray's *Dissolving Royal Marriages: A Documentary History, 860–1600* (Cambridge: Cambridge University Press, 2014). Against a cynical view of the Church's collaboration with royalty, D'Avray points out that "naturally kings wanted to hack into the software to affect the result, but the defences of the system from the thirteenth century were surprisingly effective. Kings had their own experts, of course, to help them get the desired result within the formal rules. On monogamy and indissolubility, however, the rules were resistant" (D'Avray, *Papacy, Monarchy and Marriage*, 4). D'Avray concludes, "In later medieval papal dealings with kings, the indissolubility principle was not subject to exceptions—except of the kind that proves the rule" (ibid., 238).

[58] Rex, "Church in Doubt", 50. Douthat makes the same basic point: "If God wills the suspension of his own law when things get particularly difficult or complicated, whenever too much emotional or physical suffering would be imposed, from the point of view of every Christian who ever suffered or even died for the sake of their hardest passages, the gospels look less like a revelation than a somewhat cruel trick. And just as it is difficult to maintain an ideological regime once you decide that the ideology has been misleading people on various essential points, the idea that Catholicism can thrive by embracing a theory that makes the

The Catholic Church that for twenty centuries proclaimed both the mercy of Christ and her own institution by Christ, including her ability to teach definitively on matters of faith and morals, would be revealed to have lacked mercy (or any sense of the faith[59]) precisely in the pastoral administration and doctrinal understanding of her own sacraments.[60] This would be a shattering situation indeed.

Is the Doctrine of Marital Indissolubility Dissoluble?

The Catholic theologians Kenneth Himes and James Coriden, however, have recently argued against marital indissolubility on the grounds that it belongs to a juridicist distortion of the Church and

---

gospels' moral vision at best incomplete, at worst actively cruel, and the church's historical interpretation a further cruelty needlessly imposed ... well, let us call that theory unduly optimistic" (Douthat, To Change the Church, 180).

[59] Carlos Caffarra notes—in accord with Vatican II's Lumen Gentium—that "the faithful [clergy and laity together] are gifted with the supernatural sensus fidei (sense of the faith), which does not consist solely or necessarily in the consensus of the faithful" (Carlos Cardinal Caffarra, "Sacramental Ontology and the Indissolubility of Marriage", in Dodaro, Remaining in the Truth of Christ, 169). For a different view, favoring the fluidity of marriage doctrine, see Peter Black and James F. Keenan, S.J., "The Evolving Self-Understanding of the Moral Theologian: 1900–2000", Studia Moralia 39 (2001): 319. See also William V. D'Antonio et al., "American Catholics and Church Authority", in The Crisis of Authority in Catholic Modernity, ed. Michael J. Lacey and Francis Oakley (Oxford: Oxford University Press, 2011), 273–92. Their polling data and interviews indicate that a majority of Catholics consider the Church (and/or Scripture) to be wrong about abortion, fornication, homosexual acts, and contraception, as well as divorce and remarriage.

[60] It should be noted that Rex holds that "the Church enjoys, in a very restricted context, a privilege of guidance by the Holy Spirit that protects it against defining what is false in Christian doctrine or morality as a truth to be held by all Christians. It cannot require Catholics to believe what is false, but that does not prevent it from committing countless other kinds of errors. The dreadful revelations of the abuse crisis put that beyond doubt. The definition (and hence limitation) of infallibility is most helpfully seen as a providential dispensation that has allowed the Church to admit its numerous mistakes and crimes in the vast areas of human endeavor not guaranteed by infallibility" (Rex, "Church in Doubt", 49). Like myself, Rex therefore considers it possible that the "traditional teaching on marriage will be compromised in practice by pastoral concessions" (ibid.), without this constituting a fundamental doctrinal rupture. Ignace Berten, who advocates the possibility of such rupture and who seeks to redefine Catholic marriage as dissoluble, argues that "Francis seeks deliberately to break with this tendency to dogmatize or infallibilize the expression of the Magisterium" (Ignace Berten, O.P., Les divorcés remariés peuvent-ils communier?: Enjeux ecclésiaux des débats autour du Synode sur la famille et d'Amoris laetitia [Namur, Belgium: Lessius, 2017], 339).

of marriage. They state, "The language of indissolubility related to marriage is not biblical, nor is it patristic. It was not the language of the classic medieval canonists, or of the councils of the Middle Ages."[61] The language of "indissolubility", they contend, "is juridical language, legal terminology, not the language of moral obligation".[62] Himes and Coriden also suggest that there is a major distinction between papal and conciliar teaching that *marriage* is indissoluble, and papal and conciliar teaching that the *marriage bond* is indissoluble. They argue that if it is solely marriage (as distinct from the marriage bond) that is indissoluble, then, as a *covenant of love*, marriage's indissolubility

[61] Kenneth R. Himes, O.F.M., and James A. Coriden, "The Indissolubility of Marriage: Reasons to Reconsider", *Theological Studies* 65 (2004): 457–58. See also their "Notes on Moral Theology: Pastoral Care of the Divorced and Remarried", *Theological Studies* 57 (1996): 97–123. For a cognate view, see Michael Lawler, "Divorce and Remarriage in the Catholic Church: Ten Theses", *New Theology Review* 12 (1999): 48–63. Himes and Coriden attempt to hold to some limits: "In Russian Orthodoxy, during the 16th and 17th centuries, a degree of permissiveness developed that countenanced even divorce by mutual consent. How such a practice can be reconciled with the thrust of both traditions, East and West, to promote the value of permanence and fidelity in marital love is not readily discernible" ("Indissolubility of Marriage", 473). They could have added that the sixteenth and seventeenth centuries are not the only instances of this permissiveness in Orthodox theology, at least de facto.

[62] Himes and Coriden, "Indissolubility of Marriage", 458. I note that even if the term "indissolubility" is not used, the reality is fully present in Scripture, the Fathers, and the medieval canonists and councils. The Joint Committee of Orthodox and Catholic Bishops' "Pastoral Statement on Orthodox/Roman Catholic Marriages" similarly asserts that the Second Vatican Council, in its treatment of marriage in *Gaudium et Spes*, "implicitly recognized that teaching on marriage had frequently proceeded from a biological and juridical point of view rather than from an interpersonal and existential one". This is an erroneous claim, even if "biological" and "juridical" elements (and sometimes emphases) have been present. See chapter 4 below for discussion of Aquinas' theology of marriage. See also Peter F. Ryan, S.J., and Germain Grisez, "Indissoluble Marriage: A Reply to Kenneth Himes and James Coriden", *Theological Studies* 72 (2011): 369–415. Responding to the work of Fransen and others, Ryan and Grisez emphasize that "Trent's canon five solemnly defines, as a truth of faith, the proposition that marriage cannot be dissolved on three grounds other than adultery; and canon seven solemnly defines that the Church has not erred and does not err in teaching that marriage cannot be dissolved on the ground of adultery. Since any proposition is either true or false, if the Church has not erred in teaching that proposition, it must be true. Moreover, canon seven ... is self-referential, and it is now clear that 'in accordance with evangelical and apostolic doctrine' means that canon seven is itself a dogma had from Scripture—a dogma to be accepted as revealed truth and held with divine and Catholic faith" (ibid., 409–10). In their view, "If *dogma* means a solemnly defined proposition, then there is no dogma that *ratum et consummatum* marriages as such are absolutely indissoluble. Nevertheless, that teaching was proposed as divinely revealed by the ordinary and universal magisterium and held as such by the whole Church. Teachings of that sort are no more open to revision than are solemnly defined propositions" (ibid., 414).

is based upon the subjective commitment and love of the couple; and if these elements fade away, the indissolubility dissolves.

On this view, the earlier teaching about the objectivity of marital indissolubility had to do with the "bond" of marriage, but the language of a "bond" is juridicist and impersonal, inappropriate for marriage. Himes and Coriden contend that when the Second Vatican Council and more recent popes steer relatively clear of the language of a marital "bond", the meaning of this decision about language is, at least implicitly, to acknowledge that the ground of "indissolubility" has always been subjective rather than objective: namely, as a covenant of love, marriage is "indissoluble" unless the couple falls out of love— and thus marriage has never been *objectively* indissoluble, despite the fact that the Church taught this. Himes and Coriden also argue that the pope's power to dissolve marriages between a baptized person and an unbaptized person indicates that the "Church's doctrine on the indissolubility of marriage" is in fact already "shot through with exceptions, privileges, and dispensations based on theologically questionable authority".[63] They add that, due to the burgeoning number of annulments (which they support), "the Church's witness to the permanence of the marriage covenant is badly blurred."[64]

I note that when the *Catechism of the Catholic Church*—in its section on "The Effects of the Sacrament of Matrimony"—teaches that "*the marriage bond* has been established by God himself in such a way that a

---

[63] Himes and Coriden, "Indissolubility of Marriage", 462. They draw upon John T. Noonan's *The Power to Dissolve: Lawyers and Marriages in the Court of the Roman Curia* (Cambridge, MA: Harvard University Press, 1972), which sought to make the same point in the heated ecclesiastical climate of the early 1970s. Himes and Coriden state, "We believe, contrary to Ratzinger, that it is not plausible in the face of the data to assert that the present teaching of marital indissolubility is a matter to be considered as definitive dogma or definitive doctrine. Certainly it is authoritative Catholic doctrine and to be acknowledged as such, but that does not rule out further development and reform" (Himes and Coriden, "Indissolubility of Marriage", 465). They have in view a 1986 letter from Joseph Cardinal Ratzinger, then prefect of the Congregation for the Doctrine of the Faith, to Charles Curran. The exchange between Curran and Ratzinger is published in Charles Curran, *Faithful Dissent* (Kansas City, MO: Sheed and Ward, 1986), 267–76. For their analysis of the teachings of the Council of Trent, Himes and Coriden rely upon Fransen's work, which has been ably critiqued by Christian Brugger and which does not stand up to the actual texts of Trent, as I have indicated above. Besides, it is difficult to "reform" the doctrine of marital indissolubility, without turning it into its opposite: dissoluble marriage. Development is possible for all doctrines of the Church, but development is one thing and rupture (or corruption) another.

[64] Himes and Coriden, "Indissolubility of Marriage", 462.

marriage concluded and consummated between baptized persons can never be dissolved" and also that this marriage "bond, which results from the free human act of the spouses and their consummation of the marriage, is a reality, henceforth irrevocable, and gives rise to a covenant guaranteed by God's fidelity", the *Catechism* provides a response to arguments such as that of Himes and Coriden.[65] What the *Catechism* teaches about the marriage bond is none other than what Catholics celebrating this sacrament have been taught authoritatively and solemnly by Trent as well as by later popes and Vatican II: a valid and consummated marriage between two baptized persons cannot be dissolved, because it is objectively indissoluble.

Himes and Coriden contend that Jesus' teaching on divorce—or, as they put it, "the Synoptics' teaching on divorce", which express "various traditions subsequent to Jesus that emerged from the situations of the New Testament churches"—belongs to the "radicalized Torah" of an "eschatological prophet" whose teachings made sense "within a community of disciples who expected an imminent end of the world and a transformation of the created order".[66] With this large caveat in mind, Himes and Coriden grant that "all agree that Jesus opposed divorce" and that "scholars affirm that Jesus opposed divorce and considered remarriage to be adultery."[67] But they emphasize that these teachings of Jesus should "not be taken out of context and read as legal norms or even as moral maxims".[68] They assume that eschatological fervor and halakhic or legal teaching are opposed, an assumption that biblical scholars such as Dale Allison and Jonathan Pennington have shown to be mistaken.[69] For Himes and Coriden,

---

[65] *Catechism of the Catholic Church*, no. 1640; emphasis in original.

[66] Himes and Coriden, "Indissolubility of Marriage", 466–67.

[67] Ibid., 466.

[68] Ibid.

[69] See Dale C. Allison, *Constructing Jesus: Memory, Imagination, and History* (Grand Rapids, MI: Baker Academic, 2010), and Jonathan T. Pennington, *The Sermon on the Mount and Human Flourishing: A Theological Commentary* (Grand Rapids, MI: Baker Academic, 2017). See also the theologian Christoph Theobald, S.J.,'s contention that Jesus, in his teaching upon marriage, establishes "*fidelity* as the norm of conscience", while operating not "on the terrain of concrete norms of *halakhah*" but rather on the terrain of an " 'eschatological' prophet and not as a scribe or doctor of the law" (Christoph Theobald, *Urgences pastorales du moment présent: Pour une pédagogie de la réform* [Paris: Bayard, 2017], 218). In their biblical analysis, Himes and Coriden are drawing upon Raymond F. Collins, *Divorce in the New Testament* (Collegeville,

"the historical Jesus" simply taught that "divorce is wrong and *ought not occur*"—which would be a mere platitude, even if an ideal.[70]

Himes and Coriden argue with respect to Ephesians 5 that "it is the committed, faithful love of a man and woman that embodies the sacrament.... Their love is the symbolic presentation of the love between Christ and his body."[71] Recall that Paul states, " 'For this reason a man shall leave his father and mother and be joined to his wife, and the two shall become one flesh.' This is a great mystery, and I mean in reference to Christ and the Church" (Eph 5:31–32). I note that by recalling that "the two shall become one", Ephesians 5:31 indicates that there is more to the union than simply the ongoing subjective affectivity of the husband and wife. But for Himes and Coriden, it is the subjective love alone that "embodies the sacrament" (the covenant of marriage), and if this love goes away, nothing is left. They ask rhetorically, "What is it that continues to symbolize the Christ-Church union once the tragedy of marital breakdown occurs?"[72]

MN: Liturgical Press, 1992), as well as Mary Rose D'Angelo, "Remarriage and the Divorce Sayings Attributed to Jesus", in *Divorce and Remarriage: Religious and Psychological Perspectives*, ed. William P. Roberts (Kansas City, MO: Sheed and Ward, 1990), 78–106; John Donahue, "Divorce—New Testament Perspectives", in *Marriage Studies: Reflection on Canon Law and Theology*, vol. 2, ed. Thomas Doyle (Washington, D.C.: Canon Law Society of America, 1982), 1–19; George McRae, "New Testament Perspectives on Marriage and Divorce", in *Divorce and Remarriage in the Catholic Church*, ed. Lawrence G. Wrenn (New York: Newman Press, 1973), 1–15; Pheme Perkins, "Marriage in the New Testament and Its World", in *Commitment to Partnership: Explorations of the Theology of Marriage*, ed. William Roberts (New York: Paulist, 1987), 5–30; and Bruce Vawter, "Divorce and the New Testament", *Catholic Biblical Quarterly* 39 (1977): 528–42. These materials are now quite dated.

[70] Himes and Coriden, "Indissolubility of Marriage", 468. Highlighting the difference between Jesus' day and later epochs, Himes and Coriden add that "if we are to suppose that Jesus was proclaiming what the Church at the present time teaches, he would have had to mean that no divorce is possible once the couple has been baptized, given consent according to the proper canonical form, and engaged subsequently in sexual intercourse" (ibid.). I consider that if such a standard for receiving Jesus' teaching were correct, Jesus could no longer speak to us, and doctrinal development would distance us from Jesus rather than illumining his teachings. Himes and Coriden go on to argue that Paul and Matthew felt free to modify Jesus' authoritative teaching, but the insights of Luz and Bockmuehl (noted above) cast doubt upon such a claim.

[71] Ibid., 497.

[72] Ibid. Taking matters further, they agree with the view of Rudolf Schnackenburg that Ephesians 5:32 does not even refer to marriage; see Rudolf Schnackenburg, *Ephesians: A Commentary*, trans. Helen Heron (Edinburgh: T&T Clark, 1991), 255–56. The biblical scholar Margaret Y. MacDonald takes a more balanced position in her analysis of Ephesians 5:32: "There is some uncertainty as to what exactly constitutes the mystery here. Does it refer

The Church's answer, as they recognize, is that the man has been "joined to his wife" and the two have "become one" sacramentally and objectively.[73] Put simply, Ephesians 5:31 refers to an objective bond that endures indissolubly while both spouses live. Himes and Coriden know this argument, but they insist that even if it were so, "the bond of marriage is nothing more nor less than a human relationship", inhering in "the human persons who make up the relationship".[74] In their view, it follows that "when the relationship is terminated", it is clear that "the bond has ended" and is no more.[75] In saying this, they assume that a "relationship" as intimate as a valid and consummated marriage can simply be "ended" when a couple falls out of love and divorces. On the contrary, I observe that a sacramental marriage objectively unites the two into one while they both live. As John Paul II says, "the Christian conjugal bond" can therefore be "a typically Christian communion of two persons because it represents the mystery of Christ's incarnation and the mystery of His covenant".[76]

---

to marriage between man and woman, only to Christ and the church, or to both? The apparent lack of clarity may be due to the close association between the two in the author's own mind. Given the use of the marriage metaphor throughout 5:22–33, it seems best to assume that the term 'mystery' encompasses both human marriage (seen as a reflection of divine reality) and the relationship between Christ and the church" (Margaret Y. McDonald, *Colossians and Ephesians* [Collegeville, MN: Liturgical Press, 2000], 331).

[73] They complain that on this view, "No longer a moral exhortation to husbands to love their wives, Ephesians was read [by the medievals] as a doctrinal claim that marriage was indissoluble" (Himes and Coriden, "Indissolubility of Marriage", 493). But this contrast between a "moral exhortation" and a "doctrinal claim" is a fallacious one, because the reason for the moral exhortation is that Paul thinks that marriage has a specific nature, which he grounds in Genesis 2 (and which is the ground of the "doctrine"). They also criticize the value of Ephesians 5 on the grounds that Paul (or the author of Ephesians) "left unchallenged" the hierarchical and patriarchal "social customs of marriage" (ibid., 491). The indissoluble nature of the marital bond, however, does not depend upon patriarchal oppression for its truth or goodness. See also, for a perspective in line with Himes and Coriden's, Theodore Mackin, "Ephesians 5:21–33 and Radical Indissolubility", in *Marriage Studies: Reflections in Canon Law and Theology*, vol. 3, ed. Thomas Doyle (Washington, D.C.: Canon Law Society of America, 1985), 1–45.

[74] Himes and Coriden, "Indissolubility of Marriage", 485. See also Ladislas Örsy, S.J., *Marriage in Canon Law: Texts and Comments, Reflections and Questions* (Collegeville, MN: Liturgical Press, 1990), 271, and Michael Lawler, "Blessed Are Spouses Who Love, For Their Marriages Will Be Permanent: A Theology of the Bonds of Marriage", *Jurist* 55 (1995): 218–42.

[75] Himes and Coriden, "Indissolubility of Marriage", 486.

[76] Pope John Paul II, *Familiaris Consortio*, no. 13.

Himes and Coriden conclude by arguing that the Church's teaching on marital indissolubility is an example of realized eschatology, whereas in fact the kingdom has been inaugurated but not consummated. They propose that Jesus' teachings on marriage are equivalent to his teachings on nonviolence, which in their view indicate an eschatological ideal that can justly be broken in the fallen world. In my view, although there is no doubt that the world is fallen and the kingdom has only been inaugurated, Jesus never speaks as though his precept—"What therefore God has joined together, let no man put asunder" (Mt 19:6)—is an ideal that his followers will not be expected to follow. Jesus expects his followers, by the grace of the Spirit, to be able to observe difficult commandments such as "You shall not kill, You shall not commit adultery, You shall not steal, You shall not bear false witness, Honor your father and mother, and 'You shall love your neighbor as yourself' [Lev 19:18]" (Mt 19:18–19). Likewise, Paul believes that not committing adultery will be within the power of Jesus' followers due to the grace of the Holy Spirit (see 1 Cor 6:9–11).

For Himes and Coriden, without retreating "from the radical demand upon a couple to continue to grow throughout their lifetimes in a faithful, committed, loving union", the Catholic Church must jettison her teaching that a valid and consummated marriage between two baptized persons is indissoluble.[77] They consider that an "exceptionless norm for all consummated, sacramental marriages is unrealistic, incoherent, and injurious".[78] Their insistence that the Church reject her solemn and oft-repeated teaching—and thereby reject her pledge to Catholic couples that the marriage bond is indeed objectively indissoluble, a divine gift that has been and is treasured by most Catholic couples—is in fact a call for the Catholic Church to abandon Jesus' firm rejection of divorce and remarriage and to deny her own solemn and consistently repeated teaching about the nature of the Sacrament of Matrimony.

Of course, there are a number of Catholic theologians who agree with them. For example, Ladislas Örsy argues that it is possible both to hold that "there is no doubt that the law of indissolubility

---

[77] Himes and Coriden, "Indissolubility of Marriage", 498.
[78] Ibid., 498–99.

has been proclaimed by the Lord as part of the new laws of the Kingdom" and to affirm that the Church possesses "radical power to dissolve the bond", thus making all "indissoluble" Christian marriages into contingently dissolvable ones.[79] Likewise, Michael Lawler asserts that because the historical Jesus' teaching was not strictly the same as the Church's teaching (since, for instance, Jesus did not mention anything about canon law), the overturning of the doctrine of marital indissolubility is within the power of "the same agent that introduced the teaching in the first place, namely, the magisterial Church".[80]

Thus, for Himes, Coriden, Örsy, and Lawler (among others), the Church can and should now deny marital indissolubility by adopting a view that allows for the dissolution of valid and consummated Christian marriages. The purpose of the present chapter's presentation of the teaching of Council of Trent, Vatican II, and various popes has been to show that the Church cannot deny marital indissolubility without undercutting her ability to teach any doctrinal truth about the contents of the Gospel. Having pledged that the marriages of Catholics are strictly indissoluble—and having taught this repeatedly and solemnly on the basis of Jesus' own teaching—the Church cannot inform married couples that in fact, in the case of a valid and consummated marriage, the sacrament confers only a contingent dissolubility. Such a grave doctrinal rupture, were it possible, would undermine the trustworthiness of the Church's teaching about the nature of any of the sacraments, including the nature of the Sacrament of Holy Orders and the Petrine office itself (and many other realities of faith), which generally have less explicit support in

---

[79] Örsy, *Marriage in Canon Law*, 276–77.

[80] Lawler, "Blessed Are Spouses Who Love", 239. This claim helps to explain why, as Ross Douthat observes, "After years of using 'the magisterium has spoken, the case is closed' as an argument ender, conservative Catholics now [in the midst of the media debate surrounding the event of the 2015 Synod] sided with the reluctant rebels, insisting on the limits of papal power, and generally covering synodal politics with a focus on the politics—a style that implicitly conceded the possibility of the very changes that theologically they considered impossible. Meanwhile, liberal Catholics had suddenly turned ultramontane: They were papal supremacists who found interventions like the cardinals' letter impertinent, absolute believers in the Holy Spirit's tight control of doctrinal deliberation, and firm clericalists when it came to any objections raised to Kasper's proposal or the synod proceedings from outside the papacy and hierarchy" (Douthat, *To Change the Church*, 120–21).

Scripture and tradition than does the Church's teaching on the absolute indissolubility of Christian marriage.[81]

Fortunately, however, the Church today continues to affirm the doctrine of marital indissolubility, despite the strong efforts to undermine it. Let me now turn to the most recent magisterial teaching on this subject, *Amoris Laetitia*.

---

[81] This point is well articulated by José Granados when he remarks that "anyone who denies the indissolubility of marriage ... denies in turn the unity of tradition down through the ages" (José Granados, "From Flesh to Flesh: On the Sacramental Meaning of Tradition", *Communio* 44 [2017]: 645). As Granados perceives, the key point is the following: "The sacraments ... are supporting elements in the concept of tradition. This means that not only does tradition say something about the sacraments, but also the sacraments are the channel or vehicle of the same tradition that the Gospel transmits to us. They are not only what is transmitted, but also an integral part of the transmitting subject herself, which is the Church. Therefore, if central elements of the sacraments were called into question, this would damage the very channel through which tradition flows" (ibid.). This point can hardly be emphasized enough.

Chapter 3

Pope Francis' *Amoris Laetitia* and Marital Indissolubility

In his apostolic exhortation *Evangelii Gaudium*, Pope Francis states that "a preacher has to contemplate the word, but he also has to contemplate his people.... He needs to be able to link the message of a biblical text to a human situation, to an experience which cries out for the light of God's word."[1] The reality of divorce and remarriage is well known by people who grew up, as I did, in the 1970s. I watched my three best friends endure, in heartbreaking ways, the divorce (and in some cases remarriage) of each of their sets of parents. My life as a teenager was marked by the experience of additional friends whose parents were divorcing or whose parents had married new partners. I am close to persons—Protestants, lapsed Catholics, and Catholics— who had dreadful first marriages and wonderful second marriages. Like most persons who have reached their late forties, I know what failure, chronic pain, discouragement, exclusion, and starting anew feel like.

In my forthcoming *Engaging the Doctrine of Marriage*, I explore how the lived experience of marriage relates to believers' sharing in Christ and the holy Trinity, as well as to the whole of God's plan of salvation. Although the present chapter does not repeat this discussion, in the background of this chapter is the way in which the sacramental reality of indissoluble marriage pertains to the experience of continuing to hope in Christ even in the midst of sin and sorrow. Since life involves living with suffering in one way or another, each person must carry his cross unto salvation, by the grace of the Holy Spirit

---

[1] *Apostolic Exhortation of the Holy Father Francis, The Joy of the Gospel (Evangelii Gaudium)*, Vatican trans. (Boston: Pauline Books & Media, 2013), no. 154.

who guides Christ's followers along the "narrow" and "hard" way "that leads to life" (Mt 7:14).

Pope Francis recognizes that in contemporary Western society, however, many people consider the Church's and Christ's teachings on marriage to be unreal and out of touch. In response, as the philosopher Thibaud Collin has noted, Pope Francis pastorally seeks "to make the conjugal morality of the Church more bearable and attractive".[2] The pastoral reception of *Amoris Laetitia* has been an unusually complex one, with different bishops' conferences and individual bishops permitted to interpret it in mutually contradictory ways.[3] Although Gerhard Cardinal Müller, as head of the Congregation for the Doctrine of the Faith, insisted that the Church has not changed her traditional sacramental discipline in any way,[4] Pope Francis shed

---

[2] Thibaud Collin, *Le mariage chrétien a-t-il encore un avenir? Pour en finir avec les malentendus* (Paris: Artège, 2018), 268. In discussing the implementation proposed by the bishops of the Buenos Aires pastoral region, Collin identifies a potential problem: "Access to the sacraments is scandalous, in the ecclesial sense of the term, when it happens while certain injustices remain. But is not the new union in itself intrinsically an injustice, since it violates the right of the spouse? Can one imagine that the sole injustices to avoid or to repair are in a certain way peripheral to the state of adultery, while the adultery could be seen as not being an injustice, an immediate cause of a scandal, for those who, in this state, publically come forward to eucharistic communion?" (ibid., 177). He indicates a further problem: "There is, certainly, maturation and historicity in human life, but should not the progress in question be rightly seen as the progressive realization of the person by his choices? Now, certain choices are contrary to a person's true good and, as such, they cannot be regarded as that which renders possible the person's future good acts. Each kilometer that I travel between Paris and Lyon draws me closer to Lyon. But all the acts that I commit do not draw me closer to God, because God is not at the end of a road; God draws me now, and only my free response to his call enables me to remain in communion with him" (ibid., 176).

[3] For the reception in the United States, see, for example, the United States Conference of Catholic Bishops, "Report on Reception and Implementation of *Amoris Laetitia* in the United States", September 27, 2016, http://www.usccb.org/issues-and-action/marriage-and-family/upload/Report-on-Reception-and-Implementation-of-Amoris-Laetitia-in-the-United-States.pdf. For discussion of the international reception of the document through October 4, 2016, from a perspective supportive of fundamental change, see Ignace Berten, O.P., *Les divorcés remariés peuvent-ils communier?: Enjeux ecclésiaux des débats autour du Synode sur la famille et d'*Amoris laetitia (Namur, Belgium: Lessius, 2017), 243–99.

[4] See Gerhard Cardinal Müller, "Was dürfen wir von der Familie erwarten?: Eine Kultur der Hoffnung für die Familie ausgehend vom Nachsynodalen Apostolischen Schreiben Amoris laetitia?", *Die Tagespost*, May 6, 2016, http://www.collationes.org/component/k2/item/2310-was-duerfen-wir-von-der-familie-erwarten, and included in *Zum Gelingen von Ehe und Familie: Ermutigung aus Amoris laetitia: Für Walter Kardinal Kasper*, ed. George Augustin (Freiburg: Herder, 2018), 77–95. See also, along the same lines, Müller's "Warum 'Amoris laetitia' orthodox verstanden warden kann und muss", in *Zum Gelingen von Ehe und Familie*, 263–81.

light on his own interpretation of *Amoris Laetitia* when he included within his official Magisterium his originally private letter to the bishops of the Buenos Aires pastoral region. In this letter, Pope Francis commends the bishops for laying out a path for divorced and remarried persons, bound by a prior sacramental marriage, to return to Eucharistic Communion through pastoral discernment and the Sacrament of Penance, without needing to separate or to abstain from sexual intercourse. This is the path commended by Walter Cardinal Kasper (among many others) in a series of publications since the early 1970s,[5] and it conforms in certain ways to the approach taken by the Orthodox Church for centuries. Kasper maintains that in such cases, the original Christian marriage is not dissolved, but rather remains permanently valid.[6]

[5] For an influential statement of his views published right before the Synod of Bishops, see Walter Kasper, *The Gospel of the Family*, trans. William Madges (New York: Paulist Press, 2014). See also Walter Kasper, *Pope Francis' Revolution of Tenderness and Love: Theological and Pastoral Perspectives*, trans. William Madges (New York: Paulist Press, 2015).

[6] See Cardinal Kasper's remarks on this point in "Merciful God, Merciful Church: An Interview with Cardinal Walter Kasper", by Matthew Boudway and Grant Gallicho, *Commonweal*, published electronically May 7, 2014, https://www.commonwealmagazine.org/kasper -interview-popefrancis-vatican. See also Louis Roy, O.P., "In and Out of Communion", *Tablet* (April 7, 2018): 13. For Roy, Cardinal Kasper's proposal, as adopted by Pope Francis, does not represent doctrinal development because it does not change doctrine. Instead, "the doctrinal essentials are understood to be non-negotiable, but they must be applied according to many concrete and varied factors" (ibid.). Roy sums up the pastoral change as "no longer maintaining a rigid, static attitude to sinners", but now "adopting instead an inductive, dynamic approach that begins with particular situations and asks how best to respond. The Church then redefines the practical rules susceptible of guiding the way that she can and must mediate mercy to sinners. This is the meaning of the 'paradigm shift'; something profound is happening in this papacy, but, rather than involving a change in the Church's teaching that Christian marriage is indissoluble, it is a process that is helping bishops, priests and lay catechists more deeply to interiorise the Church's traditional doctrines on marriage" (ibid.). Roy argues that bishops and theologians who are opposed to Kasper's (and Pope Francis') position are trapped in what Bernard Lonergan called "classicism", meaning a nostalgic clinging to a supposedly unchanging past. As Roy states, "Since nothing significant is permitted to change within a classicist framework, theologians and Church leaders who are mentally imprisoned in it reject any significant modification of pastoral rules. And they have little patience with the meanings and values that characterise any new epoch. I cannot detect in their declarations a real openness to judicious changes of pastoral rules, which they wrongly identify with changes in doctrine.... Some Catholics have always found it difficult to renounce the dream of a Church whose robustness, power and credibility would consist in never changing" (ibid.). I think that Roy is here very unfair to his opponents, but I am glad that he insists that the doctrine of marital indissolubility has not been affected (or, for that matter, the doctrine of marital exclusivity). In Nicholas J. Healy, Jr.'s view, a more promising alternative to Kasper's

The purpose of this chapter, therefore, is to examine *Amoris Laetitia* in light of its interpretation by Pope Francis and by other leading figures. My purpose is to highlight the affirmation of marital indissolubility in *Amoris Laetitia*, but I do not shy away from articulating the tensions that have arisen. Angelo Scola remarks, "Indissolubility is ultimately what makes Christian marriage a sacrament.... In fact, only by its being indissoluble does marriage participate in the nuptial sacrifice that the Word incarnate makes of himself on the cross."[7] Indissolubility and the Sacrament of Matrimony are inseparable.

The Bishops of the Buenos Aires Pastoral Region, Pope Francis, and the Interpretation of *Amoris Laetitia*

In 2016, the bishops of the Buenos Aires pastoral region wrote a letter to the region's priests explaining how to implement chapter 8 of *Amoris Laetitia*, and they forwarded this letter to Pope Francis for his approval. In their letter to the priests of the region, the bishops comment that the pastoral path of accompanying divorced and remarried persons who are still bound by a prior sacramental marriage "does not necessarily finish in the sacraments; it may also lead to other ways of

---

position—an alternative noted by Kasper himself, and already undertaken in a certain way by Pope Francis—would be to undertake an "expansion of the annulment process. As confirmed by the Council of Trent and subsequent doctrine and practice, the Church does have considerable authority over the form of marriage; concretely, she can determine the conditions for validity or the impediments to marriage" (Nicholas J. Healy, Jr., "The Merciful Gift of Indissolubility and the Question of Pastoral Care for Civilly Divorced and Remarried Catholics", *Communio* 41 [2014]: 325). In a 1998 essay, republished with new footnotes on November 30, 2011 in *L'Osservatore Romano*, Joseph Ratzinger raised the question of whether a baptized person who, at the time of his or her marriage, lacks faith can really possess a sacramental marriage; see "The Pastoral Approach to Marriage Must Be Founded on Truth", http://www.osservatoreromano.va/en/news/the-pastoral-approach-to-marriage-must-be-founded-. He answered his own question as Pope Benedict XVI, in his Address to the Roman Rota of January 26, 2013. Pope Benedict XVI's conclusion, in agreement with the position of Pope John Paul II, is that lack of faith only removes the supernatural dimension of marriage if, in a particular circumstance, it can also be shown to have invalidated the natural dimension of marriage. See also José Granados, "The Sacramental Character of Faith: Consequences for the Debate on the Relation between Faith and Marriage", *Communio* 41 (2014): 245–68, and Lawrence J. Welch and Perry Cahall, "An Examination of the Role of Faith in Matrimonial Consent and the Consequences for the Sacrament of Marriage", *Nova et Vetera* 16 (2018): 311–42.

[7] Angelo Cardinal Scolá, *The Nuptial Mystery*, trans. Michelle K. Borras (Grand Rapids, MI: Eerdmans, 2005), 104–5.

achieving further integration into the life of the Church".[8] This statement indicates that the sacraments should not be thought of as the last step in the integration, as though no integration other than sacramental integration were necessary. The bishops then observe that "whenever feasible depending on the specific circumstances of a couple", the traditional position that the couple should live together in sexual abstinence should be proposed. But the bishops state that in certain concrete cases, where "there are limitations that mitigate responsibility and culpability (cf. [Amoris Laetitia] 301–302), especially when a person believes he/she would incur a subsequent fault by harming the children of the new union, Amoris laetitia offers the possibility of having access to the sacraments of Reconciliation and Eucharist (cf. [Amoris Laetitia] footnotes 336 and 351)."[9] In his letter to the

---

[8] "Guidelines of Buenos Aires Bishops on Divorced/Remarried", Crux, September 18, 2016, https://cruxnow.com/global-church/2016/09/18/guidelines-buenos-aires-bishops-divorcedremarried. The quotations that follow all come from this source. For the original Spanish text of the bishops' letter and Pope Francis' letter to the bishops, see https://w2.vatican.va/content/francesco/es/letters/2016/documents/papa-francesco_20160905_regione-pastorale-buenos-aires.html. See also Porte aperte: Accompagnare, discernere, integrare vissuti di separazione, divorzio, o nuova unione alla luce di Amoris Laetitia, ed. Eugenio Zanetti (Milan: Ancora, 2016).

[9] See also Monique Baujard's description of the implementation of Amoris Laetitia by Archbishop Dominique Lebrun of Rouen (France): "He wrote a letter inviting divorced, separated and/or remarried persons to come to the cathedral on the 1st of November, to pass the threshold of the Holy Door with him, pray Vespers together and receive his benediction/blessing before starting a period of discernment. His letter is published on the website of the diocese, but was also handed out to Catholics in person. In his letter he asks them several times for forgiveness: forgiveness if the attitude of the church hurt them, forgiveness if they experience the law as a burden or as stones cast on their lives, and forgiveness if they suffer from their exclusion from the sacraments. He has entrusted seven priests with the mission to become 'missionaries of mercy': they are to listen to anyone who is in a difficult situation with regard to marriage and family and who wants to think about his or her place in the church. The process of discernment goes through two stages: firstly, in an inner sanctum as it were, between the person or couple and the 'missionary of mercy', and only later within the wider circle of community, with the parish and its priest. The possibility of access to the sacraments is mentioned, but it is clear that it is not automatic. The document points out the diversity of situations and repeats that Amoris laetitia asks for a case-by-case approach and not for general rules" (Monique Baujard, "Existing Practices and New Initiatives for the Divorced and Remarried in France", in A Point of No Return? Amoris Laetitia on Marriage, Divorce, and Remarriage, ed. Thomas Knieps-Port le Roi [Berlin: LIT Verlag, 2017], 243).

See also the experience in presenting Amoris Laetitia described by Philippe Bordeyne, "The Newness That Priests and People Face When They Receive Amoris Laetitia: An Overview in France", in Amoris Laetitia: A New Momentum for Moral Formation and Pastoral Practice, ed. Grant Gallicho and James F. Keenan, S.J. (New York: Paulist Press, 2018), 70–76.

bishops of the Buenos Aires pastoral region, Pope Francis affirms this interpretation.

At the same time, the bishops of the Buenos Aires pastoral region insist that these concrete cases should be limited, rather than it being assumed that all divorced and remarried persons can now approach the Eucharist after receiving the Sacrament of Reconciliation. The bishops write that "it should not be understood that this possibility implies unlimited access to sacraments, or that all situations warrant such unlimited access."

What situations, then, do not warrant unlimited access to the Eucharist? The bishops offer three examples, drawn from paragraphs 297 and 298 of *Amoris Laetitia*: cases in which a new union follows soon upon a divorce, cases of persons who have consistently failed to meet their familial obligations, and cases in which persons assume that their irregular situation is equivalent to the Christian ideal. The bishops argue that the task of the discerning conscience of a divorced and remarried person will consist in asking whether the person behaved wrongly toward his or her abandoned spouse or children. Prior to approaching the sacraments, the person should seek to resolve these injustices. The bishops teach that "where there have been unresolved injustices, providing access to sacraments is particularly outrageous." The bishops also caution that it may be better "for an eventual access to sacraments to take place in a discreet manner, especially if troublesome situations can be anticipated". They do not specify the nature of such "troublesome situations", but I assume that these situations might include, for example, members of the divorced and remarried person's former family protesting in one way or another.

The bishops state that their teaching must not and should not "create confusion about the teaching of the Church on the indissoluble marriage"; there should not be confusion about the Church's teaching, even though the Church now will act in mercy rather than requiring obedience to the law's requirements. Indeed, the couple is called to an ongoing discernment: the couple has not yet reached the ideal, and the couple should be expected to continue to grow in faith and charity and to move toward the ideal "according to the 'law of gradualness' ([*Amoris Laetitia*] 295) and with confidence in the help of grace".

For the bishops of the Buenos Aires pastoral region, therefore, a valid and consummated sacramental marriage's status as indissoluble is not in doubt. Likewise, in *Amoris Laetitia*, Pope Francis affirms that to the characteristic qualities of other kinds of human friendship, marriage joins "an indissoluble exclusivity [*indissolubilem proprietatem*] expressed in the stable commitment to share and shape together the whole of life".[10] He adds that even the subjective intention of lovers shows that "it is in the very nature of conjugal love to be definitive [*in ipsa amoris coniugalis natura aliquid inesse ad consummatum quiddam perducens*]."[11] Here, in light of the grace of sacramental marriage that enables fallen humans to live out indissoluble marriage, Pope Francis approvingly cites "the words of Saint Robert Bellarmine, 'the fact that one man unites with one woman in an indissoluble bond, and that they remain inseparable despite every kind of difficulty, even when there is no longer hope for children, can only be the sign of a great mystery [cf. Eph 5:32].' "[12]

Along these lines, Pope Francis also remarks that the "words of consent" in the marriage ceremony "cannot be reduced to the present; they involve a totality that includes the future: 'until death do us part.' "[13] He notes that the man and woman, in marriage preparation, "need to be encouraged to see the sacrament not as a single moment that then becomes a part of the past and its memories, but rather as a reality that permanently influences the whole of married life".[14] If the sacrament "permanently influences the whole of married life", then the sacrament—in a valid and consummated marriage—does not and cannot dissolve. Such a marriage is indissoluble and can never be beyond the reach of the gracious power of the sacrament.

Pope Francis urges realism about marriage in a fallen world. He recognizes that "among the causes of broken marriages are unduly high expectations about conjugal life"; and he teaches that "once it becomes apparent that the reality is more limited and challenging

---

[10] Pope Francis, *The Joy of Love: On Love in the Family* (Amoris Laetitia), Vatican trans. (Frederick, MD: Word among Us Press, 2016), no. 123.

[11] Ibid.

[12] Ibid., no. 124, citing Robert Bellarmine, *De sacramento matrimonii* 1.2, in *Disputationes* 3.5.3 (Naples: Giuliano, 1858), 778.

[13] Pope Francis, post-synodal apostolic exhortation *Amoris Laetitia* (March 19, 2016), no. 214.

[14] Ibid., no. 215.

than one imagined, the solution is not to think quickly and irrespon-
sibly about separation, but to come to the sober realization that married life is a process of growth."[15] In certain instances, such as those
involving the presence or threat of physical abuse or "chronic ill-
treatment", he affirms the necessity of marital separation for the sake
of "respect for one's own dignity and the good of the children".[16]

Like popes John Paul II and Benedict XVI, Pope Francis urges
that the divorced and remarried should not be shunned or excluded
from the community of the Church. He cites the Synod Fathers'
insistence that such accompaniment of the divorced and remarried
does not in any way detract from the Church's ability to testify to
the indissolubility of marriage.[17] He also underscores his commitment to ensuring that the marriage tribunals and annulment proceedings become more accessible and quicker.[18]

---

[15] Ibid., no. 221. See also nos. 237–38: "It is becoming more and more common to think
that, when one or both partners no longer feel fulfilled, or things have not turned out the
way they wanted, sufficient reason exists to end the marriage. Were this the case, no marriage would last. At times, all it takes to decide that everything is over is a single instance of
dissatisfaction, the absence of the other when he or she was most needed, wounded pride,
or a vague fear. Inevitably, situations will arise involving human weakness and these can
prove emotionally overwhelming. One spouse may not feel fully appreciated, or may be
attracted to another person. Jealousy and tensions may emerge, or new interests that consume
the other's time and attention. Physical changes naturally occur in everyone. These, and so
many other things, rather than threatening love [though obviously they do threaten it], are
so many occasions for reviving and renewing it. In such situations, some have the maturity
needed to reaffirm their choice of the other as their partner on life's journey, despite the
limitations of the relationship."

[16] Ibid., no. 241. He later adds, "The Church, while appreciating the situations of conflict
that are part of marriage, cannot fail to speak out on behalf of those who are most vulnerable:
the children who often suffer in silence" (no. 246).

[17] See ibid., no. 243. For an accessible history of the 2014–2015 synods, laying out the
main controverted issues and the role of Pope Francis at various important stages, see Ross
Douthat, *To Change the Church: Pope Francis and the Future of Catholicism* (New York: Simon
& Schuster, 2018), 81–125.

[18] For discussion of Pope Francis' canonical reforms in this area, see the essays in *Justice and
Mercy Have Met: Pope Francis and the Reform of the Marriage Nullity Process*, ed. Kurt Martens
(Washington, D.C.: Catholic University of America Press, 2017). In his essay in this volume,
"An Analysis of Pope Francis' 2015 Reform of the General Legislation Governing Causes
of Nullity of Marriage", William L. Daniel sums up the changes: "Standing out among the
concrete norms of the reform are the principle of the celerity of the marriage nullity process
and the principle of proximity between the judge and the parties. The same norms, however,
in notable contrast with previous legislation in the matter, seem to minimize the principle
of the protection of the indissolubility of marriage, which has been stressed frequently and

In discussing the situations of divorced and remarried Catholics, Pope Francis emphasizes that pastors must help everyone to find "his or her proper way of participating in the ecclesial community"; and he affirms that "no one can be condemned for ever, because that is not the logic of the Gospel!"[19] He underlines the need to distinguish between, on the one hand, a divorced person who has contracted "a new union arising from a recent divorce, with all the suffering and confusion which this entails for children", and on the other hand "a second union consolidated over time, with new children, proven fidelity, generous self giving, Christian commitment, a consciousness of its irregularity and of the great difficulty of going back without feeling in conscience that one would fall into new sins".[20] In this latter positive light, he includes the case of persons who have been ill treated or abandoned in their marriage. He denies that it will be

---

eloquently in the pre-Francis pontifical magisterium" (63). In Archbishop Bernard A. Hebda's contribution to the volume, "Reflections on the Role of the Diocesan Bishop Envisioned by *Mitis Iudex Dominus Iesus*", Hebda underlines "Pope Francis' emphasis on the importance of putting people before things or processes.... When Pope Francis looks at the world, at those who have for example gone through the trauma of a failed marriage, he sees brothers and sisters on the periphery. We all know, especially those of us who work in tribunals, of the reality of this" (66, 69). The canon lawyer John A. Alesandro suggests approvingly that *Amoris Laetitia* may imply further expansion of the reasons for annulment, an expansion that would mean that divorce itself indicates that the marriage is null. He notes that "the unitive property of marriage (c. 1056) requires the two spouses to be 'capable' of becoming one—not one with everyone in the whole world, but specifically with one another. Marriage does not exist in the abstract; it exists only in the individual couple, and *Amoris Laetitia*'s analysis of cultural 'individualism' raises this ground again: Even if the two individuals before us are capable of marrying someone, are they really capable of marrying *one another*?" (John A. Alesandro, "How Is This Newness Read by Canon Lawyers?", in Gallicho and Keenan, *Amoris Laetitia*, 50). If annulment grounds were extended this far, of course, there would be essentially no cases of indissolubly married persons now civilly married to a new partner, and so the logical tension raised by *Amoris Laetitia* with regard to indissoluble marital obligations still owed in charity to a previous spouse would be resolved, but by means of an overly radical critique of modern human beings. More fruitfully, see *En la Salud y en la Enfermedad: Pastoral y Derecho al Servicio del Matrimonio*, ed. Nicolás Álvarez de las Asturias (Madrid: Ediciones Cristiandad, 2015).

[19] Pope Francis, *Amoris Laetitia*, no. 297.

[20] Ibid., no. 298. In paragraph 297, Pope Francis puts the word "irregular" in quotation marks: "different 'irregular' situations". Paul M. Zulehner argues that for Pope Francis, in fact, "there are only 'irregular relationships'.... In the sense of graduality, there are only human beings who are on the way, who each live only a fragmentary good, and thus who live, in the parlance of John Paul II, 'irregularly'" (Paul M. Zulehner, *Vom Gesetz zum Gesicht: Ein neuer Ton in der Kirche: Papst Franziskus zu Ehe und Familie:* Amoris Laetitia [Ostfildern: Patmos, 2016], 72).

possible to develop "a new set of general rules, canonical in nature and applicable to all cases", since what is needed instead is a careful examination of conscience by divorced and remarried persons, accompanied by their pastors.[21] He affirms that truth and charity must guide the discernment of "what hinders the possibility of a fuller participation in the life of the Church and ... what steps can foster it and make it grow".[22] He insists that such processes of careful discernment will be able to ensure that no one will think that the Church has adopted a "double standard" on indissoluble marriage.[23]

Pope Francis goes on to point out the subjective factors that, when taken into account, may show a lack of culpability on the part of couples who are living in a civil marriage without their sacramental marriage having been annulled. He argues that no set of general rules can be applied to all cases of persons living in this situation. While the general rules remain important, the complexity of certain particular cases will inevitably go beyond what the rules can handle. He explains that "because of forms of conditioning and mitigating factors, it is possible that in an objective situation of sin ... a person can be living in God's grace, can love and can also grow in the life of grace and charity, while receiving the Church's help to this end."[24]

---

[21] Pope Francis, *Amoris Laetitia*, no. 300.

[22] Ibid.

[23] Ibid. See also Rodrigo Guerra López, "The Relevance of Some Reflections by Karol Wojtyła for Understanding *Amoris Laetitia*: Creative Fidelity", *L'Osservatore Romano*, July 22, 2016, www.osservatoreromano.va/en/news/relevance-some-reflections-karol-wojtyla-understan.

[24] Pope Francis, *Amoris Laetitia*, no. 305. He earlier argues that a good conscience can approve of one's actions even if one's actions are still objectively sinful: conscience can "recognize with sincerity and honesty what for now is the most generous response which can be given to God, and come to see with a certain moral security that it is what God himself is asking amid the concrete complexity of one's limits, while yet not fully the objective ideal" (ibid., no. 303). If Pope Francis means here to say that God can ask of a person something that is still objectively sinful, and that conscience can therefore approve of objectively sinful actions, this would involve God and conscience in our sin. If Pope Francis means simply to say that God still works upon us, in gradual steps, even when we insist to some degree upon cleaving to our sins, then this is certainly true. For a defense of *Amoris Laetitia*'s teaching here, placing the discussion of conscience in the context of concrete discernment and prudence, see Jean-Miguel Garrigues, O.P., "Répondre aux *dubia* des quatre cardinaux pour developer et préciser la doctrine morale de *Veritatis Splendor*", in *Une morale souple mais non sans boussole: Répondre aux doutes des quatre Cardinaux à propos d'* Amoris laetitia, by Alain Thomasset, S.J., and Jean-Miguel Garrigues, O.P. (Paris: Cerf, 2017), 146–48. For important concerns about the notion of conscience operative in *Amoris Laetitia*, see Kevin L. Flannery, S.J., and

In footnote 351, he affirms that "in certain cases, this can include the help of the sacraments."[25] He does not specify here whether this includes reception of the Eucharist for some persons who are living in a civil marriage while being bound by a valid sacramental marriage, although his letter to the bishops of the Buenos Aires pastoral region indicates that for him this is the case.

I note that Pope Francis does not argue that broken, valid sacramental marriages have been dissolved by their brokenness. Underscoring his commitment to the indissolubility of marriage, he observes: "To show understanding in the face of exceptional situations never implies dimming the light of the fuller ideal, or proposing less than what Jesus offers to the human being."[26] But how can

---

Thomas V. Berg, "*Amoris Laetitia*, Pastoral Discernment, and Thomas Aquinas", *Nova et Vetera* 16 (2018): 93–95, 102–4. See also Eberhard Schockenhoff's "Our Understanding of Moral Sin: The Competence of Conscience of Divorced Remarried Persons", *INTAMS Review* 20 (2014), in which Schockenhoff argues—prior to *Amoris Laetitia* but along lines found in *Amoris Laetitia*—that "each person's conscience will ultimately make the final judgment about personal faults and failures in conflicts caused by dissolved relationships and divorce, and relying on a person's conscience does not call into question the ecclesial teaching of the indissolubility of marriage and the obligatory nature of the promise of marital fidelity" (249). For background, see also my "Pinckaers and Häring on Conscience", forthcoming in *Journal of Moral Theology*; as well as the significantly different teaching on conscience found in paragraphs 54–64 of Pope John Paul II's 1993 encyclical *Veritatis Splendor*. George S. Worgul remarks, "The understanding of conscience seemingly implicit in *Amoris laetitia* might be judged a return to the theological vision of conscience being articulated by moderately progressive moralists immediately prior to the Second Vatican Council and until the papacy of John Paul II. Some representatives of this interpretation were my professor Canon Louis Janssens in Leuven, Josef Fuchs and Bernard Häring in Rome or Richard McCormick and Charles Curran in the USA" (George S. Worgul, "*Amoris Laetitia*: On the Need for a Contextual Theology and Inculturation in Practice", in Knieps-Port le Roi, *Point of No Return?*, 21). See also the "fundamental option" understanding of conscience in Nadia Delicata, "Sin, Repentance and Conversion in *Amoris Laetitia*", in Knieps-Port le Roi, *Point of No Return?*, 82.

[25] Pope Francis, *Amoris Laetitia*, no. 305.

[26] Ibid., no. 307. In her discussion of *Amoris Laetitia*, Stephanie Höllinger states that the "ideal"—which she earlier calls the "doctrine"—"remains indispensable as a point of orientation, although at the same time, and this is Pope Francis' main critique, it should not become a relentless standard demanding that the perfection implied by the ideal should be necessarily and continuously accomplished without any deviation" (Stephanie Höllinger, "Do We Expect Too Much? A Reflection on Expectations and Marriage in *Amoris Laetitia*", in Knieps-Port le Roi, *Point of No Return?*, 113). Of course the "ideal" cannot be "necessarily and continuously accomplished", which is why the objective and intrinsic indissolubility of marriage is such good news; namely, marriage can and does survive the frequent trials that occur in a real marriage. If in its references to the "ideal" of indissoluble marriage, *Amoris*

one be bound by the commitments entailed in a valid sacramental marriage that one entered freely and fully—commitments whose binding character does not depend upon things being ideal—while at the same time having sexual intercourse with one's civilly married partner, without being objectively in a state of adultery and therefore being in a state that (whatever one's subjective situation) requires the merciful call to regularize one's marital situation prior to receiving the Eucharist?[27]

A central thrust of *Amoris Laetitia* is its deep concern for people who are in long-term relationships with persons who are not their indissolubly married spouse, and, correspondingly, its frustration that the Church may seem to be leaving such Catholics stranded, especially if their civil marriage has been long-standing and fruitful and

---

Laetitia meant what Höllinger means, then it would in fact be teaching that a valid and consummated Sacrament of Matrimony is dissoluble—an interpretation that neither Pope Francis nor any of his preferred interpreters have supported and that would contradict the explicit teaching of *Amoris Laetitia*. Objective indissolubility serves the process by which spouses can address the brokenness of their marriage, through the four steps promoted by Höllinger (and by *Amoris Laetitia*): "(1) abandonment of egoism, (2) acceptance of differences, (3) forgiveness and (4) hope" (ibid., 114). For discussion of *Amoris Laetitia*'s references to the "ideal" of marriage, see Angel Perez-Lopez, "*Veritatis Splendor* and *Amoris Laetitia*: Neither Lamented nor Celebrated Discontinuity", *Nova et Vetera* 16 (2018): 1199–200.

[27] Note that experience shows that the light of the "fuller ideal" can be fairly easily dimmed. See, for example, the remarks of Archbishop Cyril Vasil', S.J., "Separation, Divorce, Dissolution of the Bond, and Remarriage: Theological and Practical Approaches of the Orthodox Churches", in *Remaining in the Truth of Christ: Marriage and Communion in the Catholic Church*, ed. Robert Dodaro, O.S.A. (San Francisco: Ignatius Press, 2014), 125–26: "The Orthodox Churches, even through the expressions of their supreme authorities—oftentimes only passively—accept the sociological reality. This laxity reveals not only the inadequate expansion of the legitimate causes for divorce compared with the criteria that are indicated in the *Nomocanon*, but also the total disappearance of the differences between the divorce conceded *bona gratia* and the divorce conceded *cum damno*. We also see this laxity in the acceptance of the possibility of a second marriage for a divorced person, where the difference is practically eliminated between the party that caused the breakdown of the marriage and the innocent party, thereby creating the impression that a decree of divorce automatically concedes the right to contract a new marriage." Vasil' adds that "from the point of view of Catholic matrimonial law, we are bound to consider a marriage valid until there is certain contrary proof (cf. can. 1060 *Codex Iuris Canonici* [CIC] and can. 779 *Canonum Ecclesiarum Orientalium* [CCEO]). Many Orthodox Churches do little more than simply ratify the divorce sentence issued by the civil court. In other Orthodox Churches, as, for example, in the Middle East, in which ecclesial authorities hold exclusive competence in matrimonial matters, declarations dissolving religious marriages are issued solely by applying the principle of *oikonomia*" (ibid., 127).

if for some reason they may not be subjectively culpable.[28] In this light, Christoph Cardinal Schönborn has commented with regard to *Amoris Laetitia*, "On the level of principle, the doctrine of marriage and the sacraments is clear. Pope Francis has newly expressed it with great clarity. On the level of discipline, the pope takes account of the endless variety of concrete situations."[29] Similarly, in his recently published book on *Amoris Laetitia*, Walter Cardinal Kasper maintains

---

[28] For this emphasis, see the interview of Cardinal Schönborn by Antonio Spadaro, S.J., "Cardinal Schönborn on 'The Joy of Love': The Full Conversation", Brian McNeil, trans., *America Magazine*, August 9, 2016, https://www.americamagazine.org/issue/richness-love. Schönborn observes that Pope Francis upholds "the strength of doctrine", without weakening it in any way, while at the same time rejecting "a withdrawal into abstract pronouncements unconnected to the subject who lives and who bears witness to the encounter with the Lord that changes one's life". I agree with Schönborn that we must not withdraw into abstraction. We must insist, doctrinally and pastorally, upon helping each and every person—in the midst of the profound difficulties that afflict us—to encounter the merciful Jesus, who is the Lord and who stunned his disciples by teaching them that "whoever divorces his wife, except for unchastity, and marries another, commits adultery; and he who marries a divorced woman, commits adultery" (Mt 19:9). Perceiving that this statement of Jesus is in fact one of mercy, we must affirm with Schönborn that "before we denounce, we must announce and accompany, stimulating growth and consolidating a deeper perception." Like all sinners, I appreciate what Schönborn calls the "positive pastoral style" that is "a way of expounding doctrine in a gentle manner, linking it to the profound motivations of men and women. The totality of doctrine is expressed, but in a fresh and new way that a large public can read." It is when we are presented with Jesus' teaching in a manner that reveals to us its mercy that we are inspired to follow him. As Schönborn says, "No family is a perfect reality, since it is made up of sinners. The family is en route. I believe that this is the bedrock of the entire document.... It is biblical realism, the way of looking at human beings that Scripture gives us." Likewise, Schönborn is correct with regard to the path of conversion of life that fallen humans often take: "As one gradually grows, the invitation to follow Christ in the daily life of the family and of marriage will make it concretely possible for the rule to become the demand that love makes."

[29] See the Schönborn interview, "Joy of Love". In French, see Christoph Cardinal Schönborn, O.P., *Le Regard du Bon pasteur: Entretien avec Antonio Spadaro* (Paris: Parole et Silence, 2015). See also, for a cognate view, Marc Cardinal Ouellet, S.S., "A Missionary Gaze: Understanding 'Amoris Laetitia'", *L'Osservatore Romano*, November 8, 2017, www.osservatoreromano.va/en/news/missionary-gaze, and Marc Cardinal Ouellet, S.S., "Accompanying, Discerning, Integrating Weakness", *L'Osservatore Romano*, November 21, 2017, www.osservatoreromano.va/en/news/accompanying-discerning-integrating-weakness. As the theologian Christine Galea puts it, "Francis taps into the treasure of the church's teachings and confirms that its moral teachings have not changed" (Christine Galea, "Reflections on Commitment and the Indissolubility of Christian Marriage", in Knieps-Port le Roi, *Point of No Return?*, 178). For the view that the doctrine of marital indissolubility has not been changed, see also Vincent Mynem C. Sagandoy, "Canonical Imperatives of Pastoral Care in *Amoris Laetitia* concerning Catholics with Irregular Marital Status", in Knieps-Port le Roi, *Point of No Return?*, 181.

that "nothing in the objective norms is altered", even if there has been a *pastoral* paradigm-shift toward mercy.[30]

Along the same lines, in his commentary on chapter 8 of *Amoris Laetitia*, Francesco Cardinal Coccopalmerio observes that paragraph 292 "contains with absolute clarity all the elements of the doctrine of marriage in full compliance with and fidelity to the traditional teaching of the Church. In particular, we can highlight the affirmation of indissolubility, contained in the effective expression: 'who belong to each other until death.'"[31] Like Schönborn and Kasper, Coccopalmerio emphasizes that we are dealing not with a doctrinal change but with a pastoral development. He states, "We can say that the exhortation offers two points of view: the repeated affirmation of the firm resolve to remain faithful to the Church's teaching on marriage and the family; and the view of the Church, of pastors, and the faithful toward irregular partnerships, particularly civil marriages and de facto unions."[32] Along similar lines, the theologian Ignace Berten states

---

[30] Walter Cardinal Kasper, *Die Botschaft von Amoris laetitia: Ein freundlicher Disput* (Freiburg: Herder, 2018), 86. In his own survey of the positions of Schönborn and others, Thibaud Collin has pointed out that from the outset, the debates are a controversy between two schools of German-speaking theology, that of Schönborn (and Kasper) and that of Müller (and, implicitly, Ratzinger/Benedict); see Thibaud Collin, *Le mariage chrétien a-t-il encore un avenir? Pour en finir avec les malentendus* (Paris: Artège, 2018), 128, 138. See also Kasper's "Geschichtlichkeit der Dogmen?", in *Gesammelte Schriften*, vol. 7, *Evangelium und Dogma: Grundlegung der Dogmatik* (Freiburg: Herder, 2015), 623–44, in which Kasper identifies three criteria for the reformulation of dogma—(1) the hierarchy of truths, with all dogma pointing toward the Trinity's love for us; (2) ecumenical and ecclesial love; (3) the need to be liveable and understandable by people of today. These criteria are inadequate to sustain dogmatic truth about the revealed realities of faith, as Reinhard Hütter and Guy Mansini, O.S.B., have shown in their respective critiques of Kasper's understanding of dogma. See Hütter, *Dust Bound for Heaven: Explorations in the Theology of Thomas Aquinas* (Grand Rapids, MI: Eerdmans, 2012), 319–31; Mansini, *Fundamental Theology* (Washington, D.C.: Catholic University of America Press, 2018), 134–37.

[31] Francesco Cardinal Coccopalmerio, *A Commentary on Chapter Eight of* Amoris Laetitia, trans. Sean O'Neill (Mahwah, NJ: Paulist Press, 2017), 3. Müller underlines this same point with regard to paragraph 292's affirmation of the indissolubility of sacramental marriage; see Müller, "Warum 'Amoris laetitia'", 271.

[32] Coccopalmerio, *Commentary on Chapter Eight of* Amoris Laetitia, 7. Sagandoy describes the situation this way: "With *Amoris laetitia*, perhaps the church is being led to a point where Catholics in irregular marriages are no more an issue but an opportunity to dwell in the hearts of every faithful Christian starting from the pastors, pastoral workers, and the whole ecclesial communities. This assumption, of course, does not mean to undermine the fundamental obligation of the church to be firm in upholding the ideals of Christian marriages. The church has to teach all Christ's faithful regardless of their situation about these ideals that it firmly believes

that "Pope Francis clearly affirms that the objective of the synod [from which emerged *Amoris Laetitia*] is pastoral and not doctrinal."[33]

Regarding Schönborn's reference to "the endless variety of concrete situations", I note that in one sense the variety of situations is indeed "endless" due to the diversity of human beings and the infinity of moral acts. Yet, the concrete situation either will or will not involve a new civil marriage on top of a still-valid sacramental marriage. If one has freely bound oneself sacramentally and indissolubly to a spouse who is still alive, how can one freely choose to have sexual intercourse with another person, without falling under the ban that Jesus himself delivers?[34] Here it is not a matter of subjectively judging a person's spiritual condition, but rather it is a matter of obeying the merciful Lord's commandment and demonstrating our obedience to that commandment in terms of sacramental discipline and moral instruction.[35]

How can this tension be addressed? In accord with *Amoris Laetitia*, Schönborn proposes that a part of the answer is to recognize that subjectively speaking, there are numerous impediments to culpability for persons who are bound by a (broken) sacramental marriage but have long been living in a successful civil marriage. He rejects the rigorism fostered by "abstract casuistry" and insists that "it is possible, in certain cases, that the one who is in an objective situation of sin can receive

---

to be true. Nonetheless pastoral care remains fundamental in realizing this opportunity of God's mercy to be made more visible to every Christian faithful despite someone's unfortunate canonical situation" ("Canonical Imperatives of Pastoral Care in *Amoris laetitia*", 193–94).

[33] Berten, *Les divorcés remariés peuvent-ils communier?*, 331. Yet, Berten contends that "Francis opens the door to a practice that contradicts the doctrine [of marital indissolubility] as it was implemented and understood by John Paul II and Benedict XVI" (ibid., 334). Berten adds, "From this point of view, the contradictors of Francis and the harsher critics of his Exhortation are not wrong in denouncing a contradiction between this pastoral opening and the doctrine as it was defined by these two popes [John Paul II and Benedict XVI]" (ibid.).

[34] In its "Letter to the Bishops of the Catholic Church concerning the Reception of Holy Communion by Divorced and Remarried Members of the Faithful (September 14, 1994)", *Acta Apostolicae Sedis* 86 (1994): 974–79, the Congregation for the Doctrine of the Faith underscores the fundamental problem: persons who have once validly entered into Christian marriage, and whose spouse is still alive, still have a valid Christian marriage; divorce and civil remarriage does not dissolve the original Christian marriage. Since a Christian can only have one marriage at a time, the civil remarriage is not a Christian marriage, and therefore involves sexual intercourse with someone other than one's spouse.

[35] See also Fabrizio Meroni, "Pastoral Care of Marriage: Affirming the Unity of Mercy and Truth", *Communio* 41 (2014): 438–61.

the help of the sacraments", given that in fact all of us "come to the sacraments as beggars, like the tax collector at the back of the temple who does not dare to lift his eyes".[36] In Schönborn's view, such individual cases need not overthrow the general rules about sacramental discipline. Indeed, he warns against "creating, even by means of a norm that spoke of exceptions, a right to receive the Eucharist in an objective situation of sin".[37] He thinks that *Amoris Laetitia* calls for pastoral discernment without establishing such a "right".

Although *Amoris Laetitia* does not create a "right" to receive the Eucharist while remaining objectively in a state of sin, Schönborn makes clear that it does allow priests to arrive, in particular situations, at the decision to open the Eucharist to divorced and remarried persons who have a valid indissoluble marriage and plan to continue in sexual relations in their new civil union.[38] Schönborn

---

[36] See the Schönborn interview, "Joy of Love". For a similar approach to that taken by Schönborn in his interview, see Kasper's *Die Botschaft von Amoris laetitia*. Like Schönborn, Kasper favors Pope Benedict XVI's "hermeneutic of continuity" (with regard to Vatican II) and sets "the original Thomistic tradition" against an approach that has been "narrowed neo-Thomistically" (Kasper, *Die Botschaft von Amoris laetitia*, 87). Kasper also argues that *Amoris Laetitia* opens up "the reception of the sacrament of the Eucharist in certain limited and definite, so-called irregular situations" (ibid., 81). As Archbishop Victor Manuel Fernandez puts it, "The general canonical norm is conserved (cf. 300) even if it does not apply in certain cases in consequence of a process of discernment. In this process, the conscience of the concrete person, in his real situation in the eyes of God, in his real possibilities and limits, plays a determinative role. This conscience—accompanied by a pastor and illumined by the orientations of the Church—is in a position to furnish a judgment sufficient for discerning the possibility of returning to Eucharistic communion" (Victor Manuel Fernandez, *Chapitre VIII de* Amoris Laetitia: *Le bilan après la tourmente*, trans. Hortense de Parscau [Paris: Parole et Silence, 2018], 34). I was unable to acquire the 2017 Spanish original of this text quickly enough; see Victor Manuel Fernandez, "El capitulo VIII de *Amoris Laetitia*: lo que queda después de la tormenta", *Medellín* 43 (2017): 449–68. As is well known, Archbishop Fernandez assisted in the writing of *Amoris Laetitia*.

[37] See the Schönborn interview, "Joy of Love".

[38] Likewise emphasizing subjective conditions, Martin M. Lintner maintains that "even though remarriage after divorce may present a serious deviation from the ideal of marriage, marked by a commitment to exclusivity and stability, not every situation of remarriage after divorce automatically presents a grave sin for the involved moral subjects" (Martin M. Lintner, "Divorce and Remarriage: A Reading of *Amoris Laetitia* from a Theological-Ethical Perspective", in Knieps-Port le Roi, *Point of No Return?*, 139). Lintner affirms that "*Amoris Laetitia* is very clear and consistent in its argumentation so as to draw the conclusion that, in some cases, this document opens up the possibility for divorced and remarried persons to approach the sacraments of Reconciliation and the Eucharist. The counterargument that *Amoris laetitia* would not state this explicitly or that it would be insufficient to state such an

credits Pope Francis with broadening the Church's outlook on sacramental discipline with respect to civil marriage after a still-binding sacramental marriage. He praises the pope's "starting point in a long and authentic tradition of theoretical and practical moral theology with regard to the imputability of the subject. John Paul II did not take this directly into consideration, but he did not disown it.... Francis appeals to the praxis of the great tradition of spiritual directors whose role has always been that of discernment."[39] The key for Schönborn, then, is the pastoral discernment of subjective nonculpability. Commenting on paragraph 301, Coccopalmerio follows a similar path, identifying "reasons that would exempt the person from being in a condition of mortal sin" and arguing that there are situations in which following the moral law only gets the person "into further sin".[40]

In my view, although obeying the moral law in a particular situation can lead to suffering for a person and for his loved ones, such an act cannot cause a person to commit or cause a

---

important content ambiguously and as a footnote open to misinterpretation sounds unreasonable.... The intention and the whole argumentation of *Amoris laetitia* are clear" (ibid., 140). See also Lintner's "Geschieden und wiederverheiratet: Zur Problematik aus theologisch-ethischer Perspektive", in *Zwischen Jesu Wort und Norm: Kirchliches Handeln angesichts von Scheidung und Wiederheirat*, ed. M. Graulich and M. Seidnader (Freiburg: Herder, 2014), 193–215.

[39] See the Schönborn interview, "Joy of Love". For the argument that *Amoris Laetitia* enacts an implicit development of the doctrine of *Veritatis Splendor*, see Garrigues, "Répondre aux *dubia* des quatre cardinaux", 149–64. With regard to *Amoris Laetitia*, Garrigues differentiates between the faulty "interpretation of the Maltese bishops and, up to a certain point, that of the German bishops", and the salutary interpretation of Cardinal Schönborn and of the Argentine bishops—the key difference being "the degree to which they transform, by collective permissions, the encouragement of a 'case by case' subjective discernment advocated by *Amoris Laetitia*" (ibid., 115–16). See also the discussion of *Amoris Laetitia* in relation to *Veritatis Splendor* by Alain Thomasset in "Pour répondre aux doutes des cardinaux, préciser la juste place des norms morales universelles et leur application aux cas singuliers", in *Une morale souple mais non sans boussole*, 23–109. Thomasset's arguments are similar to Garrigues' and to others that I examine in the present chapter. Cardinal Schönborn contributed a preface to Thomasset and Garrigues' book. See also Thomasset's approach to conscience in his "Addendum d'Alain Thomasset", in *"La vocation et la mission de la famille dans l'Église et dans le monde contemporain": 26 théologiens répondent* (Paris: Bayard, 2015), 208–13, as well as the sharp line that he draws between the Church's teachings on abortion and on contraception in his "Réponse d'Alain Thomasset", 218–22, in the same volume.

[40] Coccopalmerio, *Commentary on Chapter Eight of* Amoris Laetitia, 16–17, with reference to paragraphs 298 and 301.

sin.[41] Yet, Coccopalmerio is clearly justified in adducing the troubling situation of a person for whom "abandoning the irregular situation would harm other people who are themselves innocent, namely the partner and the children, especially the latter."[42] He gives the example of "a woman who has gone to live with a man who was canonically married but was abandoned by his wife and left with three young children", an example in which the woman "has saved the man from deep despair, and probably from the temptation to commit suicide", and has had a child with the man.[43] For his part, Archbishop Victor Manuel Fernandez gives the example of a woman who, divorced from a husband to whom she is bound in indissoluble marriage, has a civil partner who is not a Christian. Fernandez points out, "The woman cannot oblige someone, who does not share her Catholic convictions, to live in perfect continence. In this case, it is not easy for a virtuous and pious woman to take the decision to abandon this man whom she loves."[44] Strengthening the example even further, he adds that the difficulty would be especially acute if the man "has protected her from an abusive husband", or "has prevented her from falling into prostitution or suicide".[45] To leave

---

[41] See Garrigues, "Répondre aux *dubia* des quatre cardinaux", 120: "The end does not justify the means." For Garrigues, in agreement with Schönborn (and with the main lines of Coccopalmerio's argument), the key is that the subjective circumstances of the acting person can "change the very object of an act that materially remains the same"—for example, the case of "a woman who takes a contraceptive because of her alcoholic, insane, or simply gravely irresponsible husband", or the case of "just war", which takes into account the likely consequences of the use of armed force (ibid., 122, 125–26, 136–37). For necessary clarifications—despite Garrigues' critique of Thomist teleology—see Stephen L. Brock, "*Veritatis Splendor* §78, St. Thomas, and (Not Merely) Physical Objects of Moral Acts", *Nova et Vetera* 6 (2008): 1–62, and Steven A. Long, "*Veritatis Splendor* §78 and the Teleological Grammar of the Moral Act", *Nova et Vetera* 6 (2008): 139–56.

[42] Coccopalmerio, *Commentary on Chapter Eight of* Amoris Laetitia, 19.

[43] Ibid., 20. Coccopalmerio adds, "The woman in question is fully aware of being in an irregular situation. She would sincerely like to change their living situation, but, evidently, cannot. In fact, if she left the union, the man would return to his former state, and the children would remain without a mother. Leaving the union would mean, therefore, not fulfilling important duties toward persons who are in themselves innocent. It is therefore evident that this could not take place 'without further sin'" (ibid.). Commenting on paragraphs 301 and 305 (as well as footnote 341), Coccopalmerio concludes, "The Church, therefore, could allow access to Penance and the Eucharist, for the faithful who find themselves in an irregular union, which, however, requires two essential conditions: they desire to change the situation, but cannot act on their desire" (ibid., 25).

[44] Fernandez, *Chapitre VIII de* Amoris Laetitia, 26.

[45] Ibid.

this man might also cause her children to be raised "without a father and without a familial environment", thereby causing grave distress to innocent children.[46] No doubt, as Fernandez says, such a situation would significantly "reduce the culpability or imputability" of the sin of having sexual relations with a person who is not one's indissoluble spouse, against the explicit teaching of Jesus Christ.[47]

While I agree as to the matter of likely reduced imputability of guilt in such extreme situations, still it must be said that on the other hand, the woman's testimony to the truth of indissoluble marriage—her act of self-sacrificial fidelity to Christ, of "losing" her life for Christ's sake (Mt 10:39)—might also, in God's plan of grace, have powerfully good effects upon her spouse from her indissoluble marriage, upon her civil partner, upon her children (from one or both unions), and upon her community. After all, in terms of its sacramental signification, marriage is a sign of the fidelity (to the point of death) of Christ for the people whom he has redeemed; and so choosing to live in a manner that is objectively contrary to this sign is contrary to the sacrament, whereas choosing to uphold the sacramental sign is a powerful testimony of grace. We cannot know all the good that graced deeds of chastity and fidelity, of carrying one's cross and following Jesus in the living out of the sacrament, may accomplish in God's plan. Nor can we assume that a relationship will not survive the adoption of sexual continence (whether voluntary or due to illness)—though in a fallen world it often may not. As Nicholas Healy observes, the fundamental point is that "truth as fidelity"—in this case fidelity to a freely entered covenantal bond of indissoluble marriage—"is not opposed to, or even in tension with, Christ's liberating love".[48]

---

[46] Ibid., 27.

[47] Ibid. Fernandez argues that in such a case, an act may remain objectively evil but it may nonetheless be "what is possible in a context proper to the given situation", and therefore may be consistent with charity (ibid., 47).

[48] Nicholas J. Healy, Jr., "Henri de Lubac on the Development of Doctrine", *Communio* 44 (2017): 688. Healy draws at length upon Gerhard Cardinal Müller's "Was dürfen wir von der Familie erwarten?" Müller cuts against the grain of Pope Francis' later interpretation of *Amoris Laetitia* in his letter to the bishops of the Buenos Aires pastoral region, but Müller does so in order to uphold certain central aspects of *Amoris Laetitia*, above all the aspect of marital indissolubility: "The key for the path of accompaniment is the harmony between the celebration of the sacraments and Christian life. Herein lie the reasons for the discipline with regard to the Eucharist, as it has always been preserved by the Church.... The principle is that no one can really want to receive a Sacrament—the Eucharist—without at the same time having the will to live according to all other Sacraments, among them the Sacrament of Marriage. Whoever

In many cases, stopping sinning does indirectly cause harm to innocent people. Nonetheless, stopping sinning must often be done, for the sake of justice and charity, trusting in the power of Christ and the Spirit. For instance, Paul insisted that Demetrius the silversmith stop making "silver shrines of Artemis" (Acts 19:24), since Demetrius' livelihood, like the livelihood of many others in the city of Ephesus, depended upon promoting idolatry. Similarly, when a struggling businessman with young children risks poverty by stopping his practice of corrupt theft, this return to Christian charity can cause grave suffering in a family. The difficulty of these circumstances dimishes culpability and demands our compassion. But even so, stopping the sin necessarily pertains to communion with the merciful Lord of love.[49]

In response to Antonio Spadaro's probing question, "How can this perspective of Francis be integrated into the classical doctrine of the church?", Schönborn reasons that there may be an analogy in the Church's practice of giving the Eucharist under specific circumstances to Orthodox Christians or (especially) to Protestants, who are not in full communion with the Catholic Church, due to the discernment of a grave spiritual situation on the part of the individual in question.[50] On this view, pastors can discern an analogous situation

---

lives in a way that contradicts the marital bond opposes the visible sign of the Sacrament of Marriage. With regard to his bodily existence, he turns himself into a 'counter-sign' of the indissolubility, even if he is not subjectively guilty. Exactly because his carnal life is in opposition to the sign, he cannot be part of the higher eucharistic sign—in which the incarnate Love of Christ is manifest—by thus receiving Holy Communion.... This is not an exaggerated conclusion drawn from the teaching, but, rather, the foundation itself of the Sacramental Constitution of the Church" (ibid., 88). Healy comments aptly, "What Cardinal Müller is trying to protect ... is not some abstract 'norm' unable to do justice to the complexity of concrete situations; rather it is the capacity of human love to image forth, and share in, Christ's loving self-gift, which is the substance both of the Church's Eucharist and of her faith. The point is simply that, in order to be faithful to the spousal covenant it is innately called to symbolize, sex has to be an expressive enactment of an indissoluble marriage—which, absent a declaration of nullity, still binds civilly divorced and remarried people with the spouses they first said 'Yes' to at the altar" (Healy, "Henri de Lubac", 688).

[49] See John Corbett, O.P., et al., "Recent Proposals for the Pastoral Care of the Divorced and Remarried: A Theological Assessment", *Nova et Vetera* 12, no. 3 (2014): 609.

[50] Here Schönborn cites Pope John Paul II, Encyclical Letter on the Eucharist in Its Relationship to the Church, *Ecclesia de Eucharistia* (April 17, 2003), no. 45. For the view that regular sharing in the Eucharist by Protestant spouses should be permitted—a view that leaves out important aspects of the reality of the Eucharist—see Corinne Bernhard-Bitaud and Thomas

on the part of some individuals living in sexually active civil marriages while being bound to an indissoluble sacramental marriage, by taking into consideration "the non-imputability, faith in the sacrament of matrimony, the search for possible paths that allow a response to the project of God in the reality of an objective significant process".[51] Appealing to "the ever more central dimension of mercy in the consciousness of the faithful" (which, I note, is often linked in contemporary Western culture to an ever-greater forgetfulness of the nature and gravity of sin[52]), Schönborn concludes that "we are witnessing here a development by means of the addition of a complementary truth, just as the 'primacy' formulated at the First Vatican Council has undeniably been developed through the addition of the 'collegiality' of the Second Vatican Council."[53]

Knieps-Port le Roi, " 'Nourishment for the Journey, not a Prize for the Perfect': Reflecting with *Amoris Laetitia* on Eucharistic Sharing in Interchurch Marriages", in Knieps-Port le Roi, *Point of No Return?*, 215–32. They argue that, in general, "Francis has broken new ground in theology which finally makes him demand that the flow of grace should not be hindered by any moral or church law" (ibid., 231). Their position implies, though, that such laws stand in the way of grace rather than marking out the paths by which God, in Christ and through his Spirit, unites his people and deepens his people in their love for God. They state, "What impedes the union between Christ and the church to be symbolized in the Eucharistic sharing of the interchurch marriage is the lack of full 'unity in faith, worship and community life' between the churches to which the spouses (and their families) belong—a fact that the spouses are not responsible for nor can do anything about" (ibid.). But the impediment is the following: one of the spouses does not believe that Christ established the Catholic Church and its faith and sacraments, and therefore freely refuses to give the assent of faith to Christ in union with the Church's faith. For further studies advocating Eucharistic Communion for the non-Catholic spouse, see, for example, *Being One at Home: Interchurch Families as Domestic Churches*, ed. Thomas Knieps-Port le Roi and R. Temmerman (Münster: LIT Verlag, 2015); P. Neuner, "Ein katholischer Vorschlag zur Eucharistiegemeinschaft", *Stimmen der Zeit* 211 (1993): 443–50; Ruth Reardon, "*Amoris Laetitia*: Comments from an Interchurch Family Perspective", *One in Christ* 50 (2016): 66–86.

[51] See the Schönborn interview, "Joy of Love".

[52] See Christian Smith et al., *Young Catholic America: Emerging Adults In, Out of, and Gone from the Church* (Oxford: Oxford University Press, 2014), and Christian Smith with Melinda Lundquist Denton, *Soul Searching: The Religious and Spiritual Lives of American Teenagers* (Oxford: Oxford University Press, 2005).

[53] See the Schönborn interview, "Joy of Love". He adds in the same vein, with broad reference to an interview given by Pope Emeritus Benedict XVI to Jacques Servais, "We touch here on some of the profound questions connected with the 'hermeneutic of reform in continuity.' In order to transmit the doctrine, to grasp it in greater depth and to present it in a way that corresponds to the demands of our time, a tremendous effort is needed to contextualize it, drawing a distinction between the truths that are contained in the deposit of faith and the

If this is "development by means of a complementary truth", then the two truths would be these: the subjectively nonculpable or unfree situation of a person who is in a successful civil union while being bound by an indissoluble marriage that truly cannot be annulled (even given the relaxed annulment rules that the Church now has), and the fact that this same person is deliberately choosing to be in a sexual relationship with someone who is not his or her indissolubly married spouse. The latter point has moral gravity, both for the person and for the person's indissolubly married spouse (and any children that they have from their indissoluble marriage).[54] In Matthew 19, Jesus not only warns in verse 9 that "whoever divorces his wife, except for unchastity, and marries another, commits adultery; and he who marries a divorced woman, commits adultery", but also in verse 18 Jesus names "You shall not commit adultery" among the commandments that the young man must obey in order

---

way in which they are enunciated. This is particularly relevant in the areas of anthropology and of the relationship between the church and today's world, where, at first sight, there may seem to be some discontinuity. One could mention several examples, such as lending money at interest or religious freedom, where the church has taken a fresh look and has sometimes corrected certain historical decisions in order to grasp more deeply, across apparent discontinuities, the truth that is entrusted to it" (ibid.).

[54] The 1917 Code of Canon Law described as "bigamy" a civil marriage on top of a sacramental marriage; see *The 1917 or Pio-Benedictine Code of Canon Law in English Translation*, ed. Edward N. Peters (San Francisco: Ignatius Press, 2001). Correctly, the 1983 Code of Canon Law does not use this term, in recognition that people who divorce and (without annulment) remarry are not seeking to practice bigamy or polygamy, but rather are acting as though their first marriage had been dissolved. For a defense of polygamy, however, see Abu Ameenah Bilal Philips and Jamila Jones, *Polygamy in Islam* (Riyadh: International Islamic Publishing House, 2005), especially 48–49. By ignoring arguments against marital exclusivity (especially as advanced by Muslim thinkers), theologians neglect significant problems for pastoral responses to divorce and remarriage without annulment—a point noted by Wilfrid Cardinal Napier of South Africa, who has repeatedly warned that Eucharistic Communion for a man married to two women will become difficult to withhold if the Church goes down her present pastoral path. As Nicholas Healy points out with respect to Walter Kasper's position, "By upholding indissolubility and thus the continued existence of the bond, Kasper is forced to abandon the exclusivity at the heart of marriage both as a natural institution and as a real symbol of Christ's love for the Church" (Healy, "Merciful Gift of Indissolubility and the Question of Pastoral Care", 323). Healy comments, "The ground of indissolubility is the total and permanent self-giving of the spouses through their exchange of vows and through their one-flesh union.... If a theologian or member of the Church thinks it is possible to be indissolubly bound to another while allowing for sexual relations with someone else, he or she has not affirmed the truth of indissolubility" (ibid., 323–24).

to attain eternal life.[55] Why, then, does the path of mercy not consist—as I strongly think it does—in calling the person to recognize the objective truth of this situation (if subjectively this truth has been obscured) and to end the sexual relationship, despite the (cruciform) suffering this will cause, as a prerequisite for Eucharistic Communion with the merciful Lord of life?[56]

[55] By contrast, Martin Lintner argues that "objective standards cannot be deduced simply by the nature of the institution of marriage and of marital acts because every act has to be understood as the act of a person, i.e. of a moral subject who acts with certain motives and intentions as well as with its limitations and conditional dispositions. What really matters is not some kind of immanent morality of an institution like marriage or of marital acts but the person who acts and who is the subject of an institution" (Lintner, "Divorce and Remarriage", 130–31). Surely, however, the obligations pertaining to the institution of marriage—to which the person has freely bound himself or herself—involve "objective standards", including, for example, sexual exclusivity. Lintner affirms that marriage requires certain subjective attitudes, suggesting that when these attitudes are present, this can suffice (and presumably when they are absent, then no objective requirements—grounded in marriage as an institution—hold): "It is evident that the doctrine of marriage of *Gaudium et spes* marks a significant turning point in understanding marriage not as contract, but as a covenant of personal love. Therefore, the morality of an act has to be judged by standards of personal love like trust, mutual respect, honour, fidelity and generous self giving, etc. It is only rational to recognize—as Pope Francis does for example in AL 298—that such personal values of love and partnership can be lived and witnessed also in expressions of a relationship which does not correspond (yet or completely) to the institutional or sacramental marriage. The criterion of regularity or irregularity is not a sufficient or adequate one for an ethical discernment of the different and often very complex situations of partnership and family realities" (ibid., 131).

[56] Coccopalmerio argues that it is possible for the Church to admit "to the sacraments [including the Eucharist] some of the Christian faithful who are in an irregular union" but that this does not mean that "the union is regular and that marriage is either not necessary or not indissoluble" (Coccopalmerio, *Commentary on Chapter Eight of* Amoris Laetitia, 26). This claim hinges upon his view that not only are some persons subjectively nonculpable, but also some persons are not free to leave their new union without sinning by causing harm to others. As noted above, I think that persons who stop an objectively sinful situation are not thereby sinning, despite potential (and real) harmful consequences to others. For the significance of adultery, see also Flannery and Berg, "*Amoris Laetitia*, Pastoral Discernment, and Thomas Aquinas", 93–95. As Flannery and Berg comment toward the end of their essay, "Since the Apostolic age—and drawing upon the teaching of Jesus Christ himself—the Church has consistently taught that sexual intercourse with a person other than one's spouse is always, without exception, a gravely disordered behavior 'incapable of being ordered to God'" (ibid., 110). Pastorally, it is not good or just to leave "men and women entrusted to the Church's pastoral care in a state of perpetual moral ignorance, on the pretext that they would not be sinning formally" (ibid., 95). If a divorced person is still bound by a valid and consummated indissoluble marriage and, at the same time, is having sexual intercourse within a civil marriage, this action needs to be stopped prior to the restoration of Eucharistic Communion.

Citing paragraphs 2, 37, and 300 of *Amoris Laetitia*, the theologian Martin Lintner attempts to reply to objections of this kind. He states that without denying "the binding force of general norms", we must today recognize much more than the Church has done in the past "the impossibility of subsuming all single situations under a general rule", and we must "acknowledge the competence of the individual conscience in the process of understanding, judging and deciding how to respond as far as is possible to what God demands".[57] A fundamental question thus consists in whether the bond of indissoluble marriage imposes objective moral requirements (taught by Christ and the Church) that conscience, when rightly formed, not only can discern but also can obey. At an even deeper level, the ultimate question is whether indissoluble marriage is good for persons and communities. Have the moral teachings of Christ and the Church actually been good and salutary for human beings in the less-than-ideal circumstances of the fallen world?[58]

In light of the "law of gradualness" articulated by Pope John Paul II in paragraph 34 of *Familiaris Consortio* and affirmed by Pope Francis

---

[57] Lintner, "Divorce and Remarriage", 134. Lintner draws attention to G. Virt, "Moral Norms and the Forgotten Virtue of Epikeia in the Pastoral Care of the Divorced and Remarried", *Melita Theologica* 63 (2013): 17–34, and Michael G. Lawler and Todd A. Salzman, "In Amoris Laetitia, Francis' Model of Conscience Empowers Catholics", *National Catholic Reporter*, September 7, 2016, https://www.ncronline.org/news/theology/amoris-laetitia-francis-model-of-conscience-empowers-catholics; see also Michael G. Lawler and Todd A. Salzman's "*Amoris Laetitia* and the Development of Catholic Theological Ethics: A Reflection", in Knieps-Port le Roi, *Point of No Return?*, 30–44. Lintner urges the adoption of "a scepticism toward the attitude of deriving undue conclusions from particular theological considerations (cf. AL 2)" (Lintner, "Divorce and Remarriage", 135). At the same time, citing paragraph 307, he holds that "in *Amoris laetitia* the ideal of marriage stamped by its commitment to exclusivity and stability is not at all brushed aside" (ibid., 136).

[58] This is the bottom line, as is made clear by the rhetorical question of Thomas Knieps-Port le Roi: "Why then would we wish to load people up with excessive and unrealistic demands which they will probably never comply with, instead of inviting them to a path that promises personal development and fulfilment?" (Knieps-Port le Roi, introduction to *Point of No Return?*, 5). See also the observation of Reinhard Cardinal Marx, "Reflections on the Synod Process and *Amoris Laetitia*", in Knieps-Port le Roi, *Point of No Return?*, 12: "It is in the significance of love for people's lives that *Amoris laetitia* has its inner core, and the conceptual threads extend from this starting point. Many things are rediscovered from this new, old perspective." Marx adds, "An abstract theology, and especially standardised pastoral work, which do not take account of the biographical context in which they are situated, becomes irrelevant." For insight into the relationship of family breakdown and secularization, see Mary Eberstadt, *How the West Really Lost God* (West Conshohocken, PA: Templeton Press, 2013).

in paragraph 295 of *Amoris Laetitia*, Coccopalmerio observes that this law applies pastorally when "a person has an inability, or serious difficulty, in implementing the law, at least in its totality, in all its requirements, because of a condition of weakness."[59] In helping spouses to live in accord with the objective obligations imposed by the valid and consummated indissoluble marriage, a pastor must not come across as hectoring or as lacking appreciation for the complexity of personal situations and the weakness of will that understandably often accompanies the prospect of painful choices. This is the central message of *Amoris Laetitia*. The purpose of the law of gradualness is to allow for a pastoral way of indicating the requirements of the moral law to people in a manner that serves to "facilitate the healing of their weakness" and to "increase their ability to act".[60]

---

[59] Coccapalmerio, *Commentary on Chapter Eight of* Amoris Laetitia, 39.

[60] Ibid. However, as will be seen in the next paragraph, the question is whether Coccopalmerio (and *Amoris Laetitia*) have correctly spelled out the "law of gradualness" in distinction from the "gradualness of law". Properly understood, the law of gradualness begins with the person being aware that he is currently in a state of mortal sin. To take the example given by Branislav Kuljovsky, "the continuous development towards the full horizon of the moral good can never take the form of specific kinds of behavior considered morally evil regardless of one's circumstances and motivations. Thus, for example, one can never graduate the norm prohibiting sexual intercourse with an unwilling partner (rape) as if one could permit it as long as its brutality diminishes in time or as long as one finds oneself in a difficult life circumstance, or as long as one feels unable, due to his/her weakness, to avoid it" (Branislav Kuljovsky, "The Law of Gradualness or the Gradualness of Law? A Critical Analysis of *Amoris Laetitia*", in Knieps-Port le Roi, *Point of No Return?*, 57). Kuljovsky has put his finger upon a crucial weak point of *Amoris Laetitia*, one that will have to be corrected because, as Kuljovsky's example shows (and many others could be given), it does not make sense. As Kuljovsky goes on to explain, "Whereas 'the law of gradualness' requires us to recognize the moral evil and [do] everything possible, with the help of God's grace, to overcome it, 'the gradualness of law' would most probably remind us of our final destination and, as long as this ideal is kept in mind, for the time being, due to our weakness, immaturity or other difficult circumstances, we can 'legitimately' continue to act in contradiction to the moral absolutes" (ibid., 58). The "gradualness of law" is related to the theory of the "fundamental option", advocated by Bernard Häring and others, as well as to the widespread postconciliar denial that there are intrinsically evil acts (evil in all circumstances). For an instructive critique of such viewpoints, see Pope John Paul II's *Veritatis Splendor*. Many theologians simply reject *Veritatis Splendor*, however, as for instance Peter Hünermann's explanation of "why *Amoris laetitia* does not quote certain passages from *Familiaris consortio*, *Veritatis splendor*, and the *Catechism of the Catholic Church*: it is because these contain an erroneous interpretation of intrinsically evil actions" (Peter Hünermann, "The Sacrament of Marriage: A Dogmatic Theologian Reads *Amoris Laetitia*", in *A Point of No Return?* Amoris Laetitia *on Marriage, Divorce, and Remarriage*, ed. Thomas Knieps-Port le Roi [Berlin: LIT Verlag, 2017], 104). *Veritatis Splendor* repeatedly teaches about intrinsically evil actions and states solemnly that "theological opinions constitute

In light of paragraphs 303, 305, and 308 of *Amoris Laetitia*, Coccopalmerio adds that in certain cases it suffices, at least at a particular stage, for a person to make a forward movement morally or to
wish earnestly to do so.[61] His example is "the woman who has been
cohabiting for years, who is aware of the illegitimacy of her union,
is genuinely eager to put the end to it, however, is unable, at least at
present, to put her resolution into practice." To extend my example
above, the businessman-thief with young dependents might decide
to steal less, even while continuing to defraud his customers. Coccopalmerio supposes that "God himself requires only what is possible
and, therefore, is pleased with what is possible."[62] I agree with Coccopalmerio that pastors and others must encourage each and every
moral advance, with real love for sinners, ensuring insofar as possible
that "no one is excluded" from the life and love of the community.[63]
Recognizing that every person is "important and lovable",[64] Christians must not arrogantly "break a bruised reed or quench a smol-
dering wick" (Mt 12:20; cf. Is 42:3). Although self-righteousness and

---

neither the rule nor the norm of our teaching. Its authority is derived, by the assistance of the
Holy Spirit and in communion *cum Petro et sub Petro*, from our fidelity to the Catholic faith
which comes from the Apostles" (*Veritatis Splendor*, no. 116, in *The Encyclicals of Pope John Paul
II*, ed. J. Michael Miller, C.S.B. [Huntington, IN: Our Sunday Visitor, 2001], 658).

[61] Kuljovsky rightly points out that the manner in which the "law of gradualness" is defined
in paragraph 295 is a problem. Here, as Kuljovsky says, "while the 'gradualness of law' is
rejected, without explaining what it actually is, a completely new definition of the 'law of
gradualness' is coined. This new explanation seems to imply that as long as an individual or a
couple is 'not in a position to understand, appreciate or fully carry out' the objective demands
of the law (in this case a norm prohibiting premarital sex) it is legitimate not to ask from them
an *immediate effort* to observe the norm ... since, after all, human beings accomplish the moral
good by stages" (Kuljovsky, "Law of Gradualness or Gradualness of Law?", 59). To call persons
to observe the norm is done in accord with the "law of gradualness" not by approving sinful
actions if they represent advances, but by exercising pastoral patience and kindness. Thus, if
after the elucidation of the norm, persons try but fail to obey it "due to their weakness or other
difficult life circumstances, the law of gradualness should remind the priests or pastoral workers
not to judge or admonish the spouses, but rather to kindly and patiently encourage and inspire
them anew to follow the good protected by the norm. In no case can the law of gradualness
entitle them to license morally evil kinds of behavior" (ibid., 52). For the opposite view, see
Thomas Knieps-Port le Roi and Roger Burggraeve, "New Wine in New Wineskins: Amoris Laetitia and the Church's Teaching on Marriage and Family", *Louvain Studies* 39 (2016):
284–302, and to a certain degree Fernandez, "*Chapitre VIII de* Amoris Laetitia", 45–55.

[62] Coccapalmerio, *Commentary on Chapter Eight of* Amoris Laetitia, 42.
[63] Ibid., 53.
[64] Ibid.

judgmental haste must at all costs be avoided, however, I note that for persons who seek the aid of Christ, stopping the unjust action always belongs to "what is possible" by God's grace. Without rejecting any moral advance, God is not yet "pleased" by the action of a person whose action is objectively gravely wrong.[65] Jesus teaches that the one who does the will of the Father is the one who actually implements, rather than simply affirming, his Father's commandments (Mt 21:28–31).

Schönborn states at the end of his interview: "Love is demanding; but there is no greater joy than love."[66] The question, then, is how to manifest this demanding and joyful love when bound by an indissoluble marriage and its obligation of sexual exclusivity.[67]

---

[65] I note that insofar as paragraph 304 uses Aquinas' *Summa theologiae* I-II, q. 94, a. 4, to imply that no general norm can always and everywhere prohibit a certain kind of action, this is a mistaken interpretation of Aquinas. For the development of this interpretation, see Louis Janssens, "Ontic Evil and Moral Evil", *Louvain Studies* 4 (1972): 115–56; Louis Janssens, "A Moral Understanding of Some Arguments of Saint Thomas", *Ephemerides Theologicae Lovanienses* 63 (1987): 354–60; Franz Scholz, "Problems on Norms Raised by Ethical Borderline Situations: Beginnings of a Solution in Thomas Aquinas and Bonaventure", in *Readings in Moral Theology*, vol. 1, *Moral Norms and Catholic Tradition*, ed. Charles E. Curran and Richard A. McCormick, S.J. (New York: Paulist Press, 1979), 158–83; Karl-Wilhelm Merks, "Grenzzäune mit Löchern? Über die Allgemeingültigkeit moralischer Normen", in *Amoris laetitia—Wendepunkt für die Moraltheologie?*, ed. S. Goertz and C. Witting (Freiburg: Herder, 2016), 160–200. For Thomistic responses, see, for example, Servais Pinckaers, O.P., *Ce qu'on ne peut jamais faire. La question des actes intrinsèquement mauvais: Histoire et discussion* (Paris: Cerf, 1986), and Basil Cole, O.P., "Thomism, Moral Claim and *Amoris Laetitia*", *Anthropotes* 33 (2017): 313–26. See also Serge-Thomas Bonino, O.P., "Saint Thomas in the Apostolic Exhortation *Amoris Laetitia*", *Thomist* 80 (2016): 499–519.

[66] See the Schönborn interview, "Joy of Love".

[67] For his part, Rocco Buttiglione argues that all that is needed, in some cases, for the restoration of Eucharistic Communion is the following: "Go to confession, and the priest, once he has considered all the circumstances, will decide whether to give you absolution and admit you to the Eucharist or not" (Rocco Buttiglione, "The Joy of Love and the Consternation of Theologians: Some Comments on the Apostolic Exhortation *Amoris Laetitia*", *L'Osservatore Romano*, July 19, 2016, www.osservatoreromano.va/en/news/joy-love-and-consternation-theologians). Buttiglione states uncontroversially that "circumstances influence the moral evaluation of the one performing the action, rendering the agent more or less culpable of the objectively evil act he or she commits"; and he grants that "there is no doubt that a divorced and remarried person is objectively in a situation of grave sin" (ibid.). But his pastoral approach appears to deem a situation okay prior to the moral resolution of the situation by the Church. Unless the pastor has access to knowledge that is intrinsically unavailable to the Church's annulment process, what is needed first and foremost is the action of determining publicly whether the sacramental marriage was valid. Under normal circumstances, it does not suffice for the pastor simply to try to determine whether the person is subjectively culpable.

The Current Situation

Most importantly, in accord with earlier solemn Magisterial teaching, *Amoris Laetitia* affirms the indissolubility of a valid and consummated Christian marriage. At the same time, I have tried to give a place in this discussion to the tension in the pastoral approach taken by the bishops of the Buenos Aires pastoral region—namely, the fact that the obligations of the indissoluble marriage (including sexual exclusivity) are objectively contradicted by the sexually active new union.[68] As we have seen, Schönborn, Coccopalmerio, Kasper, Fernandez, and others contend that the new pastoral approach does not undermine in any way Catholic teaching on marital indissolubility. Yet, the theologian Thomas Knieps-Port le Roi argues approvingly that while "it was often heard that *Amoris laetitia* does not change doctrine but simply calls for a better pastoral care on the basis of that doctrine", in fact "this is an overly scrupulous way of presenting things and is, in the end, not true."[69] Knieps-Port le Roi insists that *Amoris*

---

[68] See José Granados, "La relation entre l'eucharistie et le mariage, et ses implications pour l'interprétation d'*Amoris Laetitia*", *Nova et Vetera* 92 (2017): 165–81; Scola, *Nuptial Mystery*, 290–303; John Meyendorff, *Marriage: An Orthodox Perspective*, 3rd rev. ed. (Yonkers, NY: St. Vladimir's Seminary Press, 1975), 20–24, 73–74; and Carlos Cardinal Caffarra, "Sacramental Ontology and the Indissolubility of Marriage", in Dodaro, *Remaining in the Truth of Christ*, 172–74. See also Sebastian Walshe, O.Praem., "The Formation and Exercise of Conscience in Private and Public Matters", *Nova et Vetera* 16 (2018): 275–309, especially 303–7. The case for reading *Amoris Laetitia* in accord with the traditional pastoral practice is made by José Granados, Stephan Kampowski, and Juan José Pérez-Soba, *Accompanying, Discerning, Integrating: A Handbook for the Pastoral Care of the Family According to* Amoris Laetitia, trans. Michael J. Miller (Steubenville, OH: Emmaus Road, 2017), and Perez-Lopez, "*Veritatis Splendor* and *Amoris Laetitia*". Granados raises the concern in a recent article that "some interpretations of the Apostolic Exhortation *Amoris laetitia* appear to call into question this sacramental framework of the Church. 1) For example, they question the harmony between the sacraments, specifically between marriage, on the one hand, and the Eucharist and Penance, on the other hand, saying that this harmony is a theological conclusion from which it is inadvisabe to draw exaggerated conclusions. 2) Furthermore they deny that there must be consistency between the sacraments and the way of Christian life, so that someone who lives contrary to that way could receive them. 3) They make the economy of the sacraments subjective, so that it ceases to be a visible economy in the flesh and in history and turns instead into an economy of the isolated, self-referential conscience. 4) All this happens, moreover, by calling into question the essential properties of marriage, since analogies are drawn between it and other lifestyles contrary to spousal love, such as cohabitation or a second union after a divorce" (José Granados, "From Flesh to Flesh: On the Sacramental Meaning of Tradition", *Communio* 44 [2017]: 665).

[69] Knieps-Port le Roi, introduction to *Point of No Return?*, 3.

Laetitia "does not ... abolish the church's teaching on the indissolubility of marriage, but it will necessarily have an impact on and ultimately modify Catholic understanding of that doctrine."[70] The modification that Knieps-Port le Roi has in view makes every Catholic marriage contingently dissoluble depending upon the spouses' acts and feelings over time. If the Church can welcome to the Eucharistic table persons who, despite being bound by an indissoluble marriage, are in a new (sexually active) union, then the obligations of the indissoluble sacramental marriage have in fact been dissolved in these cases—something that is possible only if indissoluble marriage is dissoluble in practice.

Going still further, Ignace Berten suggests that *Amoris Laetitia*, by contrast to the 2014 Synod's *relatio finalis*, deliberately avoids any appeal to the Church's "constant teaching". In his view, *Amoris Laetitia* does so because "the constancy of this teaching is not as clear as has been claimed (particularly as regards that which concerns ... indissolubility)", and also because the entire "teaching of the Church has been marked by ruptures over the course of its history".[71] Granting that the "great majority of the bishops" are not yet ready to recognize that a change of doctrine is "not only possible, but desirable", Berten considers that *Amoris Laetitia* prudently takes the path of ambiguity.[72] He thinks that *Amoris Laetitia* prepares the ground for the

---

[70] Ibid., 3–4.

[71] Berten, *Les divorcés remariés peuvent-ils communier?*, 319. Along a slightly different (but complementary) line, Berten comments, "On the one hand, by reason of the revelation in Jesus Christ, we have the truth: our knowledge is constant and definitive. On the other hand, we are on the way to truth: there is a truth in God, but there is no total access, and we have to understand truth through the experience of the present and through encounter with others" (ibid., 322). Berten proceeds to criticize Pope Benedict XVI sharply on this point, arguing that Benedict XVI's view of truth is "intransigent" and simplistic (ibid.). For Berten, the divide between Francis and Benedict XVI is the divide between Vatican II on the one hand, and Vatican I on the other.

[72] Ibid., 333–34. He observes in this regard that "one can neither separate nor oppose pastoral and doctrine" (ibid., 332). In his view, pastoral change is demanded by historical and cultural change, and in turn this pastoral change will demand doctrinal change: we must recognize "that when the culture has changed, as the experience in society has changed, to apply or to impose upon situations a doctrine elaborated in another context is an impasse" (ibid., 333). This is historicism—although Berten tries to save it by distinguishing between the "deposit of faith", counted as the apostolic teaching and the first seven ecumenical councils, and "doctrine as taught by the Church at a specific moment" (ibid., 336). Berten states, "An objective, honest reading of the Church's history over the past century and a half shows

future Church to teach that marital indissolubility is not a concrete norm but rather is a "call" of Christ that must then be "inculturated" in the diversity of historical, cultural, and individual situations.[73] Berten concludes that whatever the bishops might say about it, the pastoral change in fact "necessarily implies a change of doctrine".[74] If, as Berten maintains, Christ calls marriage to indissolubility without making it so through the sacrament, then every Christian marriage is actually contingently dissoluble, and no marriage has *ever* been indissoluble in the strict sense taught by Christ and promised to believers solemnly for centuries by the Catholic Church.

Such direct challenges to *Amoris Laetitia*'s teaching on marital indissolubility should encourage ongoing reflection about which pastoral approaches are adequate to the doctrine of marital indissolubility.[75] Only in this way will *Amoris Laetitia*'s merciful goals be attained

---

the evidence that doctrines affirmed in a dogmatic way have been abolished or substantially changed: liberty of conscience, democracy, the value of reference to human rights, ecumenism, the positive signification of non-Christian religions, the historicity of the biblical text. On all of these subjects, there have been solemn condemnations ... without any ambiguity" (ibid., 333; for a broadly similar, though briefer, list, see Fernandez, *Chapitre VIII de* Amoris Laetitia, 37–38, though Fernandez sees doctrinal development rather than rupture here). I maintain that in each case it can be shown that either the (usually papal) teaching was nondefinitive or that the definitive core of the teaching has indeed been preserved in later definitive teaching. Berten himself complains about the tendency to "dogmatize" everything said by a pope (*Les divorcés remariés peuvent-ils communier?*, 335), and he and I agree about this (although his above reference to "doctrines affirmed in a dogmatic way" is part of the problem). His rejection of the teaching of *Humanae Vitae* and of the prohibition of the ordination of women goes to the opposite extreme and denies that the Church, in consistent teaching over the course of centuries, can teach definitively on central topics of Christian life (such as embodied self-giving love in acts of marital intercourse, with respect to the teleological ordering of created human sexuality). See also my *Engaging the Doctrine of Revelation: The Mediation of the Gospel through Church and Scripture* (Grand Rapids, MI: Baker Academic, 2014).

[73] Berten, *Les divorcés remariés peuvent-ils communier?*, 320–21.

[74] Ibid., 339–40. Berten adds, "But things often evolve slowly" (ibid., 340). He makes clear that he is talking about marital indissolubility: "Taking into account the reality of our societies demands that one re-think the theological and pastoral meaning of the sacrament of marriage and more broadly of sexuality, along with the meaning that the Church has sought to express by the word 'indissolubility' " (ibid.).

[75] Such ongoing discussion would fit with the vision that Richard R. Gaillardetz has of Pope Francis' exercise of authority: "A more pluriform and multidirectional exercise of authority, in which genuine authority—or more accurately, authorities—contributes to the whole church as its members learn to listen to others, including those with whom they disagree" (Richard R. Gaillardetz, "Does Synodality Help the Church Live Out Her Mission Today?", in Gallicho and Keenan, *Amoris Laetitia*, 131).

along the path that Pope Francis (joined by Schönborn, Cocco-palmerio, Fernandez, Kasper, and many others) requires—namely, a path that does not jeopardize or undermine marital indissolubility as a sacramental pledge, a concrete reality, and an existential hope. Here I agree with the theologian Christoph Theobald, even though I disagree with his application of the insight: "The content of Christian faith *and* its manner of 'incarnating' itself personally in speech and actions constitute one body and form a coherent and credible unity."[76] This unity is expressed visibly most fully in the celebration of the Eucharist.

Contemporary reflection upon pastoral practice and sacramental discipline in concrete cases of divorce and remarriage needs to be deepened philosophically, theologically, and exegetically, so as to see the issues from their most profound ground. The way forward pastorally will require a reengagement with the reasons for and implications of Catholic doctrine and practice concerning the indissolubility of marriage, in light of Pope Francis' goals.[77] This

---

[76] Christoph Theobald, S.J., *Urgences pastorales du moment présent: Pour une pédagogie de la réform* (Paris: Bayard, 2017), 11. Theobald advocates changing the Church's understanding of marital indissolubility. He argues that in the New Testament texts (specifically Matthew 19:9 and 1 Corinthians 7:15) Jesus' eschatological "*announcement* of indissolubility is already integrated and 'translated' into precise pastoral situations, marked by their contingency and human limitations" (ibid., 218). In his view, marital indissolubility is an eschatological ideal that the Church must always proclaim while allowing for divorce and remarriage in practice, thus demonstrating pastoral appreciation for "the extreme diversity of situations" and for "the uniqueness of persons and their always new, unique, and contingent situation" (ibid., 220–21). Much like Knieps-Port le Roi and Berten (and many others), Theobald concludes that "the *spiritual* discernment demanded by this 'polyhedric' diversity of cultural and personal situations, often marked by very great fragility, is certainly regulated by doctrine, but, in the final analysis, frees the personal engagement of all the actors from all law and necessity, thus inevitably re-shaping their very understanding of the doctrine" (ibid., 221)—namely, by turning the doctrine of marital indissolubility into a teaching about an eschatological ideal that in all concrete instances involves nothing more than a contingently dissoluble marriage.

[77] Commenting on paragraphs 293, 294, and 297 of *Amoris Laetitia*, Coccopalmerio describes Pope Francis' pastoral intentions thusly, in a manner that makes sense to me (especially if one adds that in once-Catholic countries, many nominal Catholics often have little idea why the Church teaches what she does, but believe simply that the Church is judgmental): "when dealing with irregular unions, such as civil marriages and even de facto unions, pastors must approach them in a positive and constructive way, which I think means having three important attitudes: The first is to recognize, objectively, clearly and without preconceptions or hasty judgments, the reason that has led some believers to choose, not canonical marriage, but rather other forms of cohabitation: the reason for this is not always, or not frequently,

ressourcement, with its purpose of deepening the Church's pastoral expression of Christ's merciful teaching, will involve further effort to understand the reasons why the Church's teaching about marital indissolubility, even in its self-sacrificial aspect, is good for human persons and communities.

Catholics need to discern with increased depth how, in his teaching about the indissolubility of marriage, Christ is healing and elevating his followers, not judging or excluding them. Likewise, Catholics need to ask how it is that the Church's handing on of the Gospel, when it is a matter of positive teachings drawn from the Lord's own words,[78] stands as an enduringly true cognitive communication of divine revelation, without overlooking the historical and cultural contexts in which parts of the "good news" may seem less than good.

Catholics must also frankly ask whether Catholic teaching on marriage has simply been incoherent and thus harmful. Along these lines, the theologian Edward Schillebeeckx influentially argued that once a marriage has utterly broken down (due to the actions of the couple after the validly contracted Christian marriage), then it is obvious that there is no longer any marriage left to be labeled "indissoluble".[79] For Schillebeeckx, the ongoing hermeneutical process, not any specific cognitive content or teaching, is the sole definitive and authoritative element in the Church's tradition or interpretative handing on of

---

a denial of the value of canonical marriage, but rather some contingency, such as lack of work and therefore of secure income. The second attitude of pastors of souls must be to refrain from an immediate condemnation of irregular unions and to recognize that in many of them there are positive elements, such as stability, which can even be guaranteed by a public bond, a real affection toward the partner and toward the children, and a commitment to society or the Church. A third attitude suggested by the texts is certainly one of dialogue with these couples, which means that the pastors of souls must not simply be satisfied with the irregular situations, but must strive to make the faithful who are in that situation reflect on the possibility, indeed the beauty and the opportunity, of realizing the celebration of a marriage in its fullness, before the Church" (Coccopalmerio, *Commentary on Chapter Eight of* Amoris Laetitia, 12).

[78] As distinct, for example, from the Church's teachings on the Jewish people or on slavery, where the New Testament witness is far more varied—though in these two areas, too, there are clear principles for justifying doctrinal development.

[79] See Edward Schillebeeckx, O.P., "Christian Marriage and the Reality of Complete Marital Breakdown", in *Catholic Divorce: The Deception of Annulments*, ed. Pierre Hegy and Joseph Martos (New York: Continuum, 2000), 82–107. Schillebeeckx's essay was first published as "Het christelijk huwelijk en de menselijke realiteit van volkomen huwelijksontwrichting", *Annalen van het Thijmgenoorschap* (1970): 184–214.

texts.[80] Thus he is not worried about whether there might be a "rupture" with doctrine taught definitively by Christ and the Church, because he sees all doctrine as radically contextualized and therefore identifies the present cultural moment as the sole context in which any concrete propositional teaching can be deemed authentic. Schillebeeckx's position does not do justice to the promises of Jesus, to his status as Lord, or to the authority of the teachings of the "Church of the living God, the pillar and bulwark of the truth" (1 Tim 3:15).

[80] See Edward Schillebeeckx, O.P., "Towards a Catholic Use of Hermeneutics", in *God the Future of Man*, trans. N.D. Smith (New York: Sheed and Ward, 1968), 20–21: "Can we and may we simply go on repeating word-for-word the 'old' material, the Bible and the traditional statements, including those of the official *magisterium* of the Church in the present and the past, under the penalty of being unfaithful to the message if we do otherwise? Or is not just such a literal repetition itself unfaithful—is *development* in dogma, an interpretative contemporary translation of the 'old' material of the faith, not essentially the fidelity that follows from man's historicity.... Living orthodoxy can be attained only *within* a reinterpretative present-day understanding of faith which is faithful to the biblical interpretation of faith. We can, after all, never dispense with interpretation of a previously given (and originally, a biblical) interpretation, which becomes authentically understood precisely in the reinterpretation." See also his *Church: The Human Story of God*, trans. John Bowden (New York: Crossroad, 1990). For a kindred approach, see Karl Rahner, S.J., *The Shape of the Church to Come*, trans. Edward Quinn (New York: Seabury Press, 1974), and Karl Rahner, S.J., "Yesterday's History of Dogma and Theology for Tomorrow", in *Theological Investigations*, vol. 18, *God and Revelation*, trans. Edward Quinn (New York: Crossroad, 1983), 3–34. Rahner comments that "the history of faith and dogma will continue, since salvation history will continue in a new world history; but it will have a different character, not so much the character of a history of individual, newly articulated statements of faith and theological reflection on these, but the history of the new expression of the old basic substance of the faith confronting and assimilating the future horizons of understanding. It is obvious that this history will no longer be merely the history of dogma as formulated in the West and of its theology (to be exported to other countries), but the history of faith and dogma of a world Church, however little we can imagine its material and formal implications. What has been said does not exclude but includes the possibility that the new conception of the transposition of the substance of the Christian faith as one and whole will also have consequences for the interpretation of many or of all individual doctrines" (Rahner, "Yesterday's History of Dogma and Theology for Tomorrow", 34). This "substance" allegedly stands above all "individual doctrines", and therefore logically is unknowable via any enduring propositional formulation and "knowable" only as a nonconceptual experience of God's self-revelation. For a sympathetic study of Rahner's perspective, see Mary E. Hines, *The Transformation of Dogma: An Introduction to Karl Rahner on Doctrine* (New York: Paulist Press, 1989). See also Anthony M. Maher's appreciative study of George Tyrrell in relation to contemporary Catholic theology: Anthony M. Maher, *The Forgotten Jesuit of Catholic Modernism: George Tyrrell's Prophetic Theology* (Minneapolis, MN: Fortress Press, 2017). Andrew Meszaros has responded to viewpoints such as these in a historically sophisticated manner; see Andrew Meszaros, *The Prophetic Church: History and Doctrinal Development in John Henry Newman and Yves Congar* (Oxford: Oxford University Press, 2016).

Clearly, Pope Francis does not take such a position. As Archbishop Fernandez states, "Francis, like the Synod, upholds the existence of objective truths and norms, and he has never defended subjectivism or relativism. The project of God is marriage understood as an indissoluble union, and this point has not been called into question during the Synod or during his pontificate."[81] Instead, Pope Francis seeks to probe deeply into the enduring truth of Jesus' teaching that " 'no one has greater love than this, to lay down one's life for one's friends' (Jn 15:13)."[82] Far from denying enduringly true dogma, he grounds his teaching on marriage in Scripture as God's word and in Trinitarian dogma: "The word of God tells us that the family is entrusted to a man, a woman and their children, so that they may become a communion of persons in the image of the union of the Father, the Son and the Holy Spirit."[83]

I note that every Christian should be greatly moved by the suffering of those who are in "irregular" unions. In every way possible, we must desire to relieve their profound suffering, while at the same time recognizing that, like all of us, they have a cross to bear that we cannot remove. In the fallen world, suffering, death, and love are not only compatible, but deeply connected. The pastor is not supposed to attempt to remove *all* forms of suffering from the faithful, but the pastor must accompany his flock and suffer with his flock.

Thus, *Amoris Laetitia* challenges believers to be able to show why it is that marital indissolubility and its obligations are good *even* in the fallen world and *even* for believers who are called to make great sacrifices, in which the whole Church must share. In this light, it is necessary to ask whether the Catholic tradition of theological reflection about indissoluble marriage can help to articulate the goodness of marital indissolubility for believers and for the world today.[84] With

---

[81] Fernandez, *Chapitre VIII de* Amoris Laetitia, 31.

[82] Pope Francis, *Amoris Laetitia*, no. 27.

[83] Ibid., no. 29.

[84] Thomas Knieps-Port le Roi makes a helpful point in this regard: "No anxious and self-defensive mentality!—that is a first rule which should be taken seriously across diverging theological camps" (Knieps-Port le Roi, introduction to *Point of No Return?*, 4). I agree with this, as I do with a second dictum that he delivers: "Do not reduce complexity!" (ibid). But Knieps-Port le Roi applies his second dictum by stating, "We had to learn again in recent times how demagogues of different colours succeeded in seducing people by offering one-size-fits-all solutions for complex problems", and he goes on to suggest, rather uncharitably,

this question in mind, let me now turn to the example of Thomas Aquinas' theology of marital indissolubility.

---

that it is his theological opponents who are seducers and demagogues in this way (ibid.). For the real danger of a lack of charity toward opponents, see also Rocco D'Ambrosio, *Will Pope Francis Pull It Off? The Challenge of Church Reform*, trans. Barry Hudock (Collegeville, MN: Liturgical Press, 2017), 49: "In the case of the church today, the person the corrupt wish to silence is [Pope] Francis. In general, these processes of institutional reform become opportunities for those who are criticized, at every level of responsibility, to demonstrate their belief in justice, peace, and the common good. Often, however, they reveal themselves to be envious and untruthful critics and slanderers, ready to use violence (verbal or otherwise) to destroy those who criticize them and who seek to approve the institution." D'Ambrosio here labels his opponents as "the corrupt", "envious and untruthful", and "slanderers". Earlier, D'Ambrosio proposes that Catholic "fundamentalists" have confused faith with an ahistorical "ideology", that is, "a compact body of knowledge that is closed to discussion, the exclusive property of a group of enlightened ones who impose it on others and for whom it is the hallmark of their own identity, specifically because it is accepted *in toto* and without question; questions are not permitted; doubts or different emphases are not tolerated; intellectual investigation is stifled by the imposition of rigid and sterile patterns (one thinks of certain areas of philosophical and theological research)" (ibid., 29, 32). On the one hand, D'Ambrosio's list seems prone to become an ideology itself, by labeling and stifling his opponents and their concerns; and on the other hand, his account does not adequately specify the differences between an "ideology" and revealed dogmatic truth in faith and morals that demands "the obedience of faith" (Rom 1:5). He seeks to differentiate faith and ideology by explaining that "faith is an authentic encounter with a person, the Lord Jesus" and by linking "ideology" to "gnostic roots" (ibid., 33). But the encounter with Jesus and following Jesus are what dogmatic faith and morals teach about publicly: the Church proclaims who Jesus is and what his new commandment of love involves. By contrast, Gnosticism claimed to be a hidden knowledge for a spiritual elite who did not need to be guided by the Church's public (dogmatic) witness handed down from the apostles.

Chapter 4

Theological *Ressourcement*:
Aquinas on Marital Indissolubility

In receiving both *Amoris Laetitia*'s urgent concern for the good of the faithful burdened by a broken marriage and its affirmation of marital indissolubility, we can be aided by delving in some depth into the theology of marriage developed by Saint Thomas Aquinas. Aquinas is keenly interested in the role that marital indissolubility plays in the flourishing of believers and of societies. The Protestant theologian Don Browning, who at the time of his recent death was one of the world's leading students of marriage, frequently singled out the importance of Aquinas' insight into "the role of kin altruism in family formation and marriage ... especially in view of how similar it is to modern scientific views of family formation found in the emerging new field of evolutionary psychology".[1] In addition, Browning perceived that Aquinas places the "good of matrimony within a more inclusive principle of moral obligation involving mutual friendship and equity", contributing to "a thick, multidimensional understanding of the love ethic of equal regard".[2]

This chapter, therefore, seeks to build upon *Amoris Laetitia*'s primary concern for pastoral care for the excluded, by reflecting upon the life-giving impact of marital indissolubility upon human natural

[1] Don S. Browning, *Equality and the Family: A Fundamental, Practical Theology of Children, Mothers, and Fathers in Modern Societies* (Grand Rapids, MI: Eerdmans, 2007), 334–35.

[2] Ibid., 403. Browning argues that for Aquinas, "Nature and ethical reason push humans toward matrimony; Christ's love and our participation in it takes us the rest of the way by consolidating these natural and ethical tendencies into stable and permanent marital commitments" (ibid., 124). Browning also notes that he and his co-authors of *From Culture Wars to Common Ground* used "Aquinas as something of a model for our view of marriage and family and our understanding of love as equal regard" (*Equality and the Family*, 402). See Don S. Browning et al., *From Culture Wars to Common Ground: Religion and the American Family Debate* (Louisville, KY: Westminster John Knox, 2000).

and supernatural flourishing, a life-giving impact whose benefits are shared to varying degrees by all members of a society, including those whose indissoluble marriage has broken down. Aquinas can help us to see why it is good news that, as Perry Cahall says, "The absolute indissolubility of this communion is the reality that is brought into being through the action of Christ in the efficacious sign of the consent of marriage."[3]

In this chapter, I first explore Aquinas' arguments for the natural or created indissolubility of marriage. Second, I investigate his view of supernatural or sacramental indissolubility, especially in light of his *Commentary on Ephesians* (specifically Ephesians 5). Third, I examine his discussion of two seeming exceptions to the indissolubility of marriage. After examining his treatment of the so-called Pauline privilege, which allows the marriage of unbaptized persons to be dissolved, I explore his interpretation of Jesus' allowance for divorce in cases of *porneia* in Matthew 5:32 and 19:9—an interpretation that coheres with that of Luz and Bockmuehl above.[4]

---

[3] Perry J. Cahall, *The Mystery of Marriage: A Theology of the Body and the Sacrament* (Chicago: Hillenbrand Books, 2016), 309. See also the observation by Joseph W. Koterski, S.J.: "Aquinas concludes that matrimony, inasmuch as it is contracted in the faith of Christ, is able to confer the grace that enables us to do what Marriage requires, for wherever God gives us a faculty to do something, God also gives the helps by which one can do it well" (Joseph W. Koterski, S.J., "Aquinas on the Sacrament of Marriage", in *Rediscovering Aquinas and the Sacraments: Studies in Sacramental Theology*, ed. Matthew Levering and Michael Dauphinais [Chicago: Hillenbrand Books, 2009], 113). For further discussion of Aquinas' theology of marriage, see José Granados, *Una sola Carne en un solo Espíritu: Teología del Matrimonio* (Madrid: Ediciones Palabra, 2014), 134–39; Peter Kwasniewski, "St. Thomas on the Grandeur and Limitations of Marriage", *Nova et Vetera* 10 (2012): 415–36; Guy de Broglie, S.J., "La conception thomiste des deux finalités du mariage", *Doctor Communis* 30 (1974): 3–41. For a negative appraisal, see Colleen McCluskey, "An Unequal Relationship of Equals: Thomas Aquinas on Marriage", *History of Philosophy Quarterly* 24 (2007): 1–18. I agree, of course, that aspects of Aquinas' teaching on marriage (particularly with regard to the status of women) should be corrected. See also the breadth of historical background and the careful, though skeptical, analysis found in Philip L. Reynolds, *How Marriage Became One of the Sacraments* (Cambridge: Cambridge University Press, 2016), as well as Servais Pinckaers, O.P., "Ce que le Moyen Age pensait du mariage", *La vie spirituelle: Supplément* 82 (1967): 413–40. See also the remark of Hélène Bricout that even in the early modern period, "the freedom of consent remains largely theoretical. The real choice of a spouse is extremely restricted" (Hélène Bricout, "Réponse d'Hélène Bricout", in *"La vocation et la mission de la famille dans l'Église et dans le monde contemporain": 26 théologiens répondent* [Paris: Bayard, 2015], 249).

[4] See Ulrich Luz, *Matthew 1–7: A Commentary*, trans. James E. Crouch, ed. Helmut Koester (Minneapolis, MN: Fortress Press, 2007), and Markus Bockmuehl, *Jewish Law in Gentile Churches: Halakhah and the Beginning of Christian Public Ethics* (Grand Rapids, MI: Baker Academic, 2000).

Natural Indissolubility in the *Summa Theologiae* and the *Summa Contra Gentiles*

In his account of chastity in the *Summa Theologiae*, under the rubric of the virtue of temperance, Aquinas offers an argument for the indissolubility of marriage.[5] Asking whether fornication is a sin, he argues in the affirmative on the grounds that even when it does not result in a pregnancy, fornication tends to lessen the chances that the man and the woman will conceive a child within marital wedlock, and in turn this lessens the chances that the child will be raised by his mother and father. In Aquinas' view, which has since been borne out by studies,[6] the flourishing of a child generally is enhanced by being raised by his mother and father. Aquinas puts this point in terms of the care given by the mother and the protection and guidance given by the father. The father's presence seems much more replaceable or dispensable, since it would seem that the mother could either raise the child by herself or, if needed, a friend or neighbor could stand in for the father. For Aquinas, however, the father functions as an important "guide and guardian" assuring the child's progress "in goods both internal and external".[7] Aquinas does not here specify further why someone else could not easily take the father's place as "guide and guardian". But given the lengthy duration and high degree of difficulty involved in raising a child, he insists that the father is needed. He therefore argues that "human nature"—not a mere animal inclination, but our rational inclination rooted in the kind of creaturely flourishing that befits us—"rebels against an indeterminate union of the sexes", that is, against fornication.[8]

---

[5] For further discussion, see chapter 4 (on the virtue of chastity) of my *Aquinas's Eschatological Ethics and the Virtue of Temperance* (Notre Dame: University of Notre Dame Press, forthcoming).

[6] See David Popenoe, *Life without Father: Compelling New Evidence that Fatherhood and Marriage Are Indispensable for the Good of Children and Society* (New York: Simon & Schuster, 1996), and David Popenoe, *Families without Fathers: Fatherhood, Marriage and Children in American Society* (New York: Routledge, 2009). See also Mark Regnerus, "Parental Same-Sex Relationships, Family Instability, and Subsequent Life Outcomes for Adult Children: Answering Critics of the New Family Structures Study with Additional Analyses", *Social Science Research* 41 (2012): 1367–77.

[7] *Summa theologiae* II-II, q. 154, a. 3. All translations of the *Summa theologiae* are taken from *The Summa Theologica of St. Thomas Aquinas*, trans. Fathers of the English Dominican Province (Westminster, MD: Christian Classics, 1981).

[8] Ibid.

Aquinas is not saying here that no one ever wishes to fornicate. Rather, what Aquinas means by saying that "human nature rebels against an indeterminate union of the sexes" is that humans naturally and rationally tend to want to form families. Men naturally want to take care of their children; women naturally want the father of the child around and supportive during the raising of the child. Given our fallen nature, we can easily turn away from this. But in general our species—as distinct from dogs or from birds—tends naturally and rationally toward lengthy and public union between one male and one female. Aquinas comments, "Hence it is that in the human race the male has a natural solicitude for the certainty of offspring, because on him devolves the upbringing of the child."[9] Generally speaking, it matters to men to raise their own children, rather than to have their female partner impregnated by various other men. For this reason, human nature tends to try to ensure that "a man should be united to a determinate woman and should abide with her a long time or even a whole lifetime."[10]

This directedness of human nature explains why marriage is naturally part of human experience, and explains why the indissolubility of marriage makes sense even at a "natural" level, as Jesus indicates is the case. If in "the beginning" (Mt 19:8) divorce was not permitted, because by God's will the married couple is "no longer two but one" (Mt 19:6), then we should expect that as a created reality, marriage has indissolubility built into it. The bond between the man

---

[9] Ibid. See also, more broadly, Nicholas Orme, *Medieval Children* (New Haven, CT: Yale University Press, 2001). For theological and sociological discussion, see Don S. Browning, *Marriage and Modernization: How Globalization Threatens Marriage and What to Do about It* (Grand Rapids, MI: Eerdmans, 2003), 86–94. Browning argues that Aquinas is right that "the dependency of the infant was not enough in itself to bond males to infant and mother" (ibid., 87). Insightfully, Browning comments that "Aquinas's flexible natural law argument is not just a theory of family formation; it is more specifically a theory of why males join the mother-infant dyad" (ibid., 88). Browning adds that Aquinas' approach is quite "relevant to the global phenomenon" that Browning calls "the 'male problematic'—the growing worldwide trend for males to drift away from families" (ibid.). Browning reasons, "The cure for this problem must be found in part in recreating the establishment of these natural conditions that brought about family formation in the first place"—and therefore Aquinas provides "profound insights into certain essential features of any viable Christian theological response" (ibid.). He gives particular praise to Aquinas' attention to the similarities between humans and other animals, as well as to Aquinas' perceptivity regarding "the kinds of human needs and tendencies that marriage helps to organize", including "kin preference" (ibid., 99–100; cf. 115–17).

[10] *Summa Theologiae* II-II, q. 154, a. 3.

and the woman, in which they undertake to raise children (a work of caregiving that continues even after the children have reached adult age[11]), is a bond that cannot simply be annulled by the man or by the woman. In the raising of children, there will be difficult times, and if the man (or the woman) could legitimately walk away from the bond as if it never existed, then human flourishing across the generations would be seriously imperiled. Thus, the bond has a status that does not end when choice dictates or when the children grow old, since the needs of the family continue.

In his discussion of marriage in the *Summa Contra Gentiles*, we find a somewhat more extensive version of the above argument.[12] Aquinas contrasts the human being once again with dogs and birds, and he reiterates his point that under normal circumstances "the female in the human species is not at all able to take care of the upbringing of offspring by herself, since the needs of human life demand many things which cannot be provided by one person alone."[13] Note that the "needs of human life" are both spiritual and bodily; even if one parent can provide all that is needed for the child's body, there are spiritual needs that can be met for the child only by the other parent (whether the father or mother). Aquinas concludes that "it is appropriate to human nature that a man remain together with a woman after the generative act."[14]

He recognizes, however, that some women may be wealthy and may not want or need a man to be around. In response, he points out that human children require "education for the soul".[15] He considers that the education that parents must offer children is first and foremost an education in moral action, and thus an education in prudence. He explains that "a man lives by reason, which he must develop by lengthy, temporal experience so that he may achieve prudence. Hence, children must be instructed by parents who are

---

[11] The parents thereby hold together the societal structure of the family as an enduring institution across generations.

[12] Note that Aquinas died before he could specifically treat the Sacrament of Matrimony in his *Summa Theologiae*.

[13] *Summa Contra Gentiles* 3.122, in Thomas Aquinas, *Summa Contra Gentiles, Book Three: Providence, Part II*, trans. Vernon J. Bourke (Notre Dame: University of Notre Dame Press, 1975), pp. 144–45. All translations of book 3 of the *Summa Contra Gentiles* [*SCG*] are taken from this translation.

[14] Ibid., p. 145.

[15] Ibid.

already experienced people."[16] Ultimately, the education that parents owe their children is an education in living according to reason rather than simply giving in to the impulses of passions. Aquinas argues that this, too, requires two parents, rather than solely the woman. For one thing, the father will be particularly able, due to his extra strength, to deliver the needed correction to unruly adolescents.[17]

It follows, as Aquinas says, that "it is natural"—natural to the human being as a rational animal whose offspring need much time and care—"for the man to establish a lasting association with a designated woman, over no short period of time".[18] Among other benefits, this ensures that the man can be confident that the children he raises are his, which gives him added motivation to care for them. The woman, in turn, gains by being confident that the man will help to care for and educate the children whom she bears. Aquinas adds the point that fornication is not merely like a person choosing "to walk on his hands, or to use his feet for something usually done with the hands".[19] Such activities obviously have no moral bearing. By contrast, how we use our sexual organs has a large bearing upon the human good.

Aquinas appreciates that such arguments may not sway persons who, in the midst of erotic attraction, would simply like to have sex with each other without worrying about what might happen in terms of future children and without worrying about whether such children will have the benefits of a stable family with both parents. Therefore, he also advances some arguments based upon the authority of God's teaching in inspired Scripture. Notably, he cites Paul's exhortation, "Do you not know that the unrighteous [including adulterers] will not inherit the kingdom of God?" (1 Cor 6:9).

Reasons for the Natural Indissolubility of Marriage

After the children are raised, does the marital bond become dissoluble? Aquinas gives various reasons for why human flourishing requires that the marriage be indissoluble until the death of one of

---

[16] Ibid.

[17] Along erroneous lines, he also argues that the father will be more able to educate the children.

[18] SCG 3.122, p. 146.

[19] Ibid.

the spouses.[20] First, he argues that the marital bond should endure until the father and mother's care of the child ceases. For humans this means that "the father's solicitude for his son should endure until the end of the father's life."[21] Second, he argues that unlike in many other animals, where the female needs the male only for reproduction and for nothing else, in the case of humans a woman can benefit from the presence of a man for reasons other than reproduction. It would also be unjust for a man to bond with a woman only while she is young, and then cast her aside after the children are grown or after her youthful childbearing years are over. Aquinas holds that "if any man took a woman in the time of her youth, when beauty and fecundity were hers, and then sent her away after she had reached an advanced age, he would damage that woman contrary to natural equity."[22] The same point would apply to a woman who used a man's help during the years of his strength, and then cast him aside when he was older.

The third reason that Aquinas gives is based upon his view that "the society of husband and wife" is "an association of equals" rather than "a sort of slavery on the part of the wife".[23] In Aquinas' time, men typically had much more power than women, much more control over wealth and over decision-making (though obviously this point does not apply in the same way to the many men who lived as penniless peasants). Given this unequal power, Aquinas holds that the man should not have power to divorce the woman. In contemporary

---

[20] Some of these reasons rest upon his view of the rational superiority of the male (not due to a greater soul, but due to bodily factors through which rationality is mediated). We can discard these reasons, while appropriating the others.

[21] SCG 3.123, p. 147.

[22] Ibid., pp. 147–48.

[23] Ibid., p. 148. Aquinas resolves the question of polygamy on this ground of marital equality. Don Browning points out, "The problem with polygyny is for Aquinas even more directly ethical. It seems logical to assume that one man mating with several wives whose activity he carefully controlled could assume that the offspring of these unions would be truly his. Therefore, he might be more inclined to invest energy in their care, nurture, and development. But Aquinas, in spite of this reasoning, rejects polygyny as intrinsically unfair to women. In other words, he shifts the logic of his argument from the good coming from the father's investment in the care of his children (which polygyny might discharge with reasonable success) to the issue of the husband's just and equal treatment of the marital partner, his wife" (Browning, *Marriage and Modernization*, 89). For marriage as involving mutual love and companionship, see also the writings of the Roman Stoic philosopher Musonius Rufus, discussed by Browning at 82, 126–27. See *Musonius Rufus: The Roman Socrates*, ed. Cora Lutz (New Haven, CT: Yale University Press, 1947), 88–89.

society, of course, most divorces are initiated by women.[24] For today, the takeaway from this argument of Aquinas' is simply that the "association of equals" requires that neither spouse possess the power to end the marriage definitively.

Aquinas' fourth reason focuses on the father's care for his children, which in general happens only when they are his and when he is present in the home. Generally speaking, when a man divorces a woman and partners with another woman, the man is less interested in the well-being of the woman's existing children, and the father himself often grows more distant.[25] The well-being of the children, then, calls for an indissoluble marital bond.

Fifth, Aquinas proposes that the greater a friendship is, the longer-lasting the bond should be. He then remarks that marriage is "the greatest friendship", because husband and wife "are united not only in the act of fleshly union, which produces a certain gentle association even among beasts, but also in the partnership of the whole range of domestic activity".[26] In defense of the claim that marriage is the greatest friendship, he observes that Genesis 2:24 teaches that a man and woman choose each other over what otherwise would be their most important relationship, namely, their relationship to their parents. His conclusion is that as the greatest friendship, marriage

[24] Browning argues insightfully that "the symbolism of Christ's sacrificial love [Ephesians 5] compensates for the male inclination not to bond with child and partner. *In the case of the female, it can function to compensate for her tendency to bond with the child at the exclusion of the father.... The Ephesians analogy should apply to wife and mother just as fully as it does* to husband and father. *This is all the more true when we realize that there is a female counterpart to the male problematic. This is the tendency for mothers to reenact the primordial mammalian family, i.e., to have children and raise them by themselves or with the help of a coterie of close female relatives or friends.* Aquinas described this inclination to a degree; he seemed to understand that in most mammals, this is the situation of females.... Can we believe that the worldwide move toward the absence of fathers from homes is without some inclination on the part of mothers to have children with or without the involvement of fathers? Both men and women, in their quest for mutual love, must have the capacity for sacrificial commitment within the context of matrimony" (Browning, *Marriage and Modernization*, 94; emphasis in original).

[25] See, for example, E. Flouri, M.K. Narayanan, and E. Midouhas, "The Cross-Lagged Relationship between Father Absence and Child Problem Behaviour in the Early Years", *Child Care Health Development* 41 (2015): 1090–97, and Sara McLanahan, Laura Tach, and Daniel Schneider, "The Causal Effects of Father Absence", *Annual Review of Sociology* 39 (2013): 399–427.

[26] *SCG* 3.123, p. 148. See F. Galeotti, "Amore e amicizia coniugali secondo S. Tommaso", *Doctor Communis* 25 (1972): 39–59.

should be an indissoluble bond. Note that this reason is rooted in the personal love shared by the couple, rather than being rooted in the good of the children or in the need to avoid the injustice of one spouse being discarded in old age.

Sixth, Aquinas argues that the indissolubility of the marital union pertains to the good of both the man and the woman because it encourages both to behave in moral ways that conduce to true individual and societal flourishing. He considers that whereas a more casual bond would encourage both the man and the woman to keep an eye out for a better partner, an indissoluble bond makes it more likely that "the love of one spouse for the other will be more faithful."[27] Their indissoluble bond also makes it more likely that their domestic economy will be more prudent and frugal, since the man and the woman know that they will share possessions until they die. Furthermore, it avoids the almost inevitable animosity between the spouse who initiates the divorce and the relatives and friends of the spouse who endures the divorce, which is a serious matter especially in small localities where people all know each other.

In sum, Aquinas presents six arguments that build upon the grounds of human procreative teleology—as well as the crucial element of friendship—in order to show that for the good of the children, of the couple, of the family, and of society, marriage should be indissoluble. He caps these arguments, which stem from reasoning about the created purposes and goods of marriage, with an argument that comes from divine revelation. Well aware that fallen humans often do not want to commit permanently to each other or to their children— well aware of the family dysfunction that continues to mar human existence—the New Testament teaches that marriage is a sign "of the inseparable union between Christ and the Church, which is a union of one spouse with another (Eph. 5:24–32)".[28] In teaching that Christian marriage is a sign of the indissoluble bond between Christ and the Church, the New Testament makes clear that Christian marriage must be indissoluble. Aquinas cites Jesus' words in Matthew 5:32: "I say to you that every one who divorces his wife, except on the ground of únchastity, makes her an adulteress; and whoever marries

---

[27] *SCG* 3.123, p. 149.
[28] Ibid.

a divorced woman commits adultery."[29] He also cites Paul's words in 1 Corinthians 7:10–11, "To the married I give charge, not I but the Lord, that the wife should not separate from her husband (but if she does, let her remain single or else be reconciled to her husband)—and that the husband should not divorce his wife."[30]

Aquinas recognizes that although natural marriage *should* be indissoluble, this is a very high bar for fallen people who are not strengthened by the explicit revelation of Christ and the outpouring of his Holy Spirit. God did not give the precept about marriage's indissolubility to the Jewish people in the Torah. Aquinas even suggests that without grace, a man and a woman can be at each other's throats, ready to kill each other.[31] Therefore, because of the people's "hardness of heart" (Mt 19:8) God gave a precept in the Torah that explained the conditions for acceptable divorce. Christ's followers, by contrast, are empowered by grace to obey his precept about the indissolubility of marriage, a precept that accords with the natural indissolubility of marriage and that enables marriage to be a supernatural sign of the indissoluble union of Christ and his Church.[32]

Supernatural or Sacramental Indissolubility

Whereas in book 3 of the *Summa Contra Gentiles* Aquinas seeks generally to deal "with divine things according as the natural reason can arrive at the knowledge of divine things through creatures", in book 4 he takes "what has been passed on to us in the words of sacred Scripture" as "principles".[33] Book 4 includes a discussion of the Sacrament

---

[29] Ibid., p. 150. In the Vulgate and the RSV, Jesus' words in Matthew 5:32 and 19:9 are identical, but the RSV includes a note that indicates its awareness of the ancient manuscripts in which Matthew 19:9 lacks the final clause: "and he who marries a divorced woman, commits adultery." This final clause is missing from Matthew 19:9 in the critical text published in *The Greek New Testament*, 4th rev. ed., ed. Barbara Aland et al. (Stuttgart: Deutsche Bibelgesellschaft, 1994).

[30] SCG 3.123, p. 150.

[31] See ibid.

[32] See also J. M. Cabodevilla, *Hombre y Mujer: Estudio sobre el Matrimonio y el Amor Humano* (Madrid: BAC, 1962).

[33] SCG 4.1, in Thomas Aquinas, *Summa Contra Gentiles, Book Four: Salvation*, trans. Charles J. O'Neil (Notre Dame: University of Notre Dame Press, 1975), p. 39. All translations from book 4 of the *Summa Contra Gentiles* are taken from this translation. See also Thomas S. Hibbs, *Dialectic and Narrative in Aquinas: An Interpretation of the Summa Contra Gentiles* (Notre Dame: University of Notre Dame Press, 1995).

of Matrimony as instituted by Christ. In this discussion, Aquinas understands himself to be investigating one of "the things which surpass reason that have been done by God, such as the work of the Incarnation and what follows thereon".[34]

Why does there need to be a supernatural "sacrament" of marriage, if natural marriage—marriage as part of the created human ordering to individual, familial, and communal flourishing—is already indissoluble in itself (despite the dispensation that God allowed to the Israelites and presumably to others as well)? Aquinas answers that "when something is ordered to different ends there must be differing principles directing it to the end."[35] Marriage is ordered naturally to the flourishing of political communities (the family and the society) and to the good of the preservation of the species through the begetting and raising of children. Supernaturally, however, marriage is ultimately ordered to the good of Christ's Church, the supernatural society of the inaugurated kingdom. In begetting and raising children, Christian married couples do so not only in light of the flourishing of merely human communities, but specifically "for the worship of God".[36] The child is baptized and educated as part of Christ's Body, called to eternal union with the holy Trinity.

Furthermore, not only the procreative ordering of marriage is supernaturalized, but also the marital union itself stands as a precious and supernatural sign of Christ's union with the Church. Aquinas here cites Ephesians 5:32: "This is a great mystery [or sacrament], and I mean in reference to Christ and the church"; and he also cites further biblical passages confirming the unbreakable unity of Christ and the Church. Among these passages are Song of Songs 6:9, "My dove, my perfect one, is only one", as well as Christ's promise never to depart from his Church, "I am with you always, to the close of the age" (Mt 28:20), a promise echoed by 1 Thessalonians 4:17, "we shall always be with the Lord."[37] All this is crucial because marriage, as a sacramental sign of Christ's unity with his Church, *causes* in the man and the woman a real interior correspondence to what marriage signifies in the supernatural order, although this correspondence grows in perfection only when the

[34] SCG 4.1, p. 39.
[35] SCG 4.78, p. 295.
[36] Ibid.
[37] Ibid., p. 296.

man and the woman are in a state of grace. Aquinas explains that "because the sacraments effect that of which they are made signs, one must believe that in this sacrament a grace is conferred on those marrying, and that by this grace they are included in the union of Christ and the Church."[38]

In Christian marriage, the man and woman are incorporated into the unity of Christ and the Church in such a profound way as truly to be a living sign of this unbreakable unity, precisely in the "fleshly and earthly things" that they undertake in family life.[39] As the theologian David Cloutier says, "Marriage does not have two natural ends *plus* an additional sacramental end. Rather, marriage's natural ends are transformed from within, and given their genuine *telos* by being taken up within the larger story of communion with God."[40] Since this is so, Christian marriage, with its proper goods of offspring, fidelity, and the sacrament, must above all be indissoluble. Aquinas states, "Necessarily, then, matrimony as a sacrament of the Church is a union of one man to one woman to be held indivisibly."[41]

When in his *Commentary on Ephesians* Aquinas comments on Ephesians 5, he devotes a good bit of attention to the way in which Paul's exhortation deploys the two examples of the love of Christ for the Church and the love of a man for himself. When he reaches the crucial passage about the sacrament or mystery that is marriage, he focuses first on Paul's appeal to "the authority of Scripture"— namely, Paul's quotation of Genesis 2:24: "For this reason a man shall

---

[38] Ibid. Cahall eloquently describes the grace of the sacrament of Christian marriage: "As two baptized spouses exchange consent to forge a marital covenant, intending to do what the Church does, Christ allows them to participate in his spousal union with the Church. Thus the mutual consent of the spouses is an entrance into Christ's 'yes.' This is truly good news, because every marriage yearns to express what Christ, who is truly God and truly man, realizes in his Person. In the new and eternal covenant between God and man, Jesus utters his perfect 'yes' to the Father on behalf of humanity, and he utters his perfect 'yes' to his bride, the Church. Through the Sacrament of Marriage, Christ empowers couples to participate in his perfect 'yes' to the Father, and to be effective signs of his 'yes' to the Church in their relationship with each other" (Cahall, *Mystery of Marriage*, 300).

[39] SCG 4.78, p. 296.

[40] David Cloutier, *The Vice of Luxury: Economic Excess in a Consumer Age* (Washington, D.C.: Georgetown University Press, 2015), 122. Cloutier adds along the same lines, "Properly understood, the entire reality of marriage and family—including sexual intercourse—is understood in terms of a sacramental, and not simply natural, *telos*" (ibid.).

[41] SCG 4.78, p. 296.

leave his father and mother and be joined to his wife, and the two shall become one flesh" (Eph 5:31). Recall that Jesus, too, appeals to Genesis 2:24 in insisting upon the indissolubility of marriage against the Mosaic Law's permission of divorce (Mt 19:4–5). Why is it, Aquinas asks, that in marriage the two become *one*? It may seem a major exaggeration to claim that husband and wife become one in their lives together.

Aquinas argues that it is not an exaggeration, for three reasons. The first is that the man and woman's love is strong enough to impel them to leave father and mother. In men, Aquinas thinks that there is generally a natural instinct to unite with and care for a woman, and vice versa. The intimate love of the man and the woman, then, goes beyond even the love of children for parents or friend for friend. The second reason that Aquinas gives for the unique unity of husband and wife is the fact that they live together so intimately, and therefore have the opportunity for the deepest human friendship. The third reason given by Aquinas is sexual intercourse. Bodily speaking, sexual intercourse forms as it were one body, through the carnal joining of two bodies in one bodily act.[42]

After defending Genesis 2:24 on this basis, Aquinas observes that Paul applies Genesis 2:24 to the relationship of husband and wife by interpreting the "one flesh" unity in a mystical way. Specifically, Paul argues that mystically, Genesis 2:24's reference to the natural "one flesh" union of husband and wife points to the supernatural unity of Christ and his Church. For Paul, therefore, the "one flesh" union of husband and wife—their love, their living together, and their sexual union—is, in Aquinas' words, "the symbol of a sacred reality, namely, the union of Christ and the Church".[43]

Asking why Paul terms marriage a "great mystery" ("*sacramentum magnum*"), Aquinas observes that four sacraments are rightly called "great": Baptism, insofar as its effect of washing away sin and opening the gates of heaven; Confirmation, insofar as its minister is a

---

[42] For the material in this paragraph, see Aquinas, *Commentary on the Letter of Saint Paul to the Ephesians*, trans. Matthew L. Lamb, in Aquinas, *Commentary on the Letters of Saint Paul to the Galatians and Ephesians*, trans. Fabian R. Larcher and Matthew L. Lamb, ed. J. Mortensen and E. Alarcón (Lander, WY: Aquinas Institute for the Study of Sacred Doctrine, 2012), no. 333, pp. 325–26.

[43] Ibid., no. 334, p. 326.

bishop; the Eucharist, insofar as it contains "the whole Christ"; and lastly, Matrimony, insofar as it signifies the union of Christ and his Church.[44] The *greatness* of marriage among the other sacraments consists in the fact that it symbolizes the telos or goal for which the whole cosmos was created. Marriage symbolizes the very thing for which the whole Old Testament, and all God's work, prepared—the perfect consummation toward which the Church strives and in which the Church already participates by grace. This greatness of symbolization requires marriage to be indissoluble.

Aquinas proceeds to ask what Genesis 2:24 might look like if interpreted along mystical lines. He proposes that the "man" who "leaves his father" could be Christ, who as the divine Son comes into the world. This same Christ also leaves his "mother" in the sense that Christ, raised in the synagogue, fulfills the covenants with Israel and establishes the Messianic community united around himself. Christ "cleaves to his wife" in the sense that he clings permanently to the Church, from which he promises never to separate himself (see Mt 28:20).[45]

Aquinas also argues that some passages in the Old Testament are references to Christ alone, while other passages in the Old Testament can rightly be interpreted as referring to Christ *and* to others. Genesis 2:24 belongs to the latter group, since it can rightly be interpreted both as being about Christ and as being about others (who are thereby "types" of Christ). Here Aquinas reads Genesis 2:24 in light of Ephesians 5:33: "Let each one of you love his wife as himself." Christ cleaves to his wife, the Church, and husbands must cleave to their wives in the same way, thereby showing themselves to be "types of Christ".[46] Indissoluble marriage marks the Church's members as true "types" of Christ, configured to their Lord. Genesis 2:24 is about Christ, and it is about us—so long as we rightly perceive marriage's indissolubility.

However, what about the seeming exception to indissolubility that Jesus makes in Matthew 5:32 and 19:9, and the exception that Paul apparently makes to indissolubility in 1 Corinthians 7:15? Given

---

[44] Ibid. See also *Summa theologiae* III, q. 65, a. 4.
[45] Aquinas, *Commentary on the Letter of Saint Paul to the Ephesians*, no. 334, p. 326.
[46] Ibid., no. 335, p. 327.

Aquinas' commitment to the natural and supernatural indissolubility of marriage, how does Aquinas interpret these biblical passages?

The "Pauline Privilege" in the
Commentary on the Sentences

Let me begin with Aquinas' treatment of 1 Corinthians 7:15, the so-called Pauline privilege, in his *Commentary on the Sentences* (as included in the Supplement that his students added to his unfinished *Summa Theologiae*).[47] The text of 1 Corinthians 7:15 reads, "But if the unbelieving partner desires to separate, let it be so; in such a case the [Christian] brother or sister is not bound." In interpreting this verse, Aquinas states that the Christian spouse can certainly divorce the non-Christian (unbaptized) spouse; the only real question is whether the Christian spouse, having undertaken the divorce, is free to marry again. In answer to this question, Aquinas states that if the Christian spouse divorced a non-Christian spouse who was *not* trying to draw him or her back into unbelief, then the Christian spouse *cannot* marry again until the death of the non-Christian spouse. By contrast, if the non-Christian spouse *was* indeed trying to draw the Christian spouse back into unbelief, then the Christian spouse *can* marry again. When Aquinas describes a spouse as "unbelieving", he has in view an unbaptized person. As he comments, "if a believer marry a baptized heretic, the marriage is valid, although he sins by marrying her if he knows her to be a heretic."[48] Aquinas considers it illicit for a

---

[47] On the Supplement, see the brief note in Jean-Pierre Torrell, O.P., *Saint Thomas Aquinas*, vol. 1, *The Person and His Work*, trans. Robert Royal (Washington, D.C.: Catholic University of America Press, 1996), 333. For a more thorough treatment than I can offer here of Aquinas' theology of marriage in his *Commentary on the Sentences*, see B. M. Perrin, "L'institution du mariage dans le *Commentaire des Sentences* de saint Thomas (I)", *Revue Thomiste* 108 (2008): 423–66; B. M. Perrin, "L'institution du mariage dans le *Commentaire des Sentences* de saint Thomas (II)", *Revue Thomiste* 108 (2008): 599–646; Reynolds, *How Marriage Became One of the Sacraments*. See also Donald J. Gregory, *The Pauline Privilege: An Historical Synopsis and Commentary* (Washington, D.C.: Catholic University of America Press, 1931). Since Aquinas' commentary on 1 Corinthians 7–10 has been lost, editions of Aquinas' commentary on 1 Corinthians instead contain an excerpt from Peter of Tarentaise's commentary. I therefore limit myself to the *Commentary on the Sentences*.

[48] Suppl., q. 59, a. 1, ad 5. For the material in q. 59, a. 1, see Aquinas' *In IV Sent.*, dist. 39, a. 1.

Christian to marry a non-Christian—in his view (which is no longer held by the Church) the "disparity of worship" should be prudentially deemed an impediment to a valid marriage[49]—and so he has in view solely a case in which the couple both begin as non-Christians, but then one of them converts to Christianity.[50]

Aquinas affirms that there can be valid marriages between non-Christians (or "unbelievers"). He observes that "there is marriage between unbelievers, in so far as marriage fulfills an office of nature."[51] But if this is so, then how could a person's becoming a Christian free him from his marital bond, which—even as a natural marriage—Aquinas consistently deems to be indissoluble?[52] After all, Aquinas

[49] Suppl., q. 59, a. 1, ad 1.

[50] Christian Brugger provides a helpful overview of the Pauline privilege and its development into the Petrine privilege, in his *The Indissolubility of Marriage and the Council of Trent* (Washington, D.C.: Catholic University of America Press, 2017), 5: "When Jesus taught that Moses permitted divorce for Israel's 'hardness of heart,' but that 'from the beginning' marriage was indissoluble (Mt 19:8), he indicates that by its very nature marriage is indissoluble. But the passage from Paul (1 Cor 7) permitting a Christian convert to separate from an unbelieving spouse if the latter was unwilling to live peaceably with the Christian spouse seemed to single out a class of natural marriages susceptible to dissolution. This 'Pauline Privilege' became enshrined in Western canon law in the Middle Ages. It permitted the dissolution of a marriage between two non-baptized persons in the case that one (but not both) of the partners seeks baptism and converts to Christianity and the other partner 'departs' the marriage (i.e., is unwilling to live peacefully within the marriage). In response to the missionary growth in the New World in the sixteenth century, the popes began to extend the Pauline Privilege to polygamous unions that missionaries in the Americas encountered. As mixed cult marriages became more common in the modern period, the logic of the Pauline exception was applied to marriages between a *baptized* and a *non-baptized person*. Known as the Petrine Privilege, this type of union—a valid natural marriage between a baptized and a non-baptized person—admitted of dissolution by the pope, and him alone thus permitting both to remarry." See also, for a less sympathetic rendering of the actions of popes Paul III, Pius V, and Gregory XIII, Theodore Mackin, S.J., *Divorce and Remarriage* (New York: Paulist Press, 1984), 395–401. Mackin points to three further decisions: (1) Pope Pius XI's 1924 approval of an unbaptized man's request that his marriage to an Episcopalian woman be dissolved so that he could be baptized and marry a Catholic; (2) two cases in 1947 when Pope Pius XII dissolved a marriage between an unbaptized woman and a Catholic man, despite their having previously received a dispensation to marry in the Catholic Church; and (3) Pope John XXIII's decision in 1959 to grant dissolution to the nonsacramental marriage of an unbaptized man and a Protestant woman. I see no need to suppose that every prudential decision in such matters is infallible, but these decisions remain consistent in their refusal to dissolve a valid and consummated marriage between two baptized persons.

[51] Suppl., q. 59, a. 2, ad 3. For the material in q. 59, a. 2, see Aquinas' *In IV Sent.*, dist. 39, a. 2.

states in this very context that "no impediment that supervenes upon a true marriage dissolves it."[53] If two unbelievers can have a true marriage, then prior to one of them becoming a Christian, they were truly married to each other. Indeed, Aquinas affirms that "the marriage tie is not broken by the fact that one of them is converted to the faith."[54] How, then, could Paul be right that the Christian "brother or sister is not bound" by the existing marital bond?

On the one hand, Aquinas answers by suggesting that although the "marriage tie is not broken" when a spouse becomes Christian, nonetheless, the fact that one spouse is still an unbeliever may mean that "cohabitation and marital intercourse" is no longer appropriate, since the resulting children would not be properly educated in the faith.[55] In such a case, it is licit for the Christian spouse to ask for and obtain a divorce, even if the marital bond remains in force. Such a divorce amounts to what we would today term a legal separation: the marriage continues, but the ecclesiastically granted divorce means that the one spouse no longer owes the marriage debt (sexual intercourse) to the other spouse, and also that cohabitation is no longer requisite.

On the other hand, however, Aquinas adds that even though natural marriage is indissoluble, natural marriage is not "altogether firm and ratified".[56] Why not? He answers that Baptism is a form of death—as taught by Romans 6:3–4, where Paul exhorts, "Do you not know that all of us who have been baptized into Christ Jesus were baptized into his death? We were buried therefore with him by baptism into death, so that as Christ was raised from the dead by the glory of the Father, we too might walk in newness of life."[57]

---

[52] For Aquinas all of this is a particularly serious matter because he holds that "the chief good of marriage is the offspring to be brought up to the worship of God" (Suppl., q. 59, a. 1).

[53] Suppl., q. 59, a. 3, sed contra. For the material in q. 59, a. 3, see Aquinas' In IV Sent., dist. 39, a. 3.

[54] Suppl., q. 59, a. 3. Hence, later canonists would say that natural marriage is "intrinsically indissoluble" but "extrinsically soluble" (in the sense of being subject to extrinsic conditions from the supernatural order that produce solubility).

[55] Ibid.

[56] Suppl., q. 59, a. 5, ad 1. For the material in q. 59, a. 5, see Aquinas' In IV Sent., dist. 39, a. 5.

[57] For discussion of Aquinas' use of Romans 6:3–4 in the Summa Theologiae's treatise on Baptism, see my Paul in the Summa Theologiae (Washington, D.C.: Catholic University of America Press, 2014), chap. 3.

Aquinas argues that like bodily dying, the death that we undergo in Baptism releases us from the marital bond. He notes that a person "who dies to his former life is not bound to those things to which he was bound in his former life".[58] Does this mean that a father who receives Baptism is now freed from his duties to his children? On the contrary, says Aquinas, the children ought now to go with the Christian father, if the Christian father deems it necessary to divorce the unbelieving wife.[59]

The newly Christian spouse is not required to take advantage of the Pauline privilege. Paul states that "if any brother has a wife who is an unbeliever, and she consents to live with him, he should not divorce her" (1 Cor 7:12). As Aquinas puts it, "The believer after his conversion may remain with the unbeliever in the hope of her conversion ... and he does well in remaining with her, though not bound to do so".[60] Nonetheless, prior to Baptism, a marriage cannot be considered definitively "ratified", because Baptism is a real dying, with the result that in this specific case "marriage contracted in unbelief can be annulled."[61] He adds that the marriage is never *automatically* annulled. It is not annulled even by an ecclesiastical divorce, which involves a legal separation. Rather, it is annulled by entering into a Christian marriage. Aquinas comments that "the firmer tie always looses the weaker if it is contrary to it, and therefore the subsequent marriage contracted in the faith of Christ dissolves the marriage previously contracted in unbelief."[62] A natural marriage becomes dissoluble once a person has died in Christ through Baptism, and the dissolution happens when the perfect bond of Christian marriage comes to take the place of the imperfect bond of natural marriage.

The above points have to do with the marriage of two unbaptized people. But what about when a Christian marries a non-Christian?[63]

---

[58] Suppl., q. 59, a. 4; see in particular ad 2. For the material in q. 59, a. 4, see Aquinas' *In IV Sent.*, dist. 39, a. 4.

[59] See Suppl., q. 59, a. 4, ad 4.

[60] Suppl., q. 59, a. 3.

[61] Suppl., q. 59, a. 5, sed contra.

[62] Suppl., q. 59, a. 5, ad 1.

[63] Suppl., q. 59, a. 1, ad 1. Cahall notes that even today, "due to a concern for members of the Body of Christ to be able to continue to practice and pass on the faith to their children, Church law prevents a Catholic from marrying an unbaptized person who is thus not a member of the Church (although a dispensation can be sought [and will be freely granted]; CIC, c. 1086 §1)" (Cahall, *Mystery of Marriage*, 308).

The Church today holds that a marriage between a Christian and a non-Christian can be dissolved, though in such cases the determination of the pope, as the Vicar of Christ, is required.[64] A valid marriage between a Christian (i.e., a baptized person) and a non-Christian is potentially dissoluble by the Church because it is not a sacramental marriage, and therefore it can be superseded by a sacramental marriage, in accord with the fact that the Christian spouse has died in Christ. Such an action can only be undertaken if the pope judges that dissolving the marriage is in favor of the faith and for the salvation of souls.[65] As with the Pauline privilege, the rationale for this practice

[64] See Wojciech Kowal, O.M.I., "The Power of the Church to Dissolve the Matrimonial Bond in Favour of the Faith", *Studia canonica* 38 (2004): 411–38. For background, see the discussion in William H. Woestman, O.M.I., and Wojciech Kowal, O.M.I., *Special Marriage Cases and Procedures*, 4th ed. (Ottawa: Faculty of Canon Law, St. Paul University, 2008). See also Wojciech Kowal, O.M.I., "Quelques remarques sur la discipline de la dissolution de marriages en faveur de la foi", *Studia canonica* 43 (2009): 161–81. For the Church's canonical norms in this regard, see the Congregation for the Doctrine of the Faith's *Norms on the Preparation of the Process for the Dissolution of the Marriage Bond in Favour of the Faith* (April 30, 2001), as well as Janusz Kowal, S.J., "Nuove 'Norme per lo scioglimento del matrimonio *in favorem fidei*,'" *Periódica* 91 (2002): 459–506. With regard to what has been termed the "Petrine privilege", Wojciech Kowal cites Pope Pius XII's Allocution to the Roman Rota of October 3, 1941, in which Pius XII explains that the pope can act "in the name of God or as an instrument of God, as the vicar of Christ", and this power suffices to enable the pope to dissolve a marriage, though not a consummated sacramental marriage (Kowal, "Power of the Church to Dissolve", 414). Wojciech Kowal also cites Pope Pius XI's 1930 encyclical *Casti Connubii*, where the pope comments with reference to the Pauline and Petrine privilege: "If this stability [marital indissolubility] seems to be open to exception, however rare the exception may be, as in the case of certain natural marriages between unbelievers, or amongst Christians in the case of those marriages which though valid have not been consummated, that exception does not depend on the will of men nor on that or any merely human power, but on divine law, of which the only guardian and interpreter is the Church of Christ. However, not even this power can affect for any cause whatsoever a Christian marriage which is valid and has been consummated, for as it is plain that here the marriage contract has its full completion, so, by the will of God, there is also the greatest firmness and indissolubility which may not be destroyed by any human authority" (Pope Pius XI, *Casti Connubii*, no. 35; quoted in Kowal, "Power of the Church", 414).

[65] See also Kowal, "Power of the Church to Dissolve", 423, 428, 436. Kowal directs attention to a variety of secondary literature here, including R. Rubiyatmoko, *Competenza della Chiesa nello scioglimento del vincolo del matrimonio non sacramentale: Una ricerca sostanziale sullo scioglimento del vincolo matrimoniale* (Rome: Gregorian University Press, 1998), 218–24. See also the Congregation for the Doctrine of the Faith's *Notes Regarding Documentary and Procedural Aspects of Favour of the Faith Cases*. Again, what we are dealing with here is "the exercise of the ministerial power of the pope regarding non-sacramental marriages" (Kowal, "Power of the Church to Dissolve", 438).

is rooted in the distinctiveness of the supernatural rebirth of the baptized life.

It may seem insulting to have one standard for Christian marriages and one standard for non-Christian ones, especially if even
natural marriage is in a certain sense indissoluble. It seems to me,
however, that the Pauline privilege and Petrine privilege, when correctly understood, are defensible on the grounds that Baptism is a real
(sacramental) dying with Christ. It is this death that opens the way
for a Christian marriage to supersede the valid marriage between two
non-Christians or between a Christian and a non-Christian. But it
remains the case that, as Paul says, "if any brother has a wife who is an
unbeliever, and she consents to live with him, he should not divorce
her" (1 Cor 7:12).[66]

Indissolubility and *Porneia* (Mt 5:32; 19:9)
in the *Commentary on the Sentences* and the
Commentary on Matthew

The other biblical texts that are frequently quoted against the indissolubility of marriage are Matthew 5:32 and 19:9. Matthew 5:32
reads: "I say to you that every one who divorces his wife, except
on the ground of unchastity [*porneia*], makes her an adultress; and

---

[66] Kowal notes, however, that "in recent years, there have been some attempts to consider the vicarious power of the pope, exercised over marriages of unbaptized and the non-
consummated marriage of baptized, as equally applicable to the dissolution of ratified and
consummated marriages for reasons related to the good of the faithful" (Kowal, "Power of
the Church to Dissolve", 415). In response to such arguments, Pope John Paul II underscored
that the pope's authority cannot extend to dissolving sacramental, consummated marriages,
because in fact "no human authority", even that of a pope, "can dissolve a ratified and consummated marriage" (ibid.; see Pope John Paul II, "Allocution to the Roman Rota", January 21, 2000, *Acta Apostolicae Sedis* 92 [2000]: 353, where John Paul II states that "a ratified
and consummated sacramental marriage can never be dissolved not even by the power of the
Roman Pontiff"). As Kowal observes, John Paul II "maintains that the opposite assertion
would imply the thesis that there is no absolutely indissoluble marriage, which thesis would
be contrary to what the Church has taught and still teaches about the indissolubility of the
marital bond" (Kowal, "Power of the Church to Dissolve", 416). John Paul II makes clear
that "neither Scripture nor Tradition recognizes any faculty of the Roman Pontiff for dissolving a ratified and consummated marriage; on the contrary, the Church's constant practice
shows the certain knowledge of Tradition that such a power does not exist" (Pope John Paul
II, "Allocution to the Roman Rota", 355).

whoever marries a divorced woman commits adultery." The Gospel of Matthew is the only Gospel to include the exception clause. In the Gospel of Luke, we find that "every one who divorces his wife and marries another commits adultery, and he who marries a woman divorced from her husband commits adultery" (Lk 16:18); and the same is the case in Mark 10:11–12, which reads, "Whoever divorces his wife and marries another, commits adultery against her; and if she divorces her husband and marries another, she commits adultery."[67] With regard to the Gospel of Matthew, as I noted in chapter 1, it is important to appreciate that the disciples are shocked by Jesus' words. They conclude that it follows that "it is not expedient to marry" (Mt 19:10).

Obviously, however, a marriage that can be dissolved because one spouse sins after the marriage has been validly contracted, can never have been an "indissoluble" marriage that signifies the indissoluble unity of Christ and the Church. If a valid Christian marriage can be dissolved due to something that takes place after the marriage bond is sealed, then whatever else the Christian marriage may be, it is certainly not indissoluble. On the contrary, it has always been contingently dissoluble and can be dissolved as soon as a particular sin takes place. Jesus' exception clause in Matthew 5:32 and 19:9 may therefore seem to remove the grounds for considering marriage to be indissoluble. If so, then Paul's statement that "a married woman is bound by law to her husband as long as he lives" (Rom 7:2) would need to be revised to say clearly that not only death, but also sexual sin (*porneia*), can dissolve an otherwise binding, valid marriage.

How does Aquinas interpret this text? As we have already seen, he has no problem holding that in certain circumstances Christians can get divorced. He affirms that "one is not bound to keep faith with one who breaks his faith. But a spouse by fornication breaks the faith due to the other spouse. Therefore one can put the other away on account of fornication."[68] A man can divorce his wife on account of

---

[67] For a succinct historical-critical discussion of Luke 16:18 and Mark 10:11–12, see Paul Mankowski, S.J., "Dominical Teaching on Divorce and Remarriage: The Biblical Data", in *Remaining in the Truth of Christ*, 36–63, at 41–48.

[68] Suppl., q. 62, a. 1, sed contra. For the material in q. 62, a. 1, see Aquinas' *In IV Sent.*, dist. 35, a. 1.

fornication, and, logically, a woman can divorce her husband on the same grounds. But a legitimately divorced person cannot remarry, because Jesus goes on to say in Matthew 5:32 that "whoever marries a divorced woman commits adultery." For Aquinas, this is because the divorce does not dissolve the marriage, but instead is a legal separation. A man who has divorced his wife on the just grounds of her proven fornication is still a divorced man. When Jesus says that "whoever marries a divorced woman commits adultery", Aquinas assumes that this applies to the divorced man as well, since the marriage itself is not dissolved by divorce.

In an objection, Aquinas notes that common sense and mercy might seem to dictate otherwise: "It would seem that a husband can marry again after having a divorce. For no one is bound to perpetual continence. Now in some cases the husband is bound to put away his wife forever on account of fornication."[69] Put simply, it seems as though the Church is asking too much, beyond what is humanly possible.

Aquinas is well aware that some people will not listen to Christ or follow his way of holiness, and that we will all fall short in various ways. Yet, he also recognizes that denying marriage's indissolubility would go against the commandment of Christ and would not benefit the flourishing of the individuals and families that comprise Christ's Church. The Church cannot fix all human tragedies on earth. Aquinas gives the example of the man condemned to lifetime continence when his wife "contract[s] an incurable disease that is incompatible with carnal intercourse".[70] The Church must accompany such persons, but it cannot take away the cross-shaped suffering of a man having (in this case due to his wife's illness) to endure a lifetime of abstinence from sexual intercourse in order to be faithful to his marriage vows. The Church cannot approve of the suffering spouse's recourse to illicit modes of satisfying his or her desire for sexual intercourse. Part of the virtuous life of marriage is learning how to love your spouse even when he or she cannot undertake sexual intimacy. Here the Church must point to the deeds and sayings of Jesus and offer a Christ-centered spirituality of self-sacrifice, in which the

---

[69] Suppl., q. 62, a. 5, obj. 1. For the material in q. 62, a. 5, see Aquinas' *In IV Sent.*, dist. 35, a. 5.

[70] Suppl., q. 62, a. 5, ad 1.

believer asks for the Spirit's assistance, with recourse to the Sacrament of Penance as medicine.

When Aquinas takes up Matthew 5:32 in his *Commentary on the Gospel of St. Matthew*, he divides Matthew 5:32 into two parts: "Every one who divorces his wife, except on the ground of unchastity [Vulgate: fornication], makes her an adulteress"; and "whoever marries a divorced woman commits adultery." With respect to the first part, he asks whether divorce can in fact ever be acceptable, even on the grounds of "fornication" (i.e., adultery). After all, Paul teaches, "Repay no one evil for evil" (Rom 12:17); and Jesus commands, "Love your enemies and pray for those who persecute you" (Mt 5:44). But divorcing one's wife after she has committed adultery seems to be a clear case of repaying evil with evil. Aquinas replies that Jesus allowed divorce in such cases, not as an act of evil retaliation, but as an act of just punishment for infidelity.

With respect to the second part, "whoever marries a divorced woman commits adultery", Aquinas explains that this is because she already has a marriage. The legitimate divorce accomplishes a legal separation, but it does not dissolve the marriage. Therefore, since she is still married, if she were to be remarried, this would be a case of adultery, a further sin against her existing marriage.

When commenting upon the parallel text of Matthew 19:9, Aquinas says a bit more, because Matthew 19 conveys Jesus' broader remarks about marriage and divorce. When in Matthew 19 the Pharisees ask Jesus whether divorce is lawful, Jesus points them to Genesis 1:27 and 2:24. Jesus asks rhetorically, "Have you not read that he who made them from the beginning made them male and female, and said, 'For this reason a man shall leave his father and mother and be joined to his wife, and the two shall become one'?" (Mt 19:4–5). On this basis, Jesus forbids divorce: "So they are no longer two but one. What therefore God has joined together, let no man put asunder" (Mt 19:6). Recall that in response, the Pharisees challenge Jesus to explain why the Mosaic Law permitted divorce. Jesus answers that this was permitted by Moses because of the people's "hardness of heart" (Mt 19:8). God's plan for creation did not include divorce: "from the beginning it was not so" (Mt 19:8).

In the course of commenting on these verses, Aquinas remarks that although God could have founded the human race simply with one person, God chose to found the human race with two persons, a man and a woman. God did so, according to Aquinas, "in order that it might be indicated that the form of matrimony was from God".[71] This ensured that marriage could not be despised by Christians (as it was by Gnostics and other radical dualists), and it also grounded in creation the nuptial pattern of new creation—the marriage of Christ and his Church, or the marriage of God and mankind.

Granted that "man" cannot dissolve a true marriage joined by God (see Mt 19:6; Gen 2:24), does God ever will to dissolve a true marriage? Aquinas replies that the only possible reason for God doing so is when a couple wishes to enter into consecrated religious life. By contrast, when people want to dissolve a marriage, the reason is usually that one or both members of the couple want to contract a relationship with someone else. But "if God has joined something together, only He can separate it."[72] Aquinas argues that Jesus' way of phrasing the Mosaic permission ("For your hardness of heart Moses allowed you to divorce your wives") shows that the permission was from Moses, not from God. God inspired Moses to grant this permission, but God carefully did not confirm it "by divine authority", because God's plan was to pour out his Spirit so that the order God intended in creation could be restored in Christ.[73] Furthermore, Aquinas finds it notable that Jesus says that Moses "allowed" or permitted it, rather than commanded it. In Aquinas' view, Jesus thereby makes the point that "the permission did not derive from a precept, but rather it was permitted to avoid a greater evil."[74] The permission was not a positive command to do a good (let alone to do an evil), but rather the permission simply sought to ensure that the people would not commit a greater evil.

Turning to the verse that stands at the center of post-Reformation controversy, Aquinas observes that Jesus rules out divorce, "but fornication is excepted."[75] He notes that "fornication" can be both carnal and spiritual. In 1 Corinthians 7:15, in which the "unbelieving

[71] Thomas Aquinas, *Commentary on the Gospel of St. Matthew*, trans. Paul M. Kimball (Dolorosa Press, 2012), 631.
[72] Ibid., 632.
[73] Ibid., 633.
[74] Ibid., 634.
[75] Ibid.

partner" insists upon divorce, we find an exception regarding divorce made with respect to *spiritual* fornication. In Matthew 19:9 we find an exception regarding divorce made with respect to *carnal* fornication. But in the latter case, Aquinas emphasizes, the marriage cannot be dissolved, though a divorce (or legal separation) may legitimately take place. Aquinas underscores that "by no subsequent impediment [i.e., subsequent to the enactment of the marriage] can the bond of marriage be dissolved, because it signifies the union of Christ and the Church: hence, since the union of Christ and the Church cannot be dissolved, neither may the union of marriage."[76] Paul's remark in Ephesians 5:32 could make sense in no other way. If a valid Christian marriage could in fact be dissolved, then this would mean that a Christian marriage cannot really signify (let alone signify efficaciously) the unbreakable unity between Christ and his Church. A dissoluble bond cannot signify an indissoluble bond.

Aquinas asks why Jesus only grants an exception for fornication, given that there are many other serious sins one might commit. In reply, he reasons that fornication is opposed to the sexual fidelity that one owes to one's spouse, and therefore this particular action can be justly punished by the innocent spouse refusing any longer to have sexual intercourse (the marriage debt) with the "one who is not faithful".[77] He also suggests that since a man is loath to say that his wife has been sexually unfaithful, the exception made for carnal fornication will not tempt men to abuse it. Aquinas recognizes that marriage can be burdensome and people can desire to dissolve their marriages. In his commentary on Matthew 19, he notes that "leprosy and the like"—serious diseases—make marriage a difficult chore when one spouse is afflicted.[78] But he observes that the path of the Cross means that we cannot abandon our afflicted spouse or live unchastely.

In his commentary on Matthew 19:9, Aquinas does not even consider the notion that Jesus, in making the exception, is making an exception for divorce *and remarriage*. After all, in Matthew 19:9, Jesus says that someone who has been the subject of the exception and is now legitimately divorced cannot remarry. It is precisely the

[76] Ibid.
[77] Ibid.
[78] Ibid., 635.

legitimately "divorced woman" who, if remarried, causes the one who marries her to commit adultery. If the one who marries her commits adultery, it can only be because she is already married. She is divorced and legally separated, but her marriage has not been dissolved. Thus Jesus does not intend to permit divorce in the sense of a dissolution of a Christian marriage.

Conclusion

Most spouses hope for the stability of their marriage and welcome whatever strengthens this stability. The no-fault divorce laws of the past half-century have made clear how disastrous divorce is for the well-being of children.[79] In general, neither spouse benefits from a divorce; divorced women are much more likely to suffer from poverty, and divorced men are much more likely to become lonely and bitter. Indeed, among middle-class and upper-middle-class married couples in the United States, the divorce rate has been dropping precipitously. Over the past thirty years, the rate of college-educated married couples divorcing in the first seven years of marriage (or less) has dropped from 20 percent to 11 percent.[80] Whereas many of my parents' friends divorced, far fewer of my friends have divorced. Aquinas' six reasons for the goodness of marital indissolubility resonate with my generation and should enrich the Church's discourse about divorce and remarriage today.

In addition, Aquinas' arguments about Jesus' will for marriage, and Aquinas' interpretation of the Matthean exception clause, accord with the best of the historical-critical scholarship treated in chapter 1. Through the sacrament, the Lord Jesus is restoring the full dignity of marriage and empowering his followers to live it out by the grace of the Holy Spirit. Jesus does this not least because human marriage symbolizes the purpose for which Jesus came, namely, the inauguration of the marriage of God and his people. Through the grace

---

[79] I discuss this more fully in my *Engaging the Doctrine of Marriage*, in preparation.

[80] See Ted Khalaf, "Divorce Rates: Higher-Income and Lower-Income Families", Khalaf Law Group, July 16, 2018, https://bestdivorcelawyer.co/family-law/divorce-rates-higher income-lowerincome-families/.

of the sacrament, a particular Christian marriage's endurance does not depend upon the subjective fluctuations of the spouses, and the children do not have to go through wrenching cycles of their parents' divorcing and remarrying. The grace of the sacrament also upholds and strengthens those spouses who have been abandoned by their spouses and who, with the help of the Church, live out their vocation in cruciform fidelity, to the glory of God. Furthermore, the grace of the sacrament ensures that in cases where a separation becomes necessary (due to abuse or adultery), there always remains room for reconciliation and healing—and the innocent party receives the sustaining power of Christ. The sacrament seals marriage indissolubly, whereas, as the Pauline privilege shows, a natural marriage is not absolutely indissoluble.

Even so, if Christians do not recognize the power of Christ's appeal to God's will for marriage "from the beginning" (Mt 19:4), then Christians will be less likely to appreciate why the sacrament is such a great gift. The sacrament restores indissoluble marriage as originally willed by God. The sacrament bestows a sharing in the power of Christ's Cross so that the spouses can live out this vocation in holiness. In healing marriage and restoring its dignity as an indissoluble bond and covenantal communion in which children are best raised, Jesus also reveals its ultimate signification: the marriage of the triune God and mankind in self-sacrifical love, accomplished on the Cross and sacramentally represented in the Eucharist. In this way, marriage not only is in itself "the greatest friendship", but also is a sacred sign by which the spouses participate, by the power of Christ's Cross, in the Trinitarian communion into which Christ has called us as his "friends" (Jn 15:14–15).

CONCLUSION

In *Evangelii Gaudium*, Pope Francis observes that "in today's world there are innumerable signs, often expressed implicitly or negatively, of the thirst for God, for the ultimate meaning of life."[1] For some persons who "thirst for God", however, it may seem that Christian churches exist for a spiritual elite. This spiritual elite may frequent the sacraments and be warmly greeted, while less respected persons slip out the side door or never even make it in the door. Tragically, people may receive the impression that their lives are so disordered as to be unworthy even of entering the sanctuary.

In fact, the Church is deeply misunderstood when it is seen as existing for a spiritual elite. Jesus gave his followers an example by "eating with sinners and tax collectors" (Mk 2:16). And Jesus firmly rebuked the Pharisees: "Those who are well have no need of a physician, but those who are sick; I came not to call the righteous, but sinners" (Mk 2:17). We are all sinners in need of the divine Physician.

Yet, the divine Physician does not offer us a path free of sacrifice and suffering. The very opposite is the case. Even allowing for hyperbole, Jesus clearly makes intense demands: "If your eye causes you to sin, pluck it out; it is better for you to enter the kingdom of God with one eye than with two eyes to be thrown into hell" (Mk 9:47). He warns that we must place nothing above our relationship to him, not even our relationships with our closest family members. He states that "a man's foes will be those of his own household. He who loves father or mother more than me is not worthy of me; and he who loves son or daughter more than me is not worthy of me" (Mt 10:36–37). At the same time, he promises that if we recognize the divine Physician, we will learn that his path is the way of happiness. He teaches that "he who loses his life for my sake will find it" (Mt 10:39). He asks his followers to take on his "yoke" (Mt 11:29) of

---

[1] *Apostolic Exhortation of the Holy Father Francis, The Joy of the Gospel (Evangelii Gaudium)*, Vatican trans. (Boston: Pauline Books & Media, 2013), no. 86.

self-sacrificial love, a love that is deeply demanding but that is what fulfills us: "Come to me, all who labor and are heavy laden, and I will give you rest" (Mt 11:28). When his followers "hunger and thirst for righteousness", and even suffer "for righteousness' sake", it is precisely then that his followers will "be satisfied" and will inherit "the kingdom of heaven" (Mt 5:6, 10).

In the four chapters of this book, I have explored the teaching of Christ and the Catholic Church that marriage between Christians is indissoluble. Through the grace of the sacrament, indissolubility is intrinsic to what a Christian marriage is. As the theologian Antonio López remarks, "Indissolubility is the joyous affirmation that nuptial love is not at the mercy of spouses' moods, nor of the unforeseeable good or bad circumstances spouses may face, nor of the changing ideas of perceptions they may have."[2] Christ's gift of sacramental indissolubility means that a married Christian couple, having consummated a valid union, cannot in reality cast each other away, even if for good reasons they need to separate or even if one spouse repudiates the other. This is the fundamental Gospel of the family that the Lord Jesus, in his mercy, gave to his shocked disciples; and it is what the Catholic Church solemnly teaches as pertaining to divine revelation.

Whither the Doctrine of Marital Indissolubility?

Yet, recall Thomas Knieps-Port le Roi's contention, in his introduction to an edited volume that opens with an essay by Reinhard Cardinal Marx, that it is "not true" that *Amoris Laetitia* "does not change doctrine", because *Amoris Laetitia* will inevitably compel

---

[2] Antonio López, F.S.C.B., "Marriage's Indissolubility: An Untenable Promise?", *Communio* 41 (2014): 269. Linking mercy, self-sacrifice, and marital indissolubility, López writes: "Mercy, and what incarnates it, is what one both needs and opposes the most. When it is rejected, one stops listening to the other, spending time and doing things with him or her, and, ultimately, seeing the other for who he or she is. Here, too, what becomes intolerable is the life together as something other than one thinks, feels, or expects it to be; it is given to the spouses with a form of its own, and only within this form do their freedoms find fulfillment and peace. In other terms, the sacrifice asked of the spouses is that they accept that married love is greater than the two of them: it is itself a part and at the service of a greater love, namely, Christ's love for the Church" (ibid., 303).

modifications of the Catholic Church's understanding of marital indissolubility.[3] Given the delicacy of indissolubility—which vanishes as soon as we make it contingent—Knieps-Port le Roi's contention merits our attention. It should challenge all who, with Pope Francis, uphold the Church's teaching that a valid and consummated marriage between two baptized persons is indissoluble.

Like Knieps-Port le Roi, Edward Schillebeeckx, Kenneth Himes, James Coriden, Michael Lawler, and others noted above, the theologian Peter Hünermann argues that marriage is a "covenant" characterized by "mutual belonging", and "the accumulation of offenses against good faith can pile up to such an extent that the mutual belonging is no longer merely at risk, but in fact no longer exists."[4] In other words, the marriage dissolves. If so, then from the outset it was merely a contingently dissoluble covenant. This is not what Jesus, or the Church (including, as we have seen, *Amoris Laetitia*), teaches about marriage.

---

[3] Thomas Knieps-Port le Roi, introduction to *A Point of No Return?* Amoris Laetitia *on Marriage, Divorce, and Remarriage* (Berlin: LIT Verlag, 2017), 3.

[4] Peter Hünermann, "The Sacrament of Marriage: A Dogmatic Theologian Reads *Amoris Laetitia*", in Knieps-Port le Roi, *A Point of No Return?*, 102. Hünermann insists that the couple, through their subjective attitudes and actions, make their own indissolubility over the history of their marriage: "The living of the sacrament in people's life histories involves a realization of the covenant of life that must be deepened and renewed in the various phases and situations of life. At the beginning, there is the loving testing of the divine vocation to the covenant of life with this particular partner" (ibid., 102–3). Indissolubility here is no longer a gift that pertains intrinsically to a marriage bond, but rather it is something that depends upon the spouses' subjectivities. For discussion of a number of German-speaking theologians who hold this view, see Michaela C. Hastetter, "Between Failure and Jubilation: Contrary Tendencies in the Pastoral Care of Marriage", in *And God Saw That It Was Very Good: Reinvigorating the Sacrament of Marriage and the Christian Family in Light of the 2014 and 2015 Synods* (Heiligenkreuz bei Wien: Be&Be-Verlag, forthcoming). Hastetter points out that in 2011, Paul M. Zulehner undertook a study "of attitudes vis-à-vis the indissolubility of marriage and came to the following conclusion. When asked whether it was good for the church to insist on the indissolubility of marriage, 33% of Catholics agreed, as did 54% of Orthodox, whereas only 16% of Protestants agreed. Among Catholics the percentage of agreement increased with the age of respondents. In the group aged up to 29, a good quarter, that is 26%, agreed with the indissolubility of marriage; among the over 70s the figure was 51%, about half of all respondents. This shows that dissent regarding the indissolubility of marriage occurs not only at the level of theology and the magisterium but also among the Catholic laity" (Michaela C. Hastetter, "*Via Caritatis*—Pastoral Care of the Divorced and Remarried: An Ecumenical Comparison in the Context of *Amoris Laetitia*", trans. Graham Harrison, in Knieps-Port le Roi, *A Point of No Return?*, 200–201). See Paul M. Zulehner, *Verbuntung: Kirchen im weltanschaulichen Pluralismus: Religion im Leben der Menschen 1970–2010* (Ostfildern: Schwabenverlag, 2011), 269.

Pointing to the postconciliar rise of "new understandings of the requirement of permanence in Christian marriage", the theologian Margaret Farley observed in 1990 that that while "no one proposes eliminating this requirement", nonetheless, "ways are sought to interpret it which appear more adequate to human and Christian experience and less likely to place unjust and tragic burdens on individual persons and partnerships."[5] As she makes clear, however, these "more adequate" ways of interpreting "the requirement of permanence" should in her view end up by doing away with the requirement and making it instead into an ideal, whether juridically or de facto.[6] Farley

[5] Margaret A. Farley, "Divorce, Remarriage, and Pastoral Practice", in *Moral Theology: Challenges for the Future; Essays in Honor of Richard A. McCormick, S.J.*, ed. Charles E. Curran (New York: Paulist Press, 1990), 214. For Farley, the dissolution or "end of a marriage comes finally in a *decision* by the spouses (it does not, strictly speaking, as a marriage just 'die'); and it is this decision that can be morally justified and necessary (however unjustified it may have been to reach the point where this decision must be made)" (ibid., 238n55). Farley argues that her position "does not mean we are not called to great and noble loves that are self-sacrificing in a radical sense. But to sacrifice oneself is morally unjustifiable if it means violating one's very nature as a person" (ibid., 238n56). I do not see, however, how or why marital separation (as distinct from divorce as dissolution) violates "one's very nature as a person", even if it clearly requires profound self-sacrificial love.

[6] Farley tracks the evolving views of Richard McCormick on this topic, pointing out that in his "Notes on Moral Theology" (published regularly in the journal *Theological Studies*) "McCormick directly addressed the problem of divorce and remarriage nine times, and indirectly addressed it several more times" between 1965 and 1989 (Farley, "Divorce, Remarriage, and Pastoral Practice", 215). By 1975, McCormick had largely come to share Charles Curran's view that "marriages, even if they had been sacramental and consummated, could die—could cease to exist" (ibid., 220). In McCormick's view as reported by Farley, nonetheless, the Church can retain unchanged the doctrine of marital indissolubility, while altering pastoral practice and policy. Thus, although McCormick holds that a marriage can cease to exist, he thinks that there remains a "general prohibition against second marriages", though not an "absolute" prohibition, since "'proportionate reasons' in favor of other values may override it. These reasons will be particular to each individual (for they relate to special needs, responsibilities, concrete circumstances), so they (just like the reasons for divorce) must be weighed not by juridical institutions or officers but by the individuals concerned" (ibid., 222)—with the result that "it will not be necessary to 'institutionalize' exceptions (either to the precept of indissolubility or to the prohibition against remarriage)" (ibid.). If the prohibition can be overridden, and remarriage can be acceptable, then—whatever one might say about "proportionate reasons" and about avoiding "juridical" solutions—it is clearly the case that what we are dealing with is dissoluble marriage, unless there are two simultaneous marriages. As Farley notes, Curran recognized this point and held more cogently that once the possibility of dissolution is granted, indissoluble marriage is solely an *ideal* rather than a precept, and also that once a marriage has dissolved there can be no fundamental objection to remarriage, though the ideal remains in place. See also, for the evolution (and softening) of McCormick's position, his *The Critical Calling: Reflections on Moral Dilemmas Since Vatican II* (Washington, D.C.: Georgetown University Press, 1989).

understands marital "indissolubility" as an "intention of permanence" rather than in an objectively enduring bond accomplished by the Sacrament of Matrimony.[7] She thus favors a contingent "indissolubility" of marriage, grounded upon subjective intentions, that makes marriage dissoluble.[8] Yet, she grants that "if permanence—lifelong faithfulness in love, in sex, in sharing of the multiple dimensions and circumstances of life—can be achieved, it is the path towards the goals of marriage that are most desired."[9]

Farley is aware of the difference between her position and the Catholic Church's teaching. Were Christian marriage dissoluble on

---

[7] Farley, "Divorce, Remarriage, and Pastoral Practice", 228. Farley argues that "the picture it [the ontological view] offers of marriage as a bond in being, settled once and for all by freedom and grace, is finally misleading and potentially harmful to individuals and to the church" (ibid., 233). She gives three reasons for this critique: our self-determining choice cannot, even with the assistance of grace, bond us indissolubly to another person; the Church has historically promoted a patriarchal relationship between the spouses; and the Church's position entails that the spouses, by becoming "one flesh", lose their "autonomy in person and body" in a manner that has had deeply damaging consequences on women (ibid.). See also Margaret A. Farley, "Divorce and Remarriage", *Proceedings of the Catholic Theological Society of America* 30 (1975): 111–19; Margaret A. Farley, "Divorce and Remarriage: A Moral Perspective", in *Divorce and Remarriage: Religious and Psychological Perspectives*, ed. William P. Roberts (Kansas City, MO: Sheed and Ward, 1990), 107–27; Margaret A. Farley, "Marriage, Divorce, and Personal Commitments", in *Celebrating Christian Marriage*, ed. Adrian Thatcher (Edinburgh: T&T Clark, 2001), 355–72; and Margaret A. Farley, *Just Love: A Framework for Christian Sexual Ethics* (New York: Continuum, 2008), 296–310. Her arguments in *Just Love* are drawn almost verbatim from her "Divorce, Remarriage, and Pastoral Practice", but she is even clearer that her fundamental concern has to do with freedom, which requires that we not be locked ontologically into an indissoluble bond with another person (and indeed which here is not capable of constituting an indissoluble bond).

[8] Likewise, both McCormick and Curran advance psychological grounds for why marriage must inevitably be ontologically dissoluble rather than ontologically indissoluble (assuming that both spouses are alive and that the marriage was sacramentally valid). Farley sums up their positions: "The irretrievable death of a marriage relationship is that point at which, according to McCormick, resuscitation of it is no longer possible; it is at this point that the obligation of indissolubility is discontinued. And Curran argues that precisely where it is impossible 'for pilgrim Christians to live up to the fullness of love'—whether because of the limitation of creation, or sin, or the lack of the fullness of grace—there the obligation of indissolubility meets its limit" (Farley, "Divorce, Remarriage, and Pastoral Practice", 229). For a valid sacramental marriage to be ontologically indissoluble prior to the death of one spouse, of course, can only be affirmed if one supposes that psychological pressures cannot invalidate ontological realities. Farley cites McCormick's *Notes on Moral Theology 1965 through 1980* (Washington, D.C.: University Press of America, 1981), 558; and Curran's *Ongoing Revision: Studies in Moral Theology* (Notre Dame: Fides, 1975), 105. See also McCormick's "Indissolubility and the Right to the Eucharist: Separate Issues or One?", in *Ministering to the Divorced Catholic*, ed. James J. Young (New York: Paulist, 1979), 65–84.

[9] Farley, *Just Love*, 265.

the basis of something that occurs after the marriage has been validly covenanted and consummated, then Christian marriage would be a dissoluble reality, rather than effectively signifying sacramentally the indissoluble bond of Christ and the Church. The question then is whether Christian marriage's signification of Christ's marriage with the Church is a reality intrinsic to each Christian marriage, or dependent upon whether the married couple continues to act in loving ways toward each other and upon other subjective factors.

Stating the position of the Catholic Church, Aquinas considers that "by no subsequent impediment can the bond of marriage be dissolved, because it signifies the union of Christ and the Church: hence, since the union of Christ and the Church cannot be dissolved, neither may the union of marriage."[10] If the union of Christ and the Church depended upon how well the Church loves Christ, rather than upon an unbreakable union willed freely by Christ, then both the union of Christ and the Church and the union of Christian spouses would be contingently dissolvable. How we understand marital indissolubility will also have an impact upon how we interpret Christ's sacrificial love for the Church.[11] In his love, has Christ truly poured out his

[10] Thomas Aquinas, *Commentary on the Gospel of St. Matthew*, trans. Paul M. Kimball (Dolorosa Press, 2012), 634.

[11] For a sampling of other works that in various ways favor change in the Catholic Church's teaching and practice with regard to marriage, see, for example, Pierre L'Huillier et al., *Divorce et indissolubilité du mariage: Congrès de l'Association de théologiens pour l'étude de la morale* (Paris: Cerf, 1971); the full issue of *Recherches de science religieuse* 61 (1973): 483–624; *Recherches de science religieuse* 62 (1974): 7–116; "The Problem of Second Marriages: An Interim Pastoral Statement by the Study Committee Commissioned by the Board of Directors of the Catholic Theological Society of America", *Proceedings of the Catholic Theological Society of America* 27 (1972): 233–40; James J. Rue and Louise Shanahan, *The Divorced Catholic* (Mahwah, NJ: Paulist Press, 1972); Karl Lehmann, "Zur Sakramentalität der Ehe", in *Ehe und Ehescheidung: Diskussion Unter Christen*, ed. Franz Henrich and Volker Eid (Munich: Kösel, 1972), 57–74; Alcuin Coyle and Dismas Bonner, *The Church under Tension: Practical Life and Law in the Changing Church* (New York: Catholic Book Publishing, 1972); Lawrence G. Wrenn, ed., *Divorce and Remarriage in the Catholic Church* (New York: Newman Press, 1973); Steven Joseph Kelleher, *Divorce and Remarriage for Catholics?* (Garden City, NY: Doubleday, 1973); Richard P. McBrien, *The Remaking of the Church: An Agenda for Reform* (New York: Harper & Row, 1973), 99; Dennis Doherty, *Divorce and Remarriage* (St. Meinrad, IN: Abbey Press, 1974); Charles E. Curran, "Divorce: Catholic Theory and Practice in the United States", *The American Ecclesiastical Review* 168 (1974): 3–34, 75–95; Richard A. McCormick, "Notes on Moral Theology", *Theological Studies* 32 (1971): 107–22; Richard A. McCormick, "Notes on Moral Theology," *Theological Studies* 33 (1972): 91–100; Richard A. McCormick, "Notes on Moral Theology," *Theological Studies* 36 (1975): 100–17; Robert T. Kennedy and John T. Finnegan, "Select Bibliography on Divorce and Remarriage in the Catholic Church

Spirit in such a way that the Sacrament of Matrimony objectively and permanently unites the couple so long as both spouses are alive, giving them a unique, graced participation in the self-sacrificial union of Christ and the Church?

The answer may easily seem to be no. It is all too apparent that Christian marriages break down and that separation can prove to be necessary. Moreover, a civil marriage may bring contentment after a valid sacramental marriage has broken down. Faced with the evidence of the real world, can we really continue to insist upon a valid sacramental marriage's absolute indissolubility, trusting—as Gerhard Cardinal Müller advises—"in 'the Spirit which is from God, that we might understand the gifts bestowed on us by God' (1 Cor 2:12)"?[12] Furthermore, can we still affirm that the Holy Spirit works through the Church's discernment of the validity of the sacrament, in accord with the Church's public sacramental witness to the marriage?[13]

Today", in *Ministering to the Divorced Catholic*, ed. James J. Young (New York: Paulist, 1979), 260–73; James H. Provost, "Intolerable Marriage Situations: A Second Decade", *Jurist* 50 (1990): 573–612; Gerald D. Coleman, *Divorce and Remarriage in the Catholic Church* (New York: Paulist Press, 1988); Bernard Häring, *No Way Out? Pastoral Care of the Divorced and Remarried* (Middlegreen, England: St. Paul Publications, 1990); Kevin T. Kelly, *Divorce and Second Marriage: Facing the Challenge*, 2nd ed. (London: Geoffrey Chapman, 1996); John P. Beal, "Intolerable Marriage Situations Revisited: Continuing the Legacy of James H. Provost", *Jurist* 63 (2003): 253–311; Eberhard Schockenhoff, *Chancen zur Versöhnung? Die Kirche und die wiederverheirateten Geschiedenen* (Freiburg: Herder, 2012).

[12] Gerhard Ludwig Cardinal Müller, "Testimony to the Power of Grace: On the Indissolubility of Marriage and the Debate concerning the Civilly Remarried and the Sacraments", in *Remaining in the Truth of Christ: Marriage and Communion in the Catholic Church*, ed. Robert Dodaro, O.S.A. (San Francisco: Ignatius Press, 2014), 160.

[13] See ibid., 162. Kevin Flannery and Thomas Berg add the clarification, known to Müller, that in some rare cases "the ordinary canonical procedure is not sufficient to establish that the original 'marriage' was not a true marriage"; such cases "are resolved not in a marriage tribunal (in the external forum) but in the internal forum, employing the same logical principles employed in the external forum" (Kevin L. Flannery, S.J., and Thomas V. Berg, "*Amoris Laetitia*, Pastoral Discernment, and Thomas Aquinas", *Nova et Vetera* 16 [2018]: 101). They explain, "We have in mind, for instance, the hypothetical situation in which a person might have occult knowledge of some fact that would indicate with moral certainty the invalidity of the prior union but, for any number of reasons, is unable to prove that fact before a tribunal. If one party to a marriage, null because of the impediment 'vitiated consent,' refuses to make a judicial deposition but the other party knows with moral certainty that the other person's consent was vitiated, a solution in the internal forum is sometimes possible" (ibid., 104). But as they point out, "an individual's personal convictions 'in conscience' about the invalidity of a prior marital bond or about his or her most generous response that can be given to God at present, while these should be heard and taken into consideration in the context of pastoral

Defending the value of a remarriage after divorce (without annulment), the theologian Eberhard Schockenhoff notes that in contemporary culture, "Regardless of the reason why they have remarried—for companionship or because they have found a stable life partnership they did not have in their first marriage—most people do not experience the contraction of a second marriage as morally questionable, let alone sinful."[14] In his view, in holding this opinion, people are entirely right; the Church's centuries of consistent pastoral teaching on this topic have been rooted in a tragic mistake. At the same time, he somehow also contends that "relying on a person's conscience does not call into question the ecclesial teaching of the indissolubility of marriage and the obligatory nature of the promise of marital fidelity."[15]

Schockenhoff speaks frequently of irretrievably broken marriages as "dissolved". Like many of the authors noted above, he holds that "if the first marriage still exists as a legal fiction or spiritual torso, but no longer as a lived reality, living together with another partner can no longer be qualified as ongoing adultery", since as soon as "the earlier partners are no longer bound by a holistic life-context

---

counseling with gentleness and compassion, have, as such, no bearing on the resolution of that individual's situation with regard to the reception of the Eucharist—an event governed, in any case, by norms applicable in the external forum (see, for example, canon 915 of the Code of Canon Law). Pastoral ministers, in their capacity as pastoral ministers, are not free to apply the law of the Church as they see fit. Rather, they are obliged to remain faithful to true moral teaching as interpreted by the Church's authentic magisterium and in conformity with current Church law—none of which is at odds with a genuine pastoral concern for individuals" (ibid., 103–4). Again, neither pastors nor spouses can rely upon "the personal consciences as such of those involved", namely, "their subjective impressions regarding the invalidity of the prior bond. Any discernment would be an application of the *same principles used in the external forum*" (ibid., 105). See also Livio Melina, "Il ruolo della coscienza nell'acceso alla comunione eucaristica dei divorziati risposati", *Anthropotes* 11 (1995): 35–47.

[14] Eberhard Schockenhoff, "Our Understanding of Moral Sin: The Competence of Conscience of Divorced Remarried Persons", *INTAMS Review* 20 (2014), 256. See also Eberhard Schockenhoff, "Traditionsbruch oder notwendige Weiterbildung?: Zwei Lesarten des Nachsynodalen Schreibens Amoris laetitia", in *Zum Gelingen von Ehe und Familie: Ermutigung aus Amoris laetitia: Für Walter Kardinal Kasper*, ed. George Augustin (Freiburg: Herder, 2018), 282–96. Schockenhoff approves "the far-reaching paradigm shift" put forward by *Amoris Laetitia*, and he describes this paradigm shift as a movement "from an objectivistic doctrine of morality that is grounded on a static metaphysics of essences to a practical theology that corresponds to the Gospel", through an "inductive method" that allows for "promixity to experience" (ibid., 283–84, 289).

[15] Schockenhoff, "Our Understanding of Moral Sin", 249.

[*Lebenzvollzug*], they also no longer have the right to sexual communion."[16] He therefore considers that divorced persons involved in new relationships, without annulment of a prior indissoluble marriage, may "reach the reasonable conviction of conscience that the continuation of the new relationship, its legal legitimation and, therefore, a legal second marriage are morally required, especially if the relationship is long lasting".[17] Far from being a sinful action, entering into a new union of this kind without annulment of an indissoluble marriage should now be praised by the Church as "morally required". He contends that it is axiomatic that "if the partners of a second marriage live what is expected from married people, their reliable life partnership cannot be subjectively judged as a grave sin.... In a particular way, that standpoint contradicts the conscience of the people involved, who usually can hardly comprehend such a judgement."[18]

But I note that if divorced and remarried persons bound by a prior indissoluble marriage "can hardly comprehend such a judgment", this is because they are neglecting the fact that the valid and consummated marriage still binds, according to their own vows and according to the grace of the sacrament. There are still debts of love and sexual exclusivity that are owed to the betrayed spouse by the betrayer, and by both spouses to each other—even if the brokenness and complexities of the situation should inspire our compassion. Persons who "can hardly comprehend such a judgment", however, are in good company. Jesus' own disciples reacted with shock and dismay to his teachings. With regard to marriage between two Christians, Paul had to affirm that "to the married I give charge, not I but the Lord, that

---

[16] Schockenhoff, "Traditionsbruch oder notwendige Weiterbildung?", 292.

[17] Schockenhoff, "Our Understanding of Moral Sin", 256.

[18] Ibid. Schockenhoff grants that "purposefully disrupting a marriage in order to enter a new union could be an indication of human malice and meanness on the part of one of the partners and in fact, could entail severe culpability" (ibid., 257). He concludes his essay: "The Church established by Jesus Christ is by no means a community of the pure and immaculate who are without sin. Instead, it is the Church of Sinners, nurtured by the mercy of God who celebrates His presence with other sinners in the sacraments. Among all the Church's sacraments, the Eucharist is the quintessential sacrament of God's descending love. It reminds the Church of its everlasting origin, which is the love God communicates to all the sinful on the cross of Jesus Christ. Consequently, the Eucharist is not just a celebration for the redeemed to express their gratitude, but it is also the supper of reconciliation. It is the extended hand of God, which intends to reach every person—including the divorced and remarried members of the Church" (ibid., 259).

the wife should not separate from her husband (but if she does, let her remain single or else be reconciled to her husband)—and that the husband should not divorce his wife" (1 Cor 7:10–11). Note that he had to go out of his way to say "not I but the Lord", thereby indicating the authority on which this deeply challenging teaching was based. It is clear that divine revelation, as communicated in Scripture, takes a strong line that is meant to *form and enlighten* conscience as to the requirements of love, justice, and mercy. As Gerhard Müller states, "The entire sacramental economy is a work of divine mercy, and it cannot simply be swept aside by an appeal to the same"—even though the disciples at first did not perceive Jesus' teachings about marriage to be merciful.[19]

Schockenhoff considers that the first Christians very soon felt free to reject and modify these hard teachings of Jesus. Schockenhoff also holds that Jesus' statement in Matthew 5:32 and his unequivocal insistence upon marital indissolubility in Mark 10:11 and Luke 16:18 should not be taken as a "prescriptive obligation".[20] Citing essays published by Joseph Ratzinger in 1969 and 1972, when Ratzinger was thinking along lines that he later renounced,[21] Schockenhoff argues that Jesus' words are simply "a prophetic admonition" that "aim at pointing out the implications for marital life in the coming of God's reign".[22] The implication is that in the inaugurated kingdom, we are to take these words as an ideal or goal, but not as a commandment. In Schockenhoff's words, "Gentile Christian communities that grew as a result of the missionary work of Paul the Apostle, applied Jesus' instructions to certain situations of crisis, but they were not considered unconditionally binding."[23] According

---

[19] Müller, "Testimony to the Power of Grace", 163.

[20] Schockenhoff, "Our Understanding of Moral Sin", 252.

[21] See Joseph Ratzinger, "Zur Frage nach der Unauflöslichkeit der Ehe: Bemerkungen zum dogmengeschichtlichen Befund und zu seiner gegenwärtigen Bedeutung", in *Ehe und Ehescheidung: Diskussionen unter Christen*, ed. Franz Henrich and Volker Eid (Munich: Kösel, 1972), 35–52; Joseph Ratzinger, "Zur Theologie der Ehe", in *Theologie der Ehe*, ed. G. Krems and R. Mumm (Regensburg: Pustet, 1969), 81–115. For an English translation of the first-mentioned article, see Joseph Ratzinger, "On the Question of the Indissolubility of Marriage: Remarks on the Dogmatic-Historical State of Affairs and Its Significance for the Present", trans. J. Bolin, PathsofLove.com, March 25, 2011, https://www.pathsoflove.com/pdf/ratzinger-indissolubility-marriage.pdf.

[22] Schockenhoff, "Our Understanding of Moral Sin", 252.

[23] Ibid.

to Schockenhoff, Paul in 1 Corinthians 7 freely diverged from the word of Christ, by permitting "the divorce of a valid marriage in certain cases" and by allowing that "the innocently divorced spouse is free to remarry."[24] On this view, marital indissolubility has always remained the ideal for Christians. But "most likely … the actual practice of early Christian communities was to be open to the possibility of remarrying", thanks to "the practice of adjusting Jesus' instructions in light of exceptional adversity".[25]

For Schockenhoff, then, the solution is to affirm marital indissolubility as the ideal, while in practice operating in accord with the Eastern Orthodox tradition by permitting divorce and remarriage in a variety of cases, on the grounds that "a deviation from the norms of the Gospel can be justified if the intent is to consider human flaws with mercy."[26]

What Is at Stake

In light of the exegetical survey set forth in my first chapter, it will be clear that I consider Schockenhoff's claims to reflect his own context rather than accurately conveying anything like the teaching of Scripture. In his hands, the shocking power of Jesus' words, which led his disciples to exclaim that "it is not expedient to marry" (Mt 19:10), becomes a mere ideal, not shocking at all. If indissolubility is simply an ideal, then it is tautological—of course staying married is *ideally* better than getting divorced. Jesus thereby becomes a harmless sage, whose platitudinous wisdom points toward an ideal kingdom that he may have thought near, but that in fact is still a dream. Mercy becomes simply accepting the fact that none of us can achieve the

---

[24] Ibid.

[25] Ibid. Schockenhoff's perspective here accords broadly with traditional Protestant interpretations. See, for example, the extensive discussion in Anthony C. Thiselton, *The First Epistle to the Corinthians: A Commentary on the Greek Text* (Grand Rapids, MI: Eerdmans, 2000), 521–25, 540–43.

[26] Schockenhoff, "Our Understanding of Moral Sin", 253. Along lines that would also apply to cohabitating couples and same-sex unions, Schockenhoff comments that "a reliable personal lifetime partnership deserves to be morally appreciated due to the partners' mutual exchange of human values and their willingness to take on responsibility for each other in good times and bad on a public and legally binding level" (ibid., 257).

ideal. The Jesus who "came to cast fire upon the earth" and who teaches, "Do you think that I have come to give peace on earth? No, I tell you, but rather division" (Lk 12:49, 51), is neutered. The prayer of the tax collector, "God, be merciful to me a sinner!" (Lk 18:13), becomes mere assurance that God will overlook injustice, given that the tax collector could hardly be expected to stop practicing his unjust trade in service to the Roman Empire. The Jesus who commands that anyone who wishes to be his disciple must hate "even his own life" and must "bear his own cross and come after me" (Lk 14:26–27) is transformed into a man who wants to tell us that he loves us, without requiring us to keep our marriage vows. The Jesus who demands real repentance and change of life, precisely in order that we may flourish both now and eternally, turns into a Jesus who is okay with us doing whatever that upon serious reflection seems good to us.[27] Furthermore, the Paul who makes an exception for a Christian

---

[27] Ross Douthat puts this point into bold relief: "To read the gospels, to reenter their world, is to find a Jesus whose anger at legalism is directed against the *ritual* law of first-century Judaism—the rules related to purity, diet, Sabbath observance, and so on, all of which he insists can and must give way in the name of mercy, healing, encounter, love. But the moral law, the Ten Commandments and their corollaries, Jesus never qualifies or relativizes. He never suggests that there exists some shades-of-gray world in which apostasy or adultery (or fraud or murder or theft or gluttony or any other sin) are actually part of God's complicated plan. Instead he heightens moral demands—urging purity of heart as well as purity of action, proposing a more sweeping rule of charity toward the poor, a more sweeping warning against the temptations of great wealth, and a more exalted view of sex and marriage. Meanwhile, he often condemns the Jewish traditionalists and legalists of his time not because they are simplistic or harsh in their moral demands, but because their ritualism obscures the clarity of the moral law, or turns the law into a too clever means for people to avoid their clear moral obligations.... This doesn't mean that Jesus's mercy isn't absolute. It is more absolute, indeed, than Jewish law: The repentant sinner must be forgiven not seven times but seventy times seven, which is to say perpetually. But this absolute mercy is always linked to repentance; it is never deployed to supersede the Commandments, never used to suggest that they are too simplistic for dealing with the complexities of human situations, or that there is a landscape beyond or above them where the law does not apply. Jesus doesn't urge Peter to 'go ahead, betray me, I understand.' Jesus doesn't tell the woman taken in adultery, 'go back to your lover, because your situation is complex.' Jesus doesn't tell Zacchaeus the tax collector, 'actually, keep the money you may have unjustly taken, because you need it to support your family.' Jesus dines with sinners, he hangs out with prostitutes and publicans, he evangelizes the much married Samaritan woman, he welcomes thieves into eternity. But he never confirms them in their sins, or makes nuanced allowances for their state of life" (Ross Douthat, *To Change the Church: Pope Francis and the Future of Catholicism* [New York: Simon & Schuster, 2018], 176, 178). See also the insights of Matthew J. Thomas, *Paul's "Works of the Law" in the Perspective of Second Century Reception* (Tübingen: Mohr Siebeck, 2018).

who is married to a non-Christian in 1 Corinthians 7:12–15 is turned into a Paul who nonchalantly rejects the Lord's teaching that "the wife should not separate from her husband (but if she does, let her remain single or else be reconciled to her husband)—and that the husband should not divorce the wife" (1 Cor 7:10–11).

There is yet another reason for rejecting Schockenhoff's path, in which marital indissolubility is the ideal, though in practice remarriage after divorce may validly take place with the Church's firm approval. Namely, everyone can perceive that such "indissolubility" is not indissoluble at all; on the contrary, when this path is followed, marriage is easily dissoluble and, as a practical matter, no one thinks otherwise. After relating that the British Methodists in 1946 decided to allow church weddings for the remarriage of the innocent party of a divorce, the biblical scholar Anthony Thiselton notes that originally ministers who rejected this decision were allowed to refuse to celebrate such weddings. He finds that by 1996, "62 percent of all marriages in Methodist churches involved at least one divorced person" and "in 1998 ministers were also relieved of the task of identifying an 'innocent party' or the causes of breakdown."[28] In most contemporary Orthodox Churches, remarriage after divorce is not seen as of much significance, even if it is not celebrated in the same way. While firmly defending the Orthodox theology of marriage, Alexander Schmemann admits that in practice, the Orthodox Church over time has "had to accept many functions and duties, if not contrary, at least alien, to her nature".[29] Something similar would happen to the

---

[28] Thiselton, *First Epistle to the Corinthians*, 543.

[29] Alexander Schmemann, "The Indissolubility of Marriage: The Theological Tradition of the East", in *The Bond of Marriage: An Ecumenical and Interdisciplinary Study*, ed. William W. Bassett (Notre Dame: University of Notre Dame Press, 1968), 105. Theologically, Schmemann argues that we are dealing with an "antinomy": "The marriage *is* indissoluble, yet it *is* being dissolved all the time by sin and ignorance, passion and selfishness, lack of faith and lack of love. Yes, the Church acknowledges the divorce, but she *does not divorce!* She only acknowledges that here, in this concrete situation, this marriage has been broken, has come to an end, and in her compassion she gives permission to the innocent party to marry again" (ibid., 104). In my view, however, the question is what it means to say that the marriage "has come to an end". Is there still an indissoluble marriage between the two spouses, or is it no longer present? Schmemann's Orthodox account of "antinomy" seeks to transcend this question, but I do not think that it can really be transcended. Certainly, it cannot be transcended in the Catholic Church, given the solemnity and specificity of the teachings of the Council of Trent and later popes.

Catholic Church too, if Schockenhoff's viewpoint were accepted. People marrying in the Catholic Church would know full well that, no matter what the ideal might be, their marriages never are indissoluble but rather are quite dissoluble. Their marital promises would no longer permanently commit them until parted by death, no matter what the written and spoken vows might say. The gift of the sacrament would be tragically and unacceptably hollowed out by its ministers.

The theologian George Worgul argues that the next step is to ask: "Might it be possible to admit that we evangelized non-western cultures with the Gospel and with our western cultural understanding of marriage and this master narrative of marriage was understood to be true everywhere and for all time?"[30] Worgul raises this question despite the fact that it is mainly the Western theologians and bishops who have been fighting for a change in marriage doctrine, often against African opposition in particular. His question is helpful, however, in making clear that what is ultimately at stake is the truth of dogma "everywhere and for all time".[31]

---

[30] Worgul, *"Amoris Laetitia"*, 28.

[31] Stephan Kampowski marks out the limits of inculturated/contextual theology: "The proposal of a complete relativity of cultures without any reference to human nature is not at all plausible. To claim that there is a human nature is to claim that something true can be said about the meaning of human existence and behavior, something that has universal validity throughout all times and places. On what grounds can one claim the existence of a human nature? Insofar as this discussion is going on also within the church, among theologians and bishops, it is important to remember what is at stake here theologically speaking. Evidently, Christ can be the redeemer of humankind only if there actually *is* a humankind" (Stephan Kampowski, *Embracing Our Finitude: Exercises in a Christian Anthropology between Dependence and Gratitude* [Eugene, OR: Cascade, 2018], 76). Kampowski puts his finger on what is going on as a practical matter: "Among today's cultural relativists inside and outside the church, among those who consider the faith an essentially cultureless phenomenon that needs to be inculturated into different contexts, one notices a curious fact. Most of their relativism is limited to questions pertaining to the sixth commandment. One needs to remember, though, that the commandments are ten in number. One may at least wonder whether advocates of cultural relativism would as readily apply to the fifth or seventh commandment the cultural hermeneutic they use for the sixth. One will hope, at least, that they will not. Otherwise, what would they say about the ritual murder practiced among the Aztecs and the infanticide that was common among the Spartans? Could these 'cultural' practices ever be consistent with the faith? Do these practices give witness to the fact that the commandment 'Do not kill' does not express any universal truth about human nature, that it always needs to be interpreted within a given culture, and that it has to be concretely applied according to the context of the times?" (ibid., 81).

The theologian Michael Seewald makes these stakes even clearer. In a book framed by the questions about continuity in Church teaching raised by *Amoris Laetitia* and its reception, Seewald explains that "when dogma fails or stops working, it thus stands in the way of the Gospel and closes up the Gospel instead of disclosing it; then it must, for the sake of the goal that it serves [i.e., the Gospel's 'eschatological truth/event-character truth'], further develop."[32] Seewald grants the undesirability of an absolutely undogmatic Christianity. But he thinks that in questions of continuity and discontinuity, we must recognize that what appears to be, on logical grounds, a doctrinal rupture, may in fact be a deepening or development of the Church's broader consciousness, which surpasses and encompasses the Church's propositional judgments.

By locating identity and continuity in this "ecclesial" consciousness rather than in doctrinal formulations, Seewald proposes to be able to show that even dogmatic rupture does not rupture the deeper identity of the Church. His position, however, relies upon a sharp separation between the propositional judgments of the Church (ultimately entirely changeable) and the supposedly deeper truth or deeper identity of the "Gospel/Christ-event" or the eschatological Church as a living subject. But if Christians lack ability to determine the core cognitive content of the "Gospel" or the "Church" in enduring truth-judgments, then the "Gospel" and the "Church" are in fact unknowable entities onto which humans in different generations paint what they wish, in the name of the eschatological future. This is the path of liberal Protestantism in its Catholic form. If this path were followed, then divine revelation as understood by the entire Catholic tradition—including Vatican II's Dogmatic Constitutions *Dei Verbum* and *Lumen Gentium*—would be replaced by mere human gesturing toward the ineffable. The fact that Seewald thinks that this is what *Amoris Laetitia* justifies is dismaying. Such a position relativizes, and logically negates, both Jesus' authoritative teachings about marriage and the Church's consistent promise, in the name of Jesus, of sacramental marital indissolubility. Not only the marriage teachings of the Church would thereby be dissolved, but also the

---

[32] Michael Seewald, *Dogma im Wandel: Wie Glaubenslehren sich entwickeln* (Freiburg: Herder, 2018), 284.

foundation of all the Church's dogmatic teachings would crumble, since they could no longer be received as enduringly true judgments regarding a divinely given, cognitively accessible apostolic deposit of faith.

Benefitting from Theological *Ressourcement*

For his part, Aquinas helps us to perceive how it can be good news when Jesus shockingly says, "Whoever divorces his wife and marries another, commits adultery against her; and if she divorces her husband and marries another, she commits adultery" (Mk 10:11–12); and likewise when Paul shockingly says, "To the married, I give charge, not I but the Lord, that the wife should not separate from her husband (but if she does, let her remain single or else be reconciled to her husband)—and that the husband should not divorce his wife" (1 Cor 7:10–11). Aquinas emphasizes that this teaching not only restores what is good for personal and social human flourishing according to the needs of human nature, but also that this teaching belongs to the wondrous economy of grace. Through their free act of marital consent, in the Sacrament of Matrimony Christians receive a graced sharing in the union of Christ and the Church. This participation in the union of Christ and the Church, through indissoluble marriage, involves not simply a path of personal, familial, and social flourishing in this life due to the blessings of marriage; it also involves, if the marriage breaks down or great sacrifices have to be made, the graced ability to suffer in union with Christ.

As we saw, Aquinas affirms that Jesus teaches that a valid divorce does not dissolve a valid marriage, but instead only produces a legal separation. In every valid and consummated Christian marriage, according to Jesus, the spouses "are no longer two but one. What therefore God has joined together, let no man put asunder" (Mt 19:6). Aquinas' exegesis upholds Jesus' affirmation, while acknowledging the grave burdens placed on some spouses, including potentially the burden of lifelong sexual abstinence. Notable historical-critical exegetes agree with Aquinas' position, as do the great majority of the Church Fathers and the Catholic Church's Magisterium exemplified in solemnest form by the Council of Trent.

In his *Summa Contra Gentiles*, Aquinas reminds us that Christian marital indissolubility is not something alien to our created nature (as distinct from fallen human nature). In his providential care for human flourishing, God ordained marriage as an indissoluble state for the flourishing of human individuals, families, and communities. Marriage, as a reality of the order of creation, can only be dissolved by death or, in certain circumstances, by the sacramental sharing in Christ's death effected by Baptism. Aquinas goes to great lengths to show the reasonableness of indissoluble marriage, given the need of children for lengthy care, and given the fact that one spouse should not abandon the other, not least because of the intimacy of their relationship.

Is it possible to be bound by a Christian indissoluble marriage and, at the same time, to be encouraged by pastors to continue to have sexual relations with one's civil-marriage partner, with whom one has built deep bonds?[33] We must not be blind to the fact that an abandoned spouse inevitably has emotional, bodily, familial, and economic needs that will easily lead him or her to reach out to another person, in hopes of forming another union. Again, how can the merciful Lord Jesus, or the Church, be opposed to this?[34]

---

[33] Alexander R. Pruss has noted that "sexual union is a union as one *flesh*, not just one mind or one heart.... In sexuality, the two unite in a totality that involves them not just as persons, but also as animals" (Alexander R. Pruss, *One Body: An Essay in Christian Sexual Ethics* [Notre Dame: University of Notre Dame Press, 2013], 130). It might be better to say that we are rational animals, and so bodily union inevitably involves us as whole persons; it is a spiritual-physical act. Marital exclusivity means that in giving ourselves to the other person, we give our total selves. Marital indissolubility means that this total gift is permanent.

[34] Obviously, the very same question holds for same-sex unions, a point that has not been lost upon those seeking to turn *Amoris Laetitia* into a determinate change of the Church's moral doctrine. See Ignace Berten, O.P., *Les divorcés remariés peuvent-ils communier?: Enjeux ecclésiaux des débats autour du Synode sur la famille et d'*Amoris laetitia (Namur, Belgium: Lessius, 2017), 297–99, as well as Paul Zulehner's contention that "the process of further development of the Church's position on homosexuality has thus been initiated at the Synod on the Family" (Paul M. Zulehner, *Vom Gesetz zum Gesicht: Ein neuer Ton in der Kirche: Papst Franziskus zu Ehe und Familie:* Amoris Laetitia [Ostfildern: Patmos, 2016], 137). Against such views, see the remarks of Thibaud Collin in his *Le mariage chrétien a-t-il encore un avenir? Pour en finir avec les malentendus* (Paris: Artège, 2018), 197–217. Collin rightly notes that the problem consists in mistakenly conceiving of marriage as "divisible into many elements" and therefore as existing "in forms of union that share in the ideal of marriage to the degree that they possess some of these elements" (ibid., 197). As he notes, this application of an ecclesiological idea to the domain of marriage results in giving the impression that marriage "could be the endpoint or flowering of concubinage" or that one can "be more or less married" (ibid., 198); although

As I have already emphasized, this is the problem that motivates Pope Francis' *Amoris Laetitia*. Archbishop Victor Manuel Fernandez rightly states, "Francis has never affirmed that it is possible to receive communion if one is not in a state of grace."[35] Against the poison of moral judgmentalism, *Amoris Laetitia* focuses on warning Christians that we must not become like the Pharisee in Jesus' parable who arrogantly "prayed thus with himself, 'God, I thank you that I am not like other men, extortioners, unjust, adulterers, or even like this tax collector'" (Lk 18:11). Pope Francis has clearly caught the parable's gist. A great lesson of *Amoris Laetitia* is that those of us whose indissoluble Christian marriages are going relatively well must not lack care and compassion for our suffering brothers and sisters whose indissoluble marriages, often through no fault of their own, have broken down.

Yet, Jesus, the bridegroom, has given the human race a word about marriage that believers must obey.[36] In repenting and turning toward Jesus, believers must be willing to give up everything for his sake. Fortunately, obedience to Christ's merciful law for our true flourishing (as individuals and communities) is always made possible by the grace of the Holy Spirit. Ultimately, as Robert Cardinal Sarah

---

there may be cohabiting couples who have in fact freely given their permanent marital consent without recognizing that this is what it means to be husband and wife, and who are thereby married (even if they should formalize the marriage). For further background to the movement to change the Church's teaching on homosexual unions, see Adriano Oliva, O.P., *Amours: L'Église, les divorcés remariés, les couples homosexuels* (Paris: Cerf, 2015), a book that Collin discusses critically and at length, especially with regard to its grave misreading of Aquinas' moral theology. Collin also directs attention to how, through its rationale for changing sacramental discipline regarding the reception of the Eucharist, Bishop Jean-Paul Vesco, O.P., in his *Tout amour véritable est indissoluble* (Paris: Cerf, 2015), both opens the door to blessing homosexual unions and makes all marriages contingently dissoluble. As Collin explains, Vesco's argument "is that the Church cannot require the 'divorced remarried' to break the 'new union' that they have concluded. Why would such a demand be impossible? The reason invoked is that the second union, like 'every true conjugal love,' is indissoluble"—and it is the relationship (rather than the sacrament itself) that provides the indissolubility, so that the Church's task is simply to recognize and affirm this indissolubility of true love (Collin, *Le mariage chrétien a-t-il encore un avenir?*, 219).

[35] Victor Manuel Fernandez, *Chapitre VIII de Amoris Laetitia: Le bilan après la tourmente*, trans. Hortense de Parscau (Paris: Parole et Silence, 2018), 33.

[36] On Jesus as "bridegroom", see Jocelyn McWhorter, *The Bridegroom Messiah and the People of God: Marriage in the Fourth Gospel* (Cambridge: Cambridge University Press, 2006), and Brant Pitre, *Jesus the Bridegroom: The Greatest Story Ever Told* (New York: Penguin Random House, 2014).

says, "We cannot do without the Cross.... It is therefore necessary to present marriage to engaged couples as a spiritual journey in which the spouses follow Christ in his Paschal Mystery."[37]

Recall once more Pope Francis' remark in paragraph 52 of *Amoris Laetitia*: "No one can think that the weakening of the family as that natural society founded on marriage will prove beneficial to society as a whole.... There is a failure to realize that only the exclusive and indissoluble union between a man and a woman has a plenary role to play in society as a stable commitment that bears fruit in new life." Given that a valid and consummated Christian marriage is an "exclusive and indissoluble union", no truly pastoral approach to the divorced and (civilly) remarried can undermine the reality that Christian marriages are exclusive and indissoluble. Unlike contingently dissoluble realities, valid and consummated Christian marriages—by the grace of the sacrament—actually unite the husband and wife indissolubly, with binding mutual obligations including sexual exclusivity, however much the subjective feelings of the spouses may fluctuate over the years. Generally speaking, the sacramental gift of indissolubility is a source of great joy and security for Catholic couples, who live out their marriage in the midst of the difficulties that inevitably beset family life.

In this regard, the great Protestant theologian Dietrich Bonhoeffer offers an inspiring testimony. In "A Wedding Sermon from a Prison Cell", written for the wedding of his sister in May 1943 when he was in prison facing execution by the Nazis, Bonhoeffer observes that although the love of the couple is their "own private possession", "marriage is more than something personal—it is a status, an office."[38] Speaking directly to his sister and her bridegroom, he tells them that "love comes from you, but marriage from above, from God. As high as God is above man, so high are the sanctity, the rights, and the promise of marriage above the sanctity, the rights, and the

---

[37] Robert Cardinal Sarah, "Marriage Preparation in a Secularized World", in *Eleven Cardinals Speak on Marriage and the Family: Essays from a Pastoral Viewpoint*, ed. Winfried Aymans, trans. Michael J. Miller et al. (San Francisco: Ignatius Press, 2015), 106–7. As a recent example of living this to the full, Sarah points to the Pakistani Christian martyrs Shahbaz Misih and his wife, Shama Bibi.

[38] Dietrich Bonhoeffer, "A Wedding Sermon from a Prison Cell", in *Letters and Papers from Prison*, enlarged ed. (London: SCM Press, 1971), 43.

promise of love. It is not your love that sustains the marriage, but from now on, the marriage that sustains your love."[39]

For Bonhoeffer, then, marriage is grounded in God's ordinance, not in ever-changing human subjective states, although it is love that leads the couple to their free marital consent. Bonhoeffer therefore goes on to emphasize: "*God makes your marriage indissoluble.* 'What therefore God has joined together, let no man put asunder' (Matt. 19.6). God joins you together in marriage; it is his act, not yours. Do not confound your love for one another with God."[40] As Bonhoeffer says, this is a cause for great rejoicing. We know that human wills are fragile; but a marriage, and therefore a family, rests upon God. Bonhoeffer rejoices with his sister and her bridegroom that since "God makes your marriage indissoluble", the newlyweds can have assurance that "no power on earth, no temptation, no human frailty can dissolve what God holds together."[41] The indissolubility that God bestows upon Christian marriage frees the spouses "from all the anxiety that is always a characteristic of love", so that the spouses "can now say to each other with complete and confident assurance: We can never lose each other now; by the will of God we belong to each other till death."[42] Bonhoeffer concludes his sermon by underscoring that the center of a Christian marriage is Christ, and therefore the spouses must follow Christ's self-sacrificial path.

This self-sacrificial meaning of marriage needs further attention, not least in its relation to the Eucharist. Today, the Eucharist is often seen solely as "a communal meal of thanksgiving",[43] but it is also, and fundamentally, a sacrificial sharing in the merciful self-offering of Jesus Christ.[44] The Eucharist expresses the faith of those who obey Jesus' command to "do this in remembrance of me" (Lk 22:19), and this "remembrance" liturgically enables believers to share in the Lord's saving Passover and to be nourished by the new "manna", his embodied self-sacrificial love, which strengthens the love of believers.

---

[39] Ibid.

[40] Ibid.; emphasis in original.

[41] Ibid.

[42] Ibid.

[43] Nadia Delicata, "Sin, Repentance and Conversion in *Amoris Laetitia*", in *A Point of No Return? Amoris Laetitia on Marriage, Divorce, and Remarriage*, ed. Thomas Knieps-Port le Roi (Berlin: LIT Verlag, 2017), 83.

[44] See Matthew Levering, *Sacrifice and Community: Jewish Offering and Christian Eucharist* (Oxford: Blackwell, 2005).

In the Eucharist, we receive and commune with Jesus himself, even as we share in his Pasch. Strengthened by the Spirit in the unity of faith and love, believers advance toward the Father along the path of merciful self-sacrificial love in the new exodus led by the crucified, risen, and ascended Son.[45]

This Eucharistic path of love requires that we not "indulge in immorality", and it requires each of us to recall Saint Paul's promise that "God is faithful, and he will not let you be tempted beyond your strength, but with the temptation will always provide the way of escape" (1 Cor 10:8, 13). Paul exhorts, "You are not your own; you were bought with a price. So glorify God in your body" (1 Cor 6:19–20). Here we must recall ever more firmly that marriage, for Christians, is no merely worldly enterprise, but rather is a sacrament of Christ, ordered to Eucharistic Communion in the Body of Christ. As the theologian Matthias Scheeben remarks, "Marriage between Christians, provided it is otherwise legal, is essentially and under all circumstances a holy, mystical union, in which the bridal couple join and are joined in the name of Christ for the extension of His mystical body."[46] Marriage is a path of self-sacrificial Eucharistic life. For this reason, Pope Francis quotes the words of Jesus from the Gospel of John: " 'No one has greater love than this, to lay down one's life for one's friends'(Jn 15:13)."[47]

Moreover, the path of cruciform love is no mere eschatological ideal for Jesus' followers. John Piper reminds us that "God gives us the power we need to love each other in this covenant-keeping way."[48]

---

[45] See Brant Pitre, *Jesus and the Last Supper* (Grand Rapids, MI: Eerdmans, 2015). As John Corbett and others point out, the danger is that a pastoral injustice might be committed: "Were he [a divorced and civilly remarried Catholic, whose spouse is alive and whose first marriage is truly indissoluble] admitted to the Eucharist without renouncing the obstacle, the situation would be worse. He would make a sacramental Communion while unable to receive Christ in faith and charity, because of his ongoing attachment to grave sin or to an objectively disordered living situation. He might be lulled into thinking his situation is unproblematic" (John Corbett, O.P., et al., "Recent Proposals for the Pastoral Care of the Divorced and Remarried: A Theological Assessment", *Nova et Vetera* 12, no. 3 [2014]: 617).

[46] Matthias Joseph Scheeben, *The Mysteries of Christianity*, trans. Cyril Vollert, S.J. (New York: Crossroad, 2006), 606.

[47] Pope Francis, post-synodal apostolic exhortation *Amoris Laetitia* (March 19, 2016), no. 27.

[48] John Piper, *This Momentary Marriage: A Parable of Permanence* (Wheaton, IL: Crossway, 2009), 175. See also my "What Is the Gospel?", in *Theological Theology: Essays in Honour of John B. Webster*, ed. R. David Nelson, Darren Sarisky, and Justin Stratis (London: Bloomsbury, 2015), 149–66.

To share in the Eucharist means sharing in the Lord's self-sacrificial love and in his living out God's faithful covenantal promises. Inevitably, indissoluble marriage and the Eucharist are tightly bound in their signification. Through the grace of the Sacrament of Matrimony, the Holy Spirit calls and strengthens each married Christian as we stumble, fall, and seek to rise again in meeting our daily challenges and trials. No matter how many times we have failed to embody his cruciform love, Christ offers us his merciful grace anew, inviting us urgently to "go, and do not sin again" (Jn 8:11)—and giving us the strength to live out his demanding love.[49]

Embodying such love, every Christian must offer a "fraternal and evangelical *welcome* towards those who have lost contact with the Church" due to "an irregular [marital] situation".[50] In offering this fraternal welcome, believers should recall that the Pharisee who sought to entangle Jesus in controversy inadvertently spoke the truth when he flattered Jesus: "Teacher, we know that you are true, and teach the way of God truthfully, and care for no man; for you do not regard the position of men" (Mt 22:16). Jesus' teachings are often deeply challenging. Clearly, this is the case with regard to his

---

[49] Even if we cannot yet receive the Eucharist due to an objective state of sin, great desire for spiritual communion is always a deeply positive sign. On this point, see Paul Josef Cardinal Cordes, "Without Rupture or Discontinuity", in *Eleven Cardinals Speak on Marriage and the Family*, 30–37; but see also the rightful caution of Paul J. Keller, O.P., "Is Spiritual Communion for Everyone?", *Nova et Vetera* 12 (2014): 631–55. For further discussion of the deeper theological issues, see Thomas G. Dalzell, S.M., "Eucharist, Communion and Orthopraxis in the Theology of Joseph Ratzinger", *Irish Theological Quarterly* 78 (2013): 103–22.

[50] Address of His Holiness Pope John Paul II to the Pontifical Council for the Family, January 24, 1997, no. 4; emphasis in original. Similarly, as James Martin, S.J., emphasizes, believers must extend a real fraternal welcome to persons with same-sex attractions; see James Martin, S.J., *Building a Bridge: How the Catholic Church and the LGBT Community Can Enter into a Relationship of Respect, Compassion, and Sensitivity*, rev. ed. (New York: HarperCollins, 2018). Martin states, "When the episcopacy speaks about LGBT matters in a way that LGBT Catholics don't agree with or that angers or even offends them, LGBT Catholics are invited to challenge themselves to listen closely. Ask: 'What are they saying? Why are they saying it? What lies behind their words?' LGBT Catholics are called to listen, consider, pray, and of course use their informed consciences as they discern how to lead their lives" (ibid., 79). I share Martin's sadness about the offense caused by careless words or a lack of respect for a person's dignity as a child of God. At the same time, the listening to which believers are called is ultimately to the revealed Word of God, communicated to us in Scripture. The "obedience of faith" (Rom 1:5) is more than a matter of considering and discerning; it requires obedience to God's Word (which is not the Church's property, but rather is over and above the Church), including the teaching of the Church about human sexuality.

teaching on divorce and remarriage. The good news is that his teaching conduces to the true flourishing of spouses and children, despite (and, by his grace, through) the trials that spouses may endure in carrying their crosses. Let me therefore conclude this book with a psalm in praise of God's powerful presence: "He who dwells in the shelter of the Most High, who abides in the shadow of the Almighty, will say to the LORD, 'My refuge and my fortress; my God, in whom I trust.' For he will deliver you from the snare of the fowler, and from the deadly pestilence; he will cover you with his pinions, and under his wings you will find refuge; his faithfulness is a shield and buckler" (Ps 91:1–4).

BIBLIOGRAPHY

Adams, Jay E. *Marriage, Divorce, and Remarriage in the Bible*. Grand Rapids, MI: Zondervan, 1980.

Aland, Barbara, Kurt Aland, Johannes Karavidopoulos, Carlo M. Martini, and Bruce M. Metzger, eds. *The Greek New Testament*, 4th rev. ed. Stuttgart: Deutsche Bibelgesellschaft, 1994.

Albright, W. F., and C. S. Mann. *Matthew: Introduction, Translation, and Notes*. Garden City, NY: Doubleday, 1971.

Alesandro, John A. "How Is This Newness Read by Canon Lawyers?" In *Amoris Laetitia: A New Momentum for Moral Formation and Pastoral Practice*, edited by Grant Gallicho and James F. Keenan, S.J., 48–60. New York: Paulist Press, 2018.

Alivisatos, Hamicar S. *Marriage and Divorce in Accordance with the Canon Law of the Orthodox Church*. London: Faith Press, 1948.

Allison, Dale C. *Constructing Jesus: Memory, Imagination, and History*. Grand Rapids, MI: Baker Academic, 2010.

Altan, Angelo. "Indissolubilitá ed oikonomia nella teologia e nella disciplina orientale del matrimonio". *Sacra Doctrina* 49 (1968): 87–112.

Álvarez de las Asturias, Nicolás, ed. *En la Salud y en la Enfermedad: Pastoral y Derecho al Servicio del Matrimonio*. Madrid: Ediciones Cristiandad, 2015.

Aquinas, Thomas. *Commentary on the Gospel of St. Matthew*. Translated by Paul M. Kimball. Dolorosa Press, 2012.

———. *Commentary on the Letters of Saint Paul to the Galatians and Ephesians*. Translated by Fabian R. Larcher and Matthew L. Lamb. Edited by J. Mortensen and E. Alarcón. Lander, WY: Aquinas Institute for the Study of Sacred Doctrine, 2012.

———. *Summa Contra Gentiles, Book Three: Providence, Part II*. Translated by Vernon J. Bourke. Notre Dame: University of Notre Dame Press, 1975.

————. *Summa Contra Gentiles, Book Four: Salvation*. Translated by Charles J. O'Neil. Notre Dame: University of Notre Dame Press, 1975.

————. *The Summa Theologica of St. Thomas Aquinas*. Translated by the Fathers of the English Dominican Province. 5 vols. Westminster, MD: Christian Classics, 1981.

Aranoff, Susan, and Rivka Haut. *The Wed-Locked Agunot: Orthodox Jewish Women Chained to Dead Marriages*. Jefferson, NC: McFarland, 2015.

Athenagoras. *A Plea for the Christians*. Translated by B. P. Pratten. In *Ante-Nicene Fathers*. Vol. 2, *Fathers of the Second Century: Hermas, Tatian, Athenagoras, Theophilus, and Clement of Alexandria*, edited by Alexander Roberts and James Donaldson, revised by A. Cleveland Coxe, 129–48. Peabody, MA: Hendrickson, 1994.

Atkinson, David. *To Have and to Hold: The Marriage Covenant and the Discipline of Divorce*. Grand Rapids, MI: Eerdmans, 1979.

Augustin, George, ed. *Zum Gelingen von Ehe und Familie: Ermutigung aus Amoris laetitia: Für Walter Kardinal Kasper*. Freiburg: Herder, 2018.

Augustine. *On Faith and Works*. Translated by Gregory J. Lombardo, C.S.C. New York: Paulist Press, 1988.

————. *On Marriage and Concupiscence*. Translated by Peter Holmes. In *Nicene and Post-Nicene Fathers*. 1st series, edited by Philip Schaff. Vol. 5, *Augustine: Anti-Pelagian Writings*, 263–308. Peabody, MA: Hendrickson, 1995.

————. *St. Augustine on Marriage and Sexuality*. Edited by Elizabeth A. Clark. Washington, D.C.: Catholic University of America Press, 1996.

Aymans, Winfried, ed. *Eleven Cardinals Speak on Marriage and the Family: Essays from a Pastoral Viewpoint*. Translated by Michael J. Miller et al. San Francisco: Ignatius Press, 2015.

Barth, Karl. *Church Dogmatics*. Vol. 3, *The Doctrine of Creation*, pt. 4, translated by A. T. Mackay, T. H. L. Parker, H. Knight, H. A. Kennedy, and J. Marks, edited by G. W. Bromiley and T. F. Torrance. Edinburgh: T&T Clark, 1961.

Basil the Great. Letter 188, "To Amphilochius, concerning the Canons". In *Nicene and Post-Nicene Fathers*. 2nd series, edited by Philip Schaff and Henry Wace. Vol. 8, *Basil: Letters and Select*

Works, translated by Blomfield Jackson, 223–28. Peabody, MA: Hendrickson, 1995.

————. *On Christian Ethics*. Translated by Jacob N. Van Sickle. Yonkers, NY: St. Vladimir's Seminary Press, 2014.

Bassett, William W., ed. *The Bond of Marriage: An Ecumenical and Interdisciplinary Study*. Notre Dame: University of Notre Dame Press, 1968.

Baujard, Monique. "Existing Practices and New Initiatives for the Divorced and Remarried in France". In *A Point of No Return? Amoris Laetitia on Marriage, Divorce, and Remarriage*, edited by Thomas Knieps-Port le Roi, 242–46. Berlin: LIT Verlag, 2017.

Beal, John P. "Intolerable Marriage Situations Revisited: Continuing the Legacy of James H. Provost". *Jurist* 63 (2003): 253–311.

Beckmann, Rainer. *Das Evangelium der ehelichen Treue: Eine Antwort auf Kardinal Kasper*. Kisslegg: Fe-medienverlag, 2015.

Bellarmine, Robert. *Disputationes*. Naples: Giuliano, 1858.

Benedict XVI, Pope. *Post-Synodal Apostolic Exhortation of Benedict XVI, Sacrament of Charity* (Sacramentum Caritatis). Vatican translation. Boston: Pauline Books & Media, 2007.

Bernhard-Bitaud, Corinne, and Thomas Knieps-Port le Roi. "'Nourishment for the Journey, Not a Prize for the Perfect': Reflecting with *Amoris Laetitia* on Eucharistic Sharing in Interchurch Marriages". In *A Point of No Return? Amoris Laetitia on Marriage, Divorce, and Remarriage*, edited by Thomas Knieps-Port le Roi, 215–32. Berlin: LIT Verlag, 2017.

Berrouard, Marie-François, O.P. "Saint Augustin et l'indissolubilité du mariage. Évolution de sa pensée". *Recherches Augustiniennes et patristique* 5 (1968): 139–55.

Berten, Ignace, O.P. *Les divorcés remariés peuvent-ils communier? Enjeux ecclésiaux des débats autour du Synode sur la famille et d'Amoris laetitia*. Namur, Belgium: Lessius, 2017.

Betz, Hans Dieter. *The Sermon on the Mount*. Minneapolis, MN: Fortress Press, 1995.

Biliniewicz, Mariusz. *Amoris Laetitia and the Spirit of Vatican II: The Source of Controversy*. London: Routledge, 2018.

Black, Peter, and James F. Keenan, S.J. "The Evolving Self-Understanding of the Moral Theologian: 1900–2000". *Studia Moralia* 39 (2001): 291–327.

Blondel, Maurice. *Action (1893): Essay on a Critique of Life and a Science of Practice*. Translated by Oliva Blanchette. Notre Dame: University of Notre Dame Press, 1984.

Bockmuehl, Markus. *Jewish Law in Gentile Churches: Halakhah and the Beginning of Christian Public Ethics*. Grand Rapids, MI: Baker Academic, 2000.

Bof, Riccardo, and Conrad Leyser. "Divorce and Remarriage between Late Antiquity and the Early Middle Ages: Canon Law and Conflict Resolution". In *Making Early Medieval Societies: Conflict and Belonging in the Latin West, 300–1200*, edited by Kate Cooper and Conrad Leyser, 155–80. Cambridge: Cambridge University Press, 2016.

Bonhoeffer, Dietrich. "A Wedding Sermon from a Prison Cell". In *Letters and Papers from Prison*, enlarged ed., 41–47. London: SCM Press, 1971.

Bonino, Serge-Thomas, O.P. "Saint Thomas in the Apostolic Exhortation *Amoris Laetitia*". *Thomist* 80 (2016): 499–519.

Bonsirven, Joseph. *Le divorce dans le Nouveau Testament*. Paris: Desclée, 1948.

Bordeyne, Philippe. "The Newness That Priests and People Face When They Receive *Amoris Laetitia*: An Overview in France". In *Amoris Laetitia: A New Momentum for Moral Formation and Pastoral Practice*, edited by Grant Gallicho and James F. Keenan, S.J., 70–76. New York: Paulist Press, 2018.

Bousquet, François. "Principe dogmatique et théologie contemporaine?" *Recherches de science religieuse* 95 (2007): 545–58.

Bressan, Luigi. *Il Canone Tridentino sul Divorzio per Adulterio e L'interpretazione degli Autori*. Rome: Università Gregoriana Editrice, 1973.

Bricout, Hélène. "Réponse d'Hélène Bricout". In *"La vocation et la mission de la famille dans l'Église et dans le monde contemporain": 26 théologiens répondent*, 245–51. Paris: Bayard, 2015.

Brock, Stephen L. "*Veritatis Splendor* §78, St. Thomas, and (Not Merely) Physical Objects of Moral Acts". *Nova et Vetera* 6 (2008): 1–62.

Broglie, Guy de, S.J. "La conception thomiste des deux finalités du marriage". *Doctor Communis* 30 (1974): 3–41.

Bromiley, Geoffrey W. *God and Marriage*. Grand Rapids, MI: Eerdmans, 1980.

Browning, Don S. *Equality and the Family: A Fundamental, Practical Theology of Children, Mothers, and Fathers in Modern Societies.* Grand Rapids, MI: Eerdmans, 2007.

——. *Marriage and Modernization: How Globalization Threatens Marriage and What to Do about It.* Grand Rapids, MI: Eerdmans, 2003.

——, Bonnie Miller-McLemore, Pamela Couture, Bernie Lyon, and Robert Franklin. *From Culture Wars to Common Ground: Religion and the American Family Debate.* Louisville, KY: Westminster John Knox, 2000.

Brugger, E. Christian. *The Indissolubility of Marriage and the Council of Trent.* Washington, D.C.: Catholic University of America Press, 2017.

Burke, Cormac. *Covenanted Happiness: Love and Commitment in Marriage.* San Francisco: Ignatius Press, 1990.

Burke, Raymond Cardinal. "'Amoris Laetitia' and the Constant Teaching and Practice of the Church". *National Catholic Register*, April 12, 2016. http://www.ncregister.com/daily-news/amoris -laetitia-and-the-constant-teaching-and-practice-of-the-church /#ixzz46HheGSQ6/.

Buttiglione, Rocco. "The Joy of Love and the Consternation of Theologians: Some Comments on the Apostolic Exhortation *Amoris Laetitia*". *L'Osservatore Romano*, July 19, 2016. www .osservatoreromano.va/en/news/joy-love-and-consternation -theologians.

Cabodevilla, J.M. *Hombre y Mujer: Estudio sobre el Matrimonio y el Amor Humano.* Madrid: BAC, 1962.

Caffarra, Carlos Cardinal. "Sacramental Ontology and the Indissolubility of Marriage". In *Remaining in the Truth of Christ: Marriage and Communion in the Catholic Church*, edited by Robert Dodaro, O.S.A., 166–80. San Francisco: Ignatius Press, 2014.

Cahall, Perry J. *The Mystery of Marriage: A Theology of the Body and the Sacrament.* Chicago: Hillenbrand Books, 2016.

Cameli, Louis J. "How Is *Amoris Laetitia* Being Received?" In *Amoris Laetitia: A New Momentum for Moral Formation and Pastoral Practice*, edited by Grant Gallicho and James F. Keenan, S.J., 22–26. New York: Paulist Press, 2018.

Catechism of the Catholic Church, 2nd ed. Vatican City: Libreria Editrice Vaticana, 1997.

Cereti, Giovanni. *Divorzio, nuove nozze e penitenza nella chiesa primitive*. 3rd ed. Rome: Aracne Editrice, 2013.

―――. *Matrimonio e indissolubilitá*. 2nd ed. Bologna: Edizioni Dehoniane, 2014.

Chaput, Charles, O.F.M. Cap. "Pastoral Guidelines for Implementing *Amoris Laetitia*". *Nova et Vetera* 15 (2017): 1–7.

Cimorelli, Christopher, and Daniel Minch. "Views of Doctrine: Historical Consciousness, Asymptotic Notional Clarity, and the Challenge of Hermeneutics as Theology". *Louvain Studies* 37 (2013): 327–63.

Clément, Oliver. Foreword to *The Sacrament of Love: The Nuptial Mystery in the Light of the Orthodox Tradition*, by Paul Evdokimov, translated by Anthony P. Gythiel and Victoria Steadman, 7–13. Crestwood, NY: St. Vladimir's Seminary Press, 1985.

Clement of Alexandria. *The Stromata, or Miscellanies*. In *Ante-Nicene Fathers*. Vol. 2, *Fathers of the Second Century: Hermas, Tatian, Athenagoras, Theophilus, and Clement of Alexandria*, edited by Alexander Roberts and James Donaldson, revised by A. Cleveland Coxe, 299–379. Peabody, MA: Hendrickson, 1994.

Cloutier, David. *The Vice of Luxury: Economic Excess in a Consumer Age*. Washington, D.C.: Georgetown University Press, 2015.

Coccopalmerio, Francesco Cardinal. *A Commentary on Chapter Eight of* Amoris Laetitia. Translated by Sean O'Neill. Mahwah, NJ: Paulist Press, 2017.

Code of Canon Law: Latin-English Edition, New English Tradition *(Codex Iuris Canonici [CIC])*. Washington, D.C.: Canon Law Society of America, 1998.

Cole, Basil, O.P. "Thomism, Moral Claim and *Amoris Laetitia*". *Anthropotes* 33 (2017): 313–26.

Coleman, Gerald D. *Divorce and Remarriage in the Catholic Church*. New York: Paulist Press, 1988.

Collin, Thibaud. *Le mariage chrétien a-t-il encore un avenir? Pour en finir avec les malentendus*. Paris: Artège, 2018.

Collins, Raymond F. *Divorce in the New Testament*. Collegeville, MN: Liturgical Press, 1992.

Congar, Yves, O.P. *True and False Reform in the Church*. Translated by Paul Philibert, O.P. Collegeville, MN: Liturgical Press, 2011.

Congregation for the Doctrine of the Faith. "Letter to the Bishops of the Catholic Church concerning the Reception of Holy Communion by Divorced and Remarried Members of the Faithful (September 14, 1994)". *Acta Apostolicae Sedis* 86 (1994): 974–79.

Corbett, John, O.P.; Dominic Legge, O.P.; Andrew Hofer, O.P.; Kurt Martens; Paul J. Keller, O.P.; Thomas Petri, O.P.; Dominic Langevin, O.P.; and Thomas Joseph White, O.P. "Recent Proposals for the Pastoral Care of the Divorced and Remarried: A Theological Assessment". *Nova et Vetera* 12, no. 3 (2014): 601–30.

Cordes, Paul Josef Cardinal. "Without Rupture or Discontinuity". In *Eleven Cardinals Speak on Marriage and the Family: Essays from a Pastoral Viewpoint*, edited by Winfried Aymans, translated by Michael J. Miller et al., 17–38. San Francisco: Ignatius Press, 2015.

Coyle, Alcuin, and Dismas Bonner. *The Church under Tension: Practical Life and Law in the Changing Church*. New York: Catholic Book Publishing, 1972.

Crouzel, Henri. "A propos du Concile d'Arles: Faut-il mettre *non* devant *prohibentur nubere* dans le canon 10 (ou 11) du Concile d'Arles de 314 sur le remariage après divorce?" *Bulletin de Littérature ecclésiastique* 75 (1974): 25–40.

———. "Divorce and Remarriage in the Early Church: Some Reflections on Historical Methodology". Translated by Michelle K. Borras. *Communio* 41 (2014): 472–503.

———. "Divorce et remariage dans l'Église primitive". *Nouvelle revue théologique* 98 (1976): 891–917.

———. *L'Église primitive face au divorce. Du premier au cinquième siècle*. Paris: Beauchesne, 1971.

———. "Le marriage des chrétiens aux premiers siècles de l'Église". *Esprit et Vie* 83, no. 6 (1973): 3–13.

———. "Les Pères de l'Église ont-ils permis le remariage après separation?" *Bulletin de Littérature ecclésiastique* 70 (1969): 3–43.

———. "Le remariage après separation pour adultère selon les Pères latins". *Bulletin de Littérature ecclésiastique* 75 (1974): 189–204.

———. "Remarriage after Divorce in the Primitive Church? A Propos of a Recent Book". *Irish Theological Quarterly* 28 (1971): 21–41.

———. "Séparation et remariage selon les Pères anciens". *Gregorianum* 47 (1966): 472–94.

————. "Le texte patristique de Matthieu V, 32 et XIX, 9". *New Testament Studies* 19 (1972–1973): 98–119.

Curran, Charles E. *The Development of Moral Theology: Five Strands.* Washington, D.C.: Georgetown University Press, 2013.

————. "Divorce: Catholic Theory and Practice in the United States". *The American Ecclesiastical Review* 168 (1974): 3–34, 75–95.

————. *Faithful Dissent.* Kansas City, MO: Sheed and Ward, 1986.

————. *Ongoing Revision: Studies in Moral Theology.* Notre Dame: Fides, 1975.

Dalzell, Thomas G., S.M. "Eucharist, Communion and Orthopraxis in the Theology of Joseph Ratzinger". *Irish Theological Quarterly* 78 (2013): 103–22.

D'Ambrosio, Rocco. *Will Pope Francis Pull It Off? The Challenge of Church Reform.* Translated by Barry Hudock. Collegeville, MN: Liturgical Press, 2017.

D'Angelo, Mary Rose. "Remarriage and the Divorce Sayings Attributed to Jesus". In *Divorce and Remarriage: Religious and Psychological Perspectives*, edited by William P. Roberts, 78–106. Kansas City, MO: Sheed and Ward, 1990.

Daniel, William L. "An Analysis of Pope Francis' 2015 Reform of the General Legislation Governing Causes of Nullity of Marriage". In *Justice and Mercy Have Met: Pope Francis and the Reform of the Marriage Nullity Process*, edited by Kurt Martens, 27–64. Washington, D.C.: Catholic University of America Press, 2017.

D'Antonio, William V., James D. Davidson, Dean R. Hoge, and Mary L. Gautier. "American Catholics and Church Authority". In *The Crisis of Authority in Catholic Modernity*, edited by Michael J. Lacey and Francis Oakley, 273–92. Oxford: Oxford University Press, 2011.

Davies, W.D., and Dale C. Allison, Jr. *A Critical and Exegetical Commentary on the Gospel according to Saint Matthew.* Vol. 1, *Introduction and Commentary on Matthew I–VII.* London: T&T Clark, 1988.

————. *A Critical and Exegetical Commentary on the Gospel According to Saint Matthew.* Vol. 2, *Commentary on Matthew VIII–XVIII.* London: T&T Clark International, 2004.

D'Avray, D.L. *Dissolving Royal Marriages: A Documentary History, 860–1600.* Cambridge: Cambridge University Press, 2014.

————. *Papacy, Monarchy and Marriage, 860–1600*. Cambridge: Cambridge University Press, 2015.

Delicata, Nadia. "Sin, Repentance and Conversion in *Amoris Laetitia*". In *A Point of No Return? Amoris Laetitia on Marriage, Divorce, and Remarriage*, edited by Thomas Knieps-Port le Roi, 74–86. Berlin: LIT Verlag, 2017.

Denzinger, Heinrich. *Compendium of Creeds, Definitions, and Declarations on Matters of Faith and Morals*. 43rd ed. Revised and edited by Peter Hünermann with Helmut Hoping. English edition edited and translated by Robert Fastiggi and Anne Englund Nash. San Francisco: Ignatius Press, 2012.

Dodaro, Robert, O.S.A., ed. *Remaining in the Truth of Christ: Marriage and Communion in the Catholic Church*. San Francisco: Ignatius Press, 2014.

Doherty, Dennis. *Divorce and Remarriage*. St. Meinrad, IN: Abbey Press, 1974.

Donahue, John. "Divorce—New Testament Perspectives". In *Marriage Studies: Reflection on Canon Law and Theology*, vol. 2, edited by Thomas Doyle, 1–19. Washington, D.C.: Canon Law Society of America, 1982.

Douthat, Ross. *To Change the Church: Pope Francis and the Future of Catholicism*. New York: Simon & Schuster, 2018.

Duka, Dominik Cardinal, O.P. "Reflections on the Family". In *Eleven Cardinals Speak on Marriage and the Family: Essays from a Pastoral Viewpoint*, edited by Winfried Aymans, translated by Michael J. Miller et al., 39–43. San Francisco: Ignatius Press, 2015.

Dupont, Jacques. *Mariage et divorce dans l'évangile*. Bruges: Desclée de Brouwer, 1959.

Dvoráček, Jiří. "Il divorzio del vincolo matrimoniale nelle Chiese ortodosse e le sue conseguenze giuridiche per la Chiesa cattolica". In *Rodina, konflikt a možnosti mediace*, edited by Slávka Michančová and Lenka Pavlová, 25–67. Křtiny: Evropský smírčí institut, 2011.

Eberstadt, Mary. *How the West Really Lost God*. West Conshohocken, PA: Templeton Press, 2013.

Echeverria, Eduardo J. "The Essentialist versus Historicist Debate about the Truth Status of Dogmatic Formulations: A Critique of the Cimorelli-Minch Proposal". *Louvain Studies* 38 (2014): 356–69.

Eijk, Willem Jacobus Cardinal. "Can Divorced and Civilly Remarried Persons Receive Communion?" In *Eleven Cardinals Speak on Marriage and the Family: Essays from a Pastoral Viewpoint*, edited by Winfried Aymans, translated by Michael J. Miller et al., 45–54. San Francisco: Ignatius Press, 2015.

Erzbischöfliches Seelsorgeamt Freiburg. *Handreichung für die Seelsorge zur Begleitung von Menschen in Trennung, Scheidung und nach ziviler Wiederverheiratung*. Freiburg: Erzdiözese Freiburg, 2013, https://www.kfd-bundesverband.de/fileadmin/Bilder/Nachrichten/Widerverheiratet_broschuere_handreichung_09_2013.pdf.

Esolen, Anthony. *Reclaiming Catholic Social Teaching: A Defense of the Church's True Teachings on Marriage, Family, and the State*. Manchester, NH: Sophia Institute Press, 2014.

Evdokimov, Paul. "La grace du sacrement de mariage selon la tradition orthodoxe". *Parole et Pain* 35–36 (1969): 382–94.

———. *The Sacrament of Love: The Nuptial Mystery in the Light of the Orthodox Tradition*. Translated by Anthony P. Gythiel and Victoria Steadman. Crestwood, NY: St. Vladimir's Seminary Press, 1985.

Faber, E.-M., and Martin M. Lintner. "Theologische Entwicklungen in *Amoris laetitia* hinsichtlich der Frage der geschiedenen Wiederverheirateten". In *Amoris laetitia—Wendepunkt für die Moraltheologie?*, edited by Stephan Goertz and Caroline Witting, 279–320. Freiburg: Herder, 2016.

Farley, Margaret A. "Divorce and Remarriage". *Proceedings of the Catholic Theological Society of America* 30 (1975): 111–19.

———. "Divorce and Remarriage: A Moral Perspective". In *Divorce and Remarriage: Religious and Psychological Perspectives*, edited by William P. Roberts, 107–27. Kansas City, MO: Sheed and Ward, 1990.

———. "Divorce, Remarriage, and Pastoral Practice". In *Moral Theology: Challenges for the Future: Essays in Honor of Richard A. McCormick, S.J.*, edited by Charles E. Curran, 213–39. New York: Paulist Press, 1990.

———. *Just Love: A Framework for Christian Sexual Ethics*. New York: Continuum, 2008.

———. "Marriage, Divorce, and Personal Commitments". In *Celebrating Christian Marriage*, edited by Adrian Thatcher, 355–72. Edinburgh: T&T Clark, 2001.

———. "The Meaning of Commitment". In *Perspectives on Marriage: A Reader*, edited by Kieran Scott and Michael Warren, 344–56. Oxford: Oxford University Press, 2007.

———. *Personal Commitments: Beginning, Keeping, Changing.* Rev. ed. New York: Orbis, 2013.

Fernandez, Victor Manuel. *Chapitre VIII de* Amoris Laetitia: *Le bilan après la tourmente.* Translated by Hortense de Parscau. Paris: Parole et Silence, 2018.

Fitzmyer, Joseph A., S.J. *First Corinthians: A New Translation with Introduction and Commentary.* New Haven, CT: Yale University Press, 2008.

———. *To Advance the Gospel: New Testament Studies.* New York: Paulist Press, 1981.

Flannery, Kevin L., S.J., and Thomas V. Berg. "*Amoris Laetitia*, Pastoral Discernment, and Thomas Aquinas". *Nova et Vetera* 16 (2018): 81–111.

Flouri, E., M. K. Narayanan, and E. Midouhas. "The Cross-Lagged Relationship between Father Absence and Child Problem Behaviour in the Early Years". *Child Care Health Development* 41 (2015): 1090–97.

Ford, David C., Mary S. Ford, and Alfred Kentigern Siewers, eds. *Glory and Honor: Orthodox Christian Resources on Marriage.* Yonkers, NY: St. Vladimir's Seminary Press, 2016.

Foskett, Mary. *Moral Teachings of Jesus.* Nashville, TN: Abingdon Press, 2004.

Francis, Pope. *Apostolic Exhortation of the Holy Father Pope Francis, The Joy of the Gospel (Evangelii Gaudium).* Vatican translation. Boston: Pauline Books & Media, 2013.

———. *The Joy of Love: On Love in the Family* (Amoris Laetitia). Vatican translation. Frederick, MD: The Word Among Us Press, 2016.

Fransen, Piet F., S.J. "Divorce on the Ground of Adultery—The Council of Trent (1563)". In *The Future of Marriage as an Institution*, edited by Franz Böckle, 89–100. New York: Herder and Herder, 1970.

————. *Hermeneutics of the Councils and Other Studies*. Edited by H. E. Mertens and F. de Graeve. Leuven: Leuven University Press, 1985.

Gaillardetz, Richard R. "Does Synodality Help the Church Live Out Her Mission Today?" In *Amoris Laetitia: A New Momentum for Moral Formation and Pastoral Practice*, edited by Grant Gallicho and James F. Keenan, S.J., 130–35. New York: Paulist Press, 2018.

Galea, Christine. "Reflections on Commitment and the Indissolubility of Christian Marriage". In *A Point of No Return? Amoris Laetitia on Marriage, Divorce, and Remarriage*, edited by Thomas Knieps-Port le Roi, 173–80. Berlin: LIT Verlag, 2017.

Galeotti, F. "Amore e amicizia coniugali secondo S. Tommaso". *Doctor Communis* 25 (1972): 39–59.

Gallagher, Clarence. *Church Law and Church Order in Rome and Byzantium: A Comparative Study*. Cornwall: Ashgate, 2002.

Gallicho, Grant, and James F. Keenan, S.J., eds. *Amoris Laetitia: A New Momentum for Moral Formation and Pastoral Practice*. New York: Paulist Press, 2018.

Garijo-Guembe, Miguel M. "Unauflöslichkeit der Ehe und die gescheiterten Ehen in der Patristik". In *Geschieden Wiederverheiratet Abgewiesen? Antworten der Theologie*, edited by T. Schneider, 68–83. Freiburg: Herder, 1995.

Garrigues, Jean-Miguel, O.P. "Répondre aux *dubia* des quatre cardinaux pour developer et préciser la doctrine morale de *Veritatis Splendor*". In *Une morale souple mais non sans boussole: Répondre aux doutes des quatre Cardinaux à propos d'*Amoris laetitia, by Alain Thomasset, S.J., and Jean-Miguel Garrigues, O.P., 111–68. Paris: Cerf, 2017.

Goertz, Stephan, and Caroline. Witting, eds. *Amoris laetitia—Wendepunkt für die Moraltheologie?* Freiburg: Herder, 2016.

Granados, José. "From Flesh to Flesh: On the Sacramental Meaning of Tradition". *Communio* 44 (2017): 643–66.

————. "La relation entre l'eucharistie et le mariage, et ses implications pour l'interprétation d'*Amoris Laetitia*". *Nova et Vetera* 92 (2017): 165–81.

————. "The Sacramental Character of Faith: Consequences for the Debate on the Relation between Faith and Marriage". *Communio* 41 (2014): 245–68.

————. *Una Sola Carne en un Solo Espíritu: Teología del Matrimonio*. Madrid: Ediciones Palabra, 2014.

————. Stephan Kampowski, and Juan José Pérez-Soba. *Accompanying, Discerning, Integrating: A Handbook for the Pastoral Care of the Family According to* Amoris Laetitia. Translated by Michael J. Miller. Steubenville, OH: Emmaus Road, 2017.

Gregory, Donald J. *The Pauline Privilege: An Historical Synopsis and Commentary*. Washington, D.C.: Catholic University of America Press, 1931.

Gregory of Nazianzus. Letter 144. Edited and translated by Charles Gordon Browne and James Edward Swallow. In *Nicene and Post-Nicene Fathers*. 2nd series, edited by Philip Schaff and Henry Wace. Vol. 7, *Cyril of Jerusalem, Gregory Nazianzen*, 223–28. Peabody, MA: Hendrickson, 1994.

Gregory, Wilton D. "*Amoris Laetitia*: A New Momentum for Moral Formation and Pastoral Practice". In *Amoris Laetitia: A New Momentum for Moral Formation and Pastoral Practice*, edited by Grant Gallicho and James F. Keenan, S.J., 152–55. New York: Paulist Press, 2018.

Guerra López, Rodrigo. "The Relevance of Some Reflections by Karol Wojtyła for Understanding *Amoris Laetitia*: Creative Fidelity". *L'Osservatore Romano*, July 22, 2016. www.osservatore romano.va/en/news/relevance-some-reflections-karol-wojtyla -understan.

Gundry, Robert H. *Matthew: A Commentary on His Handbook for a Mixed Church under Persecution*. 2nd ed. Grand Rapids, MI: Eerdmans, 1994.

Harant, Franz. "In a Second Marriage before God and before Others: New Paths of the Church and in the Church in Austria". In *A Point of No Return?* Amoris Laetitia *on Marriage, Divorce, and Remarriage*, edited by Thomas Knieps-Port le Roi, 254–63. Berlin: LIT Verlag, 2017.

————. "In zweiter Ehe neu beginnen: Segensfeier bei Wiederheirat". *Diakonia* 33 (2002): 31–37.

Häring, Bernard. *No Way Out? Pastoral Care of the Divorced and Remarried*. Middlegreen, England: St. Paul Publications, 1990.

Häring, Hermann. *Keine Christen zweiter Klasse!: Wiederverheiratete Geschiedene—Ein theologischer Zwischenruf*. Freiburg: Herder, 2014.

Harrington, Joel F. *Reordering Marriage and Society in Reformation Germany*. Cambridge: Cambridge University Press, 1995.

Hastetter, Michaela C. "Between Failure and Jubilation: Contrary Tendencies in the Pastoral Care of Marriage". In *And God Saw That It Was Very Good: Reinvigorating the Sacrament of Marriage and the Christian Family in Light of the 2014 and 2015 Synods*. Heiligenkreuz bei Wien: Be&Be-Verlag, forthcoming.

————. "Ehe- und Familienpastoral von Benedikt bis Franziskus: Krise oder Kontinuität?" *Ambo* 1 (2016): 84–115.

————. "*Via Caritatis*—Pastoral Care of the Divorced and Remarried: An Ecumenical Comparison in the Context of *Amoris Laetitia*". Translated by Graham Harrison. In *A Point of No Return?* Amoris Laetitia *on Marriage, Divorce, and Remarriage*, edited by Thomas Knieps-Port le Roi, 195–214. Berlin: LIT Verlag, 2017.

Healy, Nicholas J., Jr. "Christian Personalism and the Debate Over the Nature and Ends of Marriage". *Communio* 39 (2012): 186–200.

————. "Henri de Lubac on the Development of Doctrine". *Communio* 44 (2017): 667–89.

————. "The Merciful Gift of Indissolubility and the Question of Pastoral Care for Civilly Divorced and Remarried Catholics". *Communio* 41 (2014): 306–30.

Hebda, Bernard A. "Reflections on the Role of the Diocesan Bishop Envisioned by *Mitis Iudex Dominus Iesus*". In *Justice and Mercy Have Met: Pope Francis and the Reform of the Marriage Nullity Process*, edited by Kurt Martens, 65–85. Washington, D.C.: Catholic University of America Press, 2017.

Hegy, Pierre, and Joseph Martos, eds. *Catholic Divorce: The Deception of Annulments*. New York: Continuum, 2000.

Heth, William A. "Divorce, but No Remarriage". In *Divorce and Remarriage: Four Christian Views*, edited by H. Wayne House, 73–129. Downers Grove, IL: IVP Academic, 1990.

————. "A Response to Gordon J. Wenham". In *Remarriage and Divorce in Today's Church: Three Views*, edited by Mark L. Strauss, 43–47. Grand Rapids, MI: Zondervan, 2006.

————. and Gordon J. Wenham. *Jesus and Divorce*. 3rd ed. Carlisle: Paternoster, 2002.

Hibbs, Thomas S. *Dialectic and Narrative in Aquinas: An Interpretation of the Summa Contra Gentiles*. Notre Dame: University of Notre Dame Press, 1995.

Himes, Kenneth R., O.F.M., and James A. Coriden. "The Indissolubility of Marriage: Reasons to Reconsider". *Theological Studies* 65 (2004): 453–99.

———, "Notes on Moral Theology: Pastoral Care of the Divorced and Remarried". *Theological Studies* 57 (1996): 97–123.

Hines, Mary E. *The Transformation of Dogma: An Introduction to Karl Rahner on Doctrine.* New York: Paulist Press, 1989.

Hogan, Richard M., and John M. LeVoir. *Covenant of Love: Pope John Paul II on Sexuality, Marriage, and Family in the Modern World: With a Commentary on* Familiaris Consortio. 2nd ed. San Francisco: Ignatius Press, 1992.

Höllinger, Stephanie. "Do We Expect Too Much? A Reflection on Expectations and Marriage in *Amoris Laetitia*". In *A Point of No Return?* Amoris Laetitia *on Marriage, Divorce, and Remarriage*, edited by Thomas Knieps-Port le Roi, 104–19. Berlin: LIT Verlag, 2017.

Hooker, Morna D. *The Gospel According to Saint Mark.* London: A. & C. Black, 1991.

House, H. Wayne, ed. *Divorce and Remarriage: Four Christian Views.* Downers Grove, IL: IVP Academic, 1990.

Hünermann, Peter. "The Sacrament of Marriage: A Dogmatic Theologian Reads *Amoris Laetitia*". In *A Point of No Return?* Amoris Laetitia *on Marriage, Divorce, and Remarriage*, edited by Thomas Knieps-Port le Roi, 87–104. Berlin: LIT Verlag, 2017.

Hunter, David G. "Augustine's Doubts on Divorce: Reconsiderations on Remarriage". *Augustinian Studies* 48 (2017): 161–82.

Hütter, Reinhard. *Dust Bound for Heaven: Explorations in the Theology of Thomas Aquinas.* Grand Rapids, MI: Eerdmans, 2012.

Imperatori-Lee, Natalia. "How Is *Amoris Laetitia* Being Received? Colonialism, Conscience, and Accompaniment". In *Amoris Laetitia: A New Momentum for Moral Formation and Pastoral Practice*, edited by Grant Gallicho and James F. Keenan, S.J., 3–11. New York: Paulist Press, 2018.

Instone-Brewer, David. *Divorce and Remarriage in the Bible: The Social and Literary Context.* Grand Rapids, MI: Eerdmans, 2002.

———. *Divorce and Remarriage in the 1st and 21st Century.* Cambridge: Grove, 2001.

International Theological Commission. "Propositions on the Doctrine of Christian Marriage". *Origins* 8 (1978): 235–39.

Janssens, Louis. "A Moral Understanding of Some Arguments of Saint Thomas". *Ephemerides Theologicae Lovanienses* 63 (1987): 354–60.

————. "Ontic Evil and Moral Evil". *Louvain Studies* 4 (1972): 115–56.

Jerome. *Commentary on Matthew*. Translated by Thomas P. Scheck. Washington, D.C.: Catholic University of America Press, 2008.

John Chrysostom. Homily 62. In *Nicene and Post-Nicene Fathers*. 1st series, edited by Philip Schaff. Vol. 10, *Chrysostom: Homilies on the Gospel of Saint Matthew*, translated by George Prevost, revised by M. B. Riddle, 381–86. Peabody, MA: Hendrickson, 1995.

John Paul II, Pope. "Allocution to the Roman Rota", January 21, 2000. *Acta Apostolicae Sedis* 92 (2000): 350–55.

————. *Familiaris Consortio*. Vatican translation. Boston: St. Paul Books & Media, 1981.

————. *Veritatis Splendor*. In *The Encyclicals of Pope John Paul II*, edited by J. Michael Miller, C.S.B., 583–661. Huntington, IN: Our Sunday Visitor, 2001.

Join-Lambert, Arnauld. "Accompanying, Discerning and Integrating the Fragility of Couples: Pastors and Theologians at a Crossroads". In *A Point of No Return? Amoris Laetitia on Marriage, Divorce, and Remarriage*, edited by Thomas Knieps-Port le Roi, 141–61. Berlin: LIT Verlag, 2017.

Journet, Charles. *Le mariage indissoluble*. St-Maurice: Editions St-Augustin, 1968.

Joyce, George Hayward, S.J. *Christian Marriage: An Historical and Doctrinal Study*. London: Sheed and Ward, 1933.

Justin Martyr. *First Apology of Justin Martyr*. In *Ante-Nicene Fathers*. Vol. 1, *The Apostolic Fathers, Justin Martyr, Irenaeus*, edited and translated by Alexander Roberts and James Donaldson, revised by A. Cleveland Coxe, 163–87. Peabody, MA: Hendrickson, 1994.

Kampowski, Stephan. *Embracing Our Finitude: Exercises in a Christian Anthropology between Dependence and Gratitude*. Eugene, OR: Cascade, 2018.

Kasper, Walter. *Die Botschaft von Amoris laetitia: Ein freundlicher Disput*. Freiburg: Herder, 2018.

————. "Geschichtlichkeit der Dogmen?" In *Gesammelte Schriften*. Vol. 7, *Evangelium und Dogma: Grundlegung der Dogmatik*, 623–44. Freiburg: Herder, 2015.

————. *The Gospel of the Family*. Translated by William Madges. New York: Paulist Press, 2014.

————. "Merciful God, Merciful Church: An Interview with Cardinal Walter Kasper". By Matthew Boudway and Grant Gallicho. *Commonweal*. Published electronically May 7, 2014. https://www.commonwealmagazine.org/kasper-interview -popefrancis-vatican.

————. *Pope Francis' Revolution of Tenderness and Love: Theological and Pastoral Perspectives*. Translated by William Madges. New York: Paulist Press, 2015.

————. *Theology of Christian Marriage*. Translated by David Smith. New York: Seabury Press, 1980.

Kaveny, Cathleen. "How Is *Amoris Laetitia* Being Received? Mercy and *Amoris Laetitia*: Insights from Secular Law". In *Amoris Laetitia: A New Momentum for Moral Formation and Pastoral Practice*, edited by Grant Gallicho and James F. Keenan, S.J., 27–38. New York: Paulist Press, 2018.

————. "Mercy, Justice, and Law: Can Legal Concepts Help Foster New Life?" In *Marriage and Family: Relics of the Past or Promise of the Future?*, edited by George Augustin, 75–106. Mahwah, NJ: Paulist Press, 2015.

Keenan, James F., S.J. "Receiving *Amoris Laetitia*". *Theological Studies* 78 (2017): 193–212.

Keener, Craig S. *... And Marries Another*. Peabody, MA: Hendrickson, 1991.

Kelleher, Steven Joseph. *Divorce and Remarriage for Catholics?* Garden City, NY: Doubleday, 1973.

Keller, Paul J., O.P. "Is Spiritual Communion for Everyone?" *Nova et Vetera* 12 (2014): 631–55.

Keller, Timothy, with Kathy Keller. *The Meaning of Marriage: Facing the Complexities of Commitment with the Wisdom of God*. New York: Riverhead Books, 2011.

Kelly, Kevin T. *Divorce and Second Marriage: Facing the Challenge*. 2nd ed. London: Geoffrey Chapman, 1996.

Kennedy, Robert T., and John T. Finnegan. "Select Bibliography on Divorce and Remarriage in the Catholic Church Today". In *Ministering to the Divorced Catholic*, edited by James J. Young, 260–73. New York: Paulist, 1979.

Knieps-Port le Roi, Thomas, ed. *A Point of No Return?* Amoris Laetitia *on Marriage, Divorce, and Remarriage*. Berlin: LIT Verlag, 2017.

———. and Roger Burggraeve. "New Wine in New Wineskins: Amoris Laetitia and the Church's Teaching on Marriage and Family". *Louvain Studies* 39 (2016): 284–302.

———. and R. Temmerman, eds. *Being One at Home: Interchurch Families as Domestic Churches*. Münster: LIT Verlag, 2015.

Koterski, Joseph W., S.J. "Aquinas on the Sacrament of Marriage". In *Rediscovering Aquinas and the Sacraments: Studies in Sacramental Theology*, edited by Matthew Levering and Michael Dauphinais, 102–13. Chicago: Hillenbrand Books, 2009.

Kowal, Janusz, S.J. "Nuove 'Norme per lo scioglimento del matrimonio *in favorem fidei.*'" *Periódica* 91 (2002): 459–506.

Kowal, Wojciech, O.M.I. "The Power of the Church to Dissolve the Matrimonial Bond in Favour of the Faith". *Studia canonica* 38 (2004): 411–38.

———. "Quelques remarques sur la discipline de la dissolution de marriages en faveur de la foi". *Studia canonica* 43 (2009): 161–81.

Kuljovsky, Branislav. "The Law of Gradualness or the Gradualness of Law? A Critical Analysis of *Amoris Laetitia*". In *A Point of No Return?* Amoris Laetitia *on Marriage, Divorce, and Remarriage*, edited by Thomas Knieps-Port le Roi, 45–64. Berlin: LIT Verlag, 2017.

Kwasniewski, Peter. "St. Thomas on the Grandeur and Limitations of Marriage". *Nova et Vetera* 10 (2012): 415–36.

Launoy, Johannes. *Regia in Matrimonium Potestas*. Paris: Edmundi Martini, 1674.

Lawler, Michael. "Blessed Are Spouses Who Love, For Their Marriages Will Be Permanent: A Theology of the Bonds of Marriage". *The Jurist* 55 (1995): 218–42.

———. "Divorce and Remarriage in the Catholic Church: Ten Theses". *New Theology Review* 12 (1999): 48–63.

Lawler, Michael G., and Todd A. Salzman. "*Amoris Laetitia* and the Development of Catholic Theological Ethics: A Reflection". In *A Point of No Return?* Amoris Laetitia *on Marriage, Divorce, and Remarriage*, edited by Thomas Knieps-Port le Roi, 30–44. Berlin: LIT Verlag, 2017.

————. "In Amoris Laetitia, Francis' Model of Conscience Empowers Catholics". *National Catholic Reporter*, September 7, 2016. https://www.ncronline.org/news/theology/amoris-laetitia-francis-model-conscience-empowers-catholics.

Le Courayer, Pierre François. *Histoire du Concile de Trente*. Amsterdam: 1750.

Lehmann, Karl. *Gegenwart des Glaubens*. Mainz: Matthias-Grünewald-Verlag, 1974.

————. "Zur Sakramentalität der Ehe". In *Ehe und Ehescheidung: Diskussion Unter Christen*, edited by Franz Henrich and Volker Eid, 57–74. Munich: Kösel, 1972.

Leithart, Peter J. *The Gospel of Matthew through New Eyes*. Vol. 1, *Jesus as Israel*. Monroe, LA: Athanasius Press, 2017.

Leo XIII, Pope. *Arcanum Divinae*. In *The Great Encyclical Letters of Pope Leo XIII*, 58–82, Rockford, IL: TAN Books, 1995.

Levering, Matthew. *Aquinas's Eschatological Ethics and the Virtue of Temperance*. Notre Dame: University of Notre Dame Press, forthcoming.

————. *Engaging the Doctrine of Marriage*. In preparation.

————. *Engaging the Doctrine of Revelation: The Mediation of the Gospel through Church and Scripture*. Grand Rapids, MI: Baker Academic, 2014.

————. *An Introduction to Vatican II as an Ongoing Theological Event*. Washington, D.C.: Catholic University of America Press, 2017.

————. *Paul in the* Summa Theologiae. Washington, D.C.: Catholic University of America Press, 2014.

————. *Sacrifice and Community: Jewish Offering and Christian Eucharist*. Oxford: Blackwell, 2005.

————. "What Is the Gospel?" In *Theological Theology: Essays in Honour of John B. Webster*, edited by R. David Nelson, Darren Sarisky, and Justin Stratis, 149–66. London: Bloomsbury, 2015.

L'Huillier, Pierre. "L'indissolubilité du mariage dans la droit et la pratique orthodoxes". *Studia Canonica* 21 (1987): 239–60.

L'Huillier, Pierre, et al. *Divorce et indissolubilité du mariage: Congrès de l'Association de théologiens pour l'étude de la morale*. Paris: Cerf, 1971.

Lintner, Martin M. "Divorce and Remarriage: A Reading of *Amoris Laetitia* from a Theological-Ethical Perspective". In *A Point of No Return?* Amoris Laetitia *on Marriage, Divorce, and Remarriage,* edited by Thomas Knieps-Port le Roi, 123–40. Berlin: LIT Verlag, 2017.

―――. "Geschieden und wiederverheiratet: Zur Problematik aus theologisch-ethischer Perspektive". In *Zwischen Jesu Wort und Norm: Kirchliches Handeln angesichts von Scheidung und Wiederheirat*, edited by M. Graulich and M. Seidnader, 193–215. Freiburg: Herder, 2014.

Long, Steven A. "*Veritatis Splendor* §78 and the Teleological Grammar of the Moral Act". *Nova et Vetera* 6 (2008): 139–56.

López, Antonio, F.S.C.B. "Marriage's Indissolubility: An Untenable Promise?" *Communio* 41 (2014): 269–305.

López, Rodrigo Guerra. "The Relevance of Some Reflections by Karol Wojtyła for Understanding *Amoris Laetitia*: Creative Fidelity". *L'Osservatore Romano*, July 22, 2016. https://www.osservatoreromano.va/en/news/relevance-some-reflections-karol-wojtyla-understan.

Luther, Martin. *Luther's Works*. Vol. 21, *Sermon on the Mount and the Magnificat*, edited by Helmut T. Lehmann. Philadelphia: Fortress, 1956.

―――. *Luther's Works*. Vol. 45, *Christian in Society II*, edited by Walther I. Brandt. Philadelphia: Fortress Press, 1962.

―――. *On the Babylonian Captivity of the Church*. In *Luther's Works*, vol. 36, Word and Sacrament II, edited by Helmut T. Lehmann and Abdel R. Wentz, 3–126. Philadelphia: Fortress Press, 1959.

Lutz, Cora, ed. *Musonius Rufus: The Roman Socrates*. New Haven, CT: Yale University Press, 1947.

Luz, Ulrich. *Matthew 1–7: A Commentary*. Translated by James E. Crouch. Edited by Helmut Koester. Minneapolis, MN: Fortress Press, 2007.

Mackin, Theodore, S.J. *Divorce and Remarriage*. New York: Paulist Press, 1984.

―――. "Ephesians 5:21–33 and Radical Indissolubility". In *Marriage Studies: Reflections in Canon Law and Theology*, vol. 3, edited by Thomas Doyle, 1–45. Washington, D.C.: Canon Law Society of America, 1985.

―――. *What Is Marriage?* New York: Paulist Press, 1982.

Maher, Anthony M. *The Forgotten Jesuit of Catholic Modernism: George Tyrrell's Prophetic Theology*. Minneapolis, MN: Fortress Press, 2017.

Mankowski, Paul, S.J. "Dominical Teaching on Divorce and Remarriage: The Biblical Data". In *Remaining in the Truth of Christ: Marriage and Communion in the Catholic Church*, edited by Robert Dodaro, O.S.A., 36–63. San Francisco: Ignatius Press, 2014.

Mansini, Guy, O.S.B. *Fundamental Theology*. Washington, D.C.: Catholic University of America Press, 2018.

———. *Promising and the Good*. Naples, FL: Sapientia Press, 2005.

Martelet, Gustave, S.J. "Christological Theses on the Sacrament of Marriage". *Origins* 8 (September 4, 1978): 200–204.

Martens, Kurt, ed. *Justice and Mercy Have Met: Pope Francis and the Reform of the Marriage Nullity Process*. Washington, D.C.: Catholic University of America Press, 2017.

Martin, James, S.J. *Building a Bridge: How the Catholic Church and the LGBT Community Can Enter into a Relationship of Respect, Compassion, and Sensitivity*. Rev. ed. New York: HarperCollins, 2018.

Marx, Reinhard Cardinal. "Reflections on the Synod Process and *Amoris Laetitia*". In *A Point of No Return? Amoris Laetitia on Marriage, Divorce, and Remarriage*, edited by Thomas Knieps-Port le Roi, 11–19. Berlin: LIT Verlag, 2017.

Maximos IV Sayegh. *L'Eglise Grecque Melkite au Councile: Discours et notes du patriarche Maximos IV et des prélats de son Église au Concile oecuménique Vatican II*. Beirut: Dar al-Kalima, 1967.

McBrien, Richard P. *The Remaking of the Church: An Agenda for Reform*. New York: Harper & Row, 1973.

McCluskey, Colleen. "An Unequal Relationship of Equals: Thomas Aquinas on Marriage". *History of Philosophy Quarterly* 24 (2007): 1–18.

McCormick, Richard. *The Critical Calling: Reflections on Moral Dilemmas Since Vatican II*. Washington, D.C.: Georgetown University Press, 1989.

———. "Indissolubility and the Right to the Eucharist: Separate Issues or One?" In *Ministering to the Divorced Catholic*, edited by James J. Young, 65–84. New York: Paulist, 1979.

———. *Notes on Moral Theology 1965 through 1980*. Washington, D.C.: University Press of America, 1981.

McDonald, Margaret Y. *Colossians and Ephesians*. Collegeville, MN: Liturgical Press, 2000.

McElroy, Robert W. "Diocesan Topical Synods: A Pathway for Pastoral Consultation in the Local Church". In *Amoris Laetitia: A*

New Momentum for Moral Formation and Pastoral Practice, edited by Grant Gallicho and James F. Keenan, S.J., 122–29. New York: Paulist Press, 2018.

McLanahan, Sara, Laura Tach, and Daniel Schneider. "The Causal Effects of Father Absence". *Annual Review of Sociology* 39 (2013): 399–427.

McRae, George. "New Testament Perspectives on Marriage and Divorce". In *Divorce and Remarriage in the Catholic Church*, edited by Lawrence G. Wrenn, 1–15. New York: Newman Press, 1973.

McWhorter, Jocelyn. *The Bridegroom Messiah and the People of God: Marriage in the Fourth Gospel*. Cambridge: Cambridge University Press, 2006.

Meisner, Joachim Cardinal. "Marriage Preparation—The Challenges of Today". In *Eleven Cardinals Speak on Marriage and the Family: Essays from a Pastoral Viewpoint*, edited by Winfried Aymans, translated by Michael J. Miller et al., 55–61. San Francisco: Ignatius Press, 2015.

Melina, Livio. "Il ruolo della coscienza nell'acceso alla comunione eucaristica dei divorziati risposati". *Anthropotes* 11 (1995): 35–47.

Merks, Karl-Wilhelm. "Grenzzäune mit Löchern? Über die Allgemeingültigkeit moralischer Normen". In *Amoris laetitia— Wendepunkt für die Moraltheologie?*, edited by S. Goertz and C. Witting, 160–200. Freiburg: Herder, 2016.

Meroni, Fabrizio. "Pastoral Care of Marriage: Affirming the Unity of Mercy and Truth". *Communio* 41 (2014): 438–61.

Meszaros, Andrew. *The Prophetic Church: History and Doctrinal Development in John Henry Newman and Yves Congar*. Oxford: Oxford University Press, 2016.

Meyendorff, John. *Marriage: An Orthodox Perspective*. 3rd rev. ed. Yonkers, NY: St. Vladimir's Seminary Press, 1975.

Milaš, Nikodim. *Das Kirchenrecht der morgenländischen Kirche*. Mostar: Verlag der Verlagsbuchhandlung von Parcher & Kisić, 1905.

Montague, George T., S.M. *First Corinthians*. Grand Rapids, MI: Baker Academic, 2011.

Morrisey, Francis G., O.M.I. "Some Themes to Be Found in the Annual Addresses of Pope John Paul II to the Roman Rota". *Studia Canonica* 38 (2004): 301–28.

Müller, Gerhard Ludwig Cardinal. "Testimony to the Power of Grace: On the Indissolubility of Marriage and the Debate concerning the Civilly Remarried and the Sacraments". In *Remaining in the Truth of Christ: Marriage and Communion in the Catholic Church*, edited by Robert Dodaro, O.S.A., 148–65. San Francisco: Ignatius Press, 2014.

———. "Warum 'Amoris laetitia' orthodox verstanden warden kann und muss". In *Zum Gelingen von Ehe und Familie: Ermutigung aus Amoris laetitia: Für Walter Kardinal Kasper*, edited by George Augustin, 263–81. Freiburg: Herder, 2018.

———. "Was dürfen wir von der Familie erwarten? Eine Kultur der Hoffnung für die Familie ausgehend vom Nachsynodalen Apostolischen Schreiben Amoris laetitia?" In *Zum Gelingen von Ehe und Familie: Ermutigung aus Amoris laetitia: Für Walter Kardinal Kasper*, edited by George Augustin, 77–95. Freiburg: Herder, 2018.

Munier, Charles. "L'échec du mariage dans l'église ancienne". *Revue de droit canonique* 38 (1988): 26–40.

Murphy, Gerasimos. *Maximos IV at Vatican II: A Quest for Autonomy*. Boston: Sophia Press, 2011.

Murphy-O'Connor, Jerome. "The Divorced Woman in 1 Cor 7:10–11". *Journal of Biblical Literature* 100 (1981): 601–6.

Murray, John. *Divorce*. Philadelphia: Presbyterian and Reformed, 1961.

Myers, John J. "Divorce, Remarriage, and Reception of the Holy Eucharist". *Studia Canonica* 57 (1997): 485–516.

Nautin, Pierre. "Divorce et remariage dans la tradition de l'Église latine". *Recherches de science religieuse* 62 (1974): 7–54.

Neirynck, Frans. "Huwelijk en Echtscheiding in het Evangelie". *Collationes Brugenses et Gandavenses* 6 (1960): 123–30.

Neuner, Peter. "Ein katholischer Vorschlag zur Eucharistiegemeinschaft". *Stimmen der Zeit* 211 (1993): 443–50.

Newheiser, Jim. *Marriage, Divorce, and Remarriage: Critical Questions and Answers*. Phillipsburg, NJ: P&R Publishing, 2017.

Noonan, John T., Jr. "Novel 22". In *The Bond of Marriage: An Ecumenical and Interdisciplinary Study*, edited by William W. Bassett, 41–96. Notre Dame: University of Notre Dame Press, 1968.

———. *The Power to Dissolve: Lawyers and Marriages in the Court of the Roman Curia*. Cambridge, MA: Harvard University Press, 1972.

Nutt, Roger W. "*Gaudium et Spes* and the Indissolubility of the Sacrament of Matrimony: The Contribution of Charles Cardinal Journet". *Nova et Vetera* 11 (2013): 619–26.

O'Connor, Michael. *Cajetan's Biblical Commentaries: Motive and Method*. Leiden: Brill, 2017.

Oliva, Adriano, O.P. *Amours: L'Église, les divorcés remariés, les couples homosexuels*. Paris: Cerf, 2015.

Olsen, V. Norskov. *The New Testament on Divorce: A Study of Their Interpretation from Erasmus to Milton*. Tübingen: Mohr, 1971.

O'Malley, John W., S.J. *Trent: What Happened at the Council*. Cambridge, MA: Harvard University Press, 2013.

Orme, Nicholas. *Medieval Children*. New Haven, CT: Yale University Press, 2001.

Örsy, Ladislas, S.J. "In Search of the Meaning of Oikonomia: Report on a Convention". *Theological Studies* 43 (1982): 312–19.

———. *Marriage in Canon Law: Texts and Comments, Reflections and Questions*. Collegeville, MN: Liturgical Press, 1990.

Ouellet, Marc Cardinal, S.S. "Accompanying, Discerning, Integrating Weakness". *L'Osservatore Romano*, November 21, 2017. www.osservatoreromano.va/en/news/accompanying-discerning-integrating-weakness.

———. "A Missionary Gaze: Understanding 'Amoris Laetitia'". *L'Osservatore Romano*, November 8, 2017. www.osservatoreromano.va/en/news/missionary-gaze.

Overbeck, Franz-Josef. "What Theological Resources Did the German Bishops Mine for Their Reception of *Amoris Laetitia*?" In *Amoris Laetitia: A New Momentum for Moral Formation and Pastoral Practice*, edited by Grant Gallicho and James F. Keenan, S.J., 139–45. New York: Paulist Press, 2018.

Ozment, Steven E. *When Fathers Ruled: Family Life in Reformation Europe*. Cambridge, MA: Harvard University Press, 1983.

Pastor of Hermas. Translated by F. Crombie. In *Ante-Nicene Fathers*. Vol. 2, *Fathers of the Second Century: Hermas, Tatian, Athenagoras, Theophilus, and Clement of Alexandria*, edited by Alexander Roberts and James Donaldson, revised by A. Cleveland Coxe, 1–58. Peabody, MA: Hendrickson, 1994.

Pelletier, Anne-Marie. "Réponse d'Anne-Marie Pelletier [I]". In *"La vocation et la mission de la famille dans l'Église et dans le monde contemporain": 26 théologiens répondent*, 56–62. Paris: Bayard, 2015.

———. "Réponse d'Anne-Marie Pelletier [II]". In *"La vocation et la mission de la famille dans l'Église et dans le monde contemporain": 26 théologiens répondent*, 72–77. Paris: Bayard, 2015.

Pennington, Jonathan T. *The Sermon on the Mount and Human Flourishing: A Theological Commentary.* Grand Rapids, MI: Baker Academic, 2017.

Perez de Guereñu, Gregorio. "*Amoris laetitia* y madurez humana y ecclesial". *Páginas* 244 (December 2016): 26–34.

Perez-Lopez, Angel. "Conjugal Charity and the Pastoral Care of the Conjugal Bond in *Amoris Laetitia*". *Scripta Fulgentia* 26 (2016): 83–119.

————. "*Veritatis Splendor* and *Amoris Laetitia*: Neither Lamented nor Celebrated Discontinuity". *Nova et Vetera* 16 (2018): 1183–1214.

Pérez-Soba, Juan José, and Stephan Kampowski. *The Gospel of the Family: Going beyond Cardinal Kasper's Proposal in the Debate on Marriage, Civil Re-Marriage, and Communion in the Church.* Translated by Michael J. Miller. San Francisco: Ignatius Press, 2014.

Perkins, Pheme. "Marriage in the New Testament and Its World". In *Commitment to Partnership: Explorations of the Theology of Marriage*, edited by William Roberts, 5–30. New York: Paulist, 1987.

Perrin, Bertrand-Marie. "L'institution du mariage dans le *Commentaire des Sentences* de saint Thomas (I)". *Revue Thomiste* 108 (2008): 423–66.

————. "L'institution du mariage dans le *Commentaire des Sentences* de saint Thomas (II)". *Revue Thomiste* 108 (2008): 599–646.

Peters, Edward N., ed. *The 1917 or Pio-Benedictine Code of Canon Law in English Translation.* San Francisco: Ignatius Press, 2001.

Petrà, Basilio. *Divorziati e risposati e seconde nozze nella Chiesa: Una via di soluzione?* Assisi: Cittadella Editrice, 2012.

————. *Divorzio e seconde nozze nella tradizione greca: Un altra via.* Assisi: Cittadella Editrice, 2014.

————. *Il matrimonio può morire? Studi sulla pastorale dei divorziati risposati.* Bologna: EDB, 1995.

Philips, Abu Ameenah Bilal, and Jamila Jones. *Polygamy in Islam.* Riyadh: International Islamic Publishing House, 2005.

Pinckaers, Servais, O.P. "Ce que le Moyen Age pensait du marriage". *La vie spirituelle. Supplément* 82 (1967): 413–40.

————. *Ce qu'on ne peut jamais faire: La question des actes intrinsèquement mauvais. Histoire et discussion.* Paris: Cerf, 1986.

Piper, John. "Divorce and Remarriage: A Position Paper". Desiring God.org, July 21, 1986. http://www.desiringgod.org/articles /divorce-remarriage-a-position-paper.

————. *This Momentary Marriage: A Parable of Permanence*. Wheaton, IL: Crossway, 2009.

————. *What Jesus Demands from the World*. Wheaton, IL: Crossway, 2006.

Pitre, Brant. *Jesus the Bridegroom: The Greatest Story Ever Told*. New York: Penguin Random House, 2014.

————. *Jesus and the Last Supper*. Grand Rapids, MI: Eerdmans, 2015.

Pius XI, Pope. *Encyclical Letter of Pius XI Christian Marriage: Casti Connubii*. Boston: St. Paul Books & Media, n.d.

Popenoe, David. *Families without Fathers: Fatherhood, Marriage and Children in American Society*. New York: Routledge, 2009.

————. *Life without Father: Compelling New Evidence that Fatherhood and Marriage Are Indispensable for the Good of Children and Society*. New York: Simon & Schuster, 1996.

Pospishil, Victor J. *Divorce and Remarriage*. New York: Herder and Herder, 1967.

Provost, James H. "Intolerable Marriage Situations: A Second Decade". *Jurist* 50 (1990): 573–612.

Pruss, Alexander R. *One Body: An Essay in Christian Sexual Ethics*. Notre Dame: University of Notre Dame Press, 2013.

Rahner, Karl, S.J. *The Shape of the Church to Come*. Translated by Edward Quinn. New York: Seabury Press, 1974.

————. "Yesterday's History of Dogma and Theology for Tomorrow". In *Theological Investigations*. Vol. 18, *God and Revelation*, translated by Edward Quinn, 3–34. New York: Crossroad, 1983.

Ratzinger, Joseph. "On the Question of the Indissolubility of Marriage: Remarks on the Dogmatic-Historical State of Affairs and Its Significance for the Present". Translated by Joseph Bolin. PathsofLove.com, March 25, 2011. https://www.pathsoflove .com/texts/ratzinger-indissolubility-marriage/

————. "Zur Frage nach der Unauflöslichkeit der Ehe: Bemerkungen zum dogmengeschichtlichen Befund und zu seiner gegenwärtigen Bedeutung". In *Ehe und Ehescheidung: Diskussion Unter Christen*, edited by Franz Henrich and Volker Eid, 35–52. Munich: Kösel, 1972.

————. "Zur Theologie der Ehe". In *Theologie der Ehe*, edited by Gerhard Krems and Reinhard Mumm, 81–115. Regensburg: Pustet, 1969.

Reardon, Ruth. "*Amoris Laetitia*: Comments from an Interchurch Family Perspective". *One in Christ* 50 (2016): 66–86.

Regnerus, Mark. "Parental Same-Sex Relationships, Family Instability, and Subsequent Life Outcomes for Adult Children: Answering Critics of the New Family Structures Study with Additional Analyses". *Social Science Research* 41 (2012): 1367–77.

Reid, Charles J., Jr. *Power over the Body, Equality in the Family: Rights and Domestic Relations in Medieval Canon Law*. Grand Rapids, MI: Eerdmans, 2004.

Rex, Richard. "A Church in Doubt". *First Things* 282 (April 2018): 47–50.

Reynolds, Philip Lyndon. *How Marriage Became One of the Sacraments*. Cambridge: Cambridge University Press, 2016.

———. *Marriage in the Western Church: The Christianization of Marriage during the Patristic and Early Medieval Periods*. Leiden: Brill, 1994.

Rist, John M. "Divorce and Remarriage in the Early Church: Some Historical and Cultural Reflections". In *Remaining in the Truth of Christ: Marriage and Communion in the Catholic Church*, edited by Robert Dodaro, O.S.A., 64–92. San Francisco: Ignatius Press, 2014.

Rodríguez Luño, Angel. "L'estinzione del matrimonio a causa della morte: Obiezioni alla tesi di B. Petrà". *Rivista di teologia morale* 130 (2001): 237–48.

Roy, Louis, O.P. "In and Out of Communion". *Tablet* (April 7, 2018): 13.

Rubio, Julie Hanlon. *Hope for Common Ground: Mediating the Personal and the Political in a Divided Church*. Washington, D.C.: Georgetown University Press, 2016.

———. "The Newness of *Amoris Laetitia*: Mercy and Truth, Truth and Mercy". In *Amoris Laetitia: A New Momentum for Moral Formation and Pastoral Practice*, edited by Grant Gallicho and James F. Keenan, S.J., 61–69. New York: Paulist Press, 2018.

Rubiyatmoko, R. *Competenza della Chiesa nello scioglimento del vincolo del matrimonio non sacramentale: Una ricerca sostanziale sullo scioglimento del vincolo matrimoniale*. Rome: Gregorian University Press, 1998.

Rue, James J., and Louise Shanahan. *The Divorced Catholic*. Mahwah, NJ: Paulist Press, 1972.

Ruini, Camillo Cardinal. "The Gospel of the Family in the Secular-
    ized West". In *Eleven Cardinals Speak on Marriage and the Family:
    Essays from a Pastoral Viewpoint*, edited by Winfried Aymans,
    translated by Michael J. Miller et al., 83–88. San Francisco:
    Ignatius Press, 2015.
Sagandoy, Vincent Mynem C. "Canonical Imperatives of Pastoral
    Care in *Amoris Laetitia* concerning Catholics with Irregular
    Marital Status". In *A Point of No Return?* Amoris Laetitia *on
    Marriage, Divorce, and Remarriage*, edited by Thomas Knieps-Port
    le Roi, 181–94. Berlin: LIT Verlag, 2017.
Sarah, Robert Cardinal. "Marriage Preparation in a Secularized
    World". In *Eleven Cardinals Speak on Marriage and the Family:
    Essays from a Pastoral Viewpoint*, edited by Winfried Aymans,
    translated by Michael J. Miller et al., 89–112. San Francisco:
    Ignatius Press, 2015.
Sarpi, Paolo. *Istoria del Concilio Tridentino*. London: 1619.
Savino, Jorge L. Cardinal. "Christian Marriage: The Reality and Pas-
    toral Care". In *Eleven Cardinals Speak on Marriage and the Family:
    Essays from a Pastoral Viewpoint*, edited by Winfried Aymans,
    translated by Michael J. Miller et al., 113–29. San Francisco:
    Ignatius Press, 2015.
Scheeben, Matthias Joseph. *The Mysteries of Christianity*. Translated by
    Cyril Vollert, S.J. New York: Crossroad, 2006.
Schembri, Kevin. "The Orthodox Tradition on Divorced and
    Remarried Faithful: What Can the Catholic Church Learn?"
    Melita Theologica 65 (2015): 121–41.
Schillebeeckx, Edward, O.P. "Christian Marriage and the Reality of
    Complete Marital Breakdown". In *Catholic Divorce: The Decep-
    tion of Annulments*, edited by Pierre Hegy and Joseph Martos,
    82–107. New York: Continuum, 2000.
———. *Church: The Human Story of God*. Translated by John
    Bowden. New York: Crossroad, 1990.
———. *God the Future of Man*. Translated by N.D. Smith. New
    York: Sheed and Ward, 1968.
Schindler, D.C. "The Crisis of Marriage as a Crisis of Meaning: On
    the Sterility of the Modern Will". *Communio* 41 (2014): 331–71.
Schmeiser, J.A. "Reception of the Eucharist by Divorced and Remar-
    ried Catholics: Three German Bishops and the Congregation

for the Doctrine of the Faith". *Liturgical Ministry* 5 (1996): 10–21.

Schmemann, Alexander. "The Indissolubility of Marriage: The Theological Tradition of the East". In *The Bond of Marriage: An Ecumenical and Interdisciplinary Study*, edited by William W. Bassett, 97–112. Notre Dame: University of Notre Dame Press, 1968.

Schnackenburg, Rudolf. *Ephesians: A Commentary*. Translated by Helen Heron. Edinburgh: T&T Clark, 1991.

———. *The Gospel of Matthew*. Translated by Robert R. Barr. Grand Rapids, MI: Eerdmans, 2002.

Schockenhoff, Eberhard. *Chancen zur Versöhnung? Die Kirche und die wiederverheirateten Geschiedenen*. Freiburg: Herder, 2012.

———. "Our Understanding of Moral Sin: The Competence of Conscience of Divorced Remarried Persons". *INTAMS Review* 20 (2014): 249–59.

———. "Traditionsbruch oder notwendige Weiterbildung? Zwei Lesarten des Nachsynodalen Schreibens Amoris laetitia". In *Zum Gelingen von Ehe und Familie: Ermutigung aus Amoris laetitia: Für Walter Kardinal Kasper*, edited by George Augustin, 282–96. Freiburg: Herder, 2018.

Scholz, Franz. "Problems on Norms Raised by Ethical Borderline Situations: Beginnings of a Solution in Thomas Aquinas and Bonaventure". In *Readings in Moral Theology*. Vol. 1, *Moral Norms and Catholic Tradition*, edited by Charles E. Curran and Richard A. McCormick, S.J., 158–83. New York: Paulist Press, 1979.

Schönborn, Christoph Cardinal, O.P. *Die Freude, Priester zu sein*. Freiburg: Herder, 2011.

———. "Cardinal Schönborn on 'The Joy of Love': The Full Conversation". Interview by Antonia Spadaro, S.J. Translated by Brian McNeil. In *America Magazine*, August 9, 2016. https://www.americamagazine.org/issue/richness-love.

———. *Le Regard du Bon pasteur: Entretien avec Antonio Spadaro*. Paris: Parole et Silence, 2015.

Scicluna, Charles Jude. "The Guidelines of the Maltese Bishops: The Theological Principles We Mined". In *Amoris Laetitia: A New Momentum for Moral Formation and Pastoral Practice*, edited by

Grant Gallicho and James F. Keenan, S.J., 146–51. New York: Paulist Press, 2018.

Scola, Angelo Cardinal. "Marriage and the Family between Anthropology and the Eucharist: Comments in View of the Extraordinary Assembly of the Synod of Bishops on the Family". Translated by Michael J. Miller. *Communio* 41 (2014): 208–25.

————. *The Nuptial Mystery.* Translated by Michelle K. Borras. Grand Rapids, MI: Eerdmans, 2005.

Seewald, Michael. *Dogma im Wandel: Wie Glaubenslehren sich entwickeln.* Freiburg: Herder, 2018.

Simonetti, Manlio, ed. *Matthew 1–13.* Ancient Christian Commentary on Scripture Series. Vol. 1a. Downers Grove, IL: InterVarsity Press, 2001.

Smith, Christian, Kyle Longest, Jonathan Hill, and Kari Christoffersen. *Young Catholic America: Emerging Adults In, Out of, and Gone from the Church.* Oxford: Oxford University Press, 2014.

Smith, Christian and Melinda Lundquist Denton. *Soul Searching: The Religious and Spiritual Lives of American Teenagers.* Oxford: Oxford University Press, 2005.

Spaemann, Robert. "Ein Bruch mit der Lehrtradition". Interview by Anian Christoph Wimmer. *CNA Deutsch*, April 28, 2016. English edition: "Interview with Robert Spaemann on Amoris Laetitia". By Anian Christoph Wimmer. Translated by Richard Andrew Krema. *CNA*, April 29, 2016. https://www.catholic newsagency.com/news/full-text-interview-with-robert-spaemann-on-amoris-laetitia-10088.

Strauss, Mark L., ed. *Remarriage after Divorce in Today's Church: Three Views.* Grand Rapids, MI: Zondervan, 2006.

Stylianopoulos, Theodore. "The Indissolubility of Marriage in the New Testament: Principle and Practice". *Greek Orthodox Theological Review* 34 (1989): 335–45.

Sullivan, Francis A., S.J. *Creative Fidelity: Weighing and Interpreting Documents of the Magisterium.* New York: Paulist Press, 1996.

Tanner, Norman P., S.J., ed. *Decrees of the Ecumenical Councils.* Vol. 1, *Nicaea I to Lateran V.* Washington, D.C.: Georgetown University Press, 1990.

————. ed. *Decrees of the Ecumenical Councils.* Vol. 2, *Trent to Vatican II.* Washington, D.C.: Georgetown University Press, 1990.

Tertullian. *Against Marcion*. Translated by Peter Holmes. In *Ante-Nicene Fathers*. Vol. 3, *Latin Christianity: Its Founder*, edited by Alexander Roberts and James Donaldson, revised by A. Cleveland Coxe, 269–475. Peabody, MA: Hendrickson, 1994.

—————. *Of Patience*. Translated by Sydney Thelwall. In *Ante-Nicene Fathers*. Vol. 3, *Latin Christianity: Its Founder*, edited by Alexander Roberts and James Donaldson, revised by A. Cleveland Coxe, 707–17. Peabody, MA: Hendrickson, 1994.

—————. *On Monogamy*. Translated by Sydney Thelwall. In *Ante-Nicene Fathers*. Vol. 4, *Fathers of the Third Century: Tertullian, Part Fourth; Minicius Felix; Commodian; Origen, Parts First and Second*, edited by Alexander Roberts and James Donaldson, revised by A. Cleveland Coxe, 59–72. Peabody, MA: Hendrickson, 1994.

Theobald, Christoph, S.J. "Postface". In *Exhortation apostolique Post-Synodale du pape François La Joie de l'Amour: Édition présentée et annotée sous la direction du Service national Famille et Société—Conférence des évêques de France—et de la Faculté de théologie du Centre Sèvres*, 321–36. Paris: Éditions Jésuites, 2016.

—————. *Urgences pastorales du moment present: Pour une pédagogie de la reform*. Paris: Bayard, 2017.

Thiselton, Anthony C. *The First Epistle to the Corinthians: A Commentary on the Greek Text*. Grand Rapids, MI: Eerdmans, 2000.

Thomas, Matthew J. *Paul's "Works of the Law" in the Perspective of Second Century Reception*. Tübingen: Mohr Siebeck, 2018.

Thomasset, Alain, S.J., and Jean-Miguel Garrigues, O.P. *Une morale souple mais non sans boussole: Répondre aux doutes des quatre Cardinaux à propos d' Amoris laetitia*. Paris: Cerf, 2017.

Tietz, Christiane. "Karl Barth and Charlotte von Kirschbaum". *Theology Today* 74 (2017): 86–111.

Torrance, Alexis. *Repentance in Late Antiquity: Eastern Asceticism and the Framing of the Christian Life, ca. 400–650*. Oxford: Oxford University Press, 2013.

Torrell, Jean-Pierre, O.P. *Saint Thomas Aquinas*. Vol. 1, *The Person and His Work*, translated by Robert Royal. Washington, D.C.: Catholic University of America Press, 1996.

Travers, Patrick. "Holy Communion and Catholics Who Have Attempted Remarriage after Divorce: A Revisitation". *Jurist* 57 (1997): 517–40.

————. "Reception of the Holy Eucharist by Catholics Attempting Remarriage after Divorce and the 1983 Code of Canon Law". *Jurist* 55 (1995): 187–217.

2012 Freiburg "Memorandum on Admitting Divorced and Remarried Persons to the Sacraments". *Memorandum "Wiederverheiratet Geschiedene in unserer Kirche"*. http://www.memorandum-priester -und-diakone-freiburg.de/?page_id=273.

United States Conference of Catholic Bishops. *Marriage: Love and Life in the Divine Plan*. Washington, D.C.: United States Conference of Catholic Bishops, 2009.

Vasil', Cyril, S.J. "Separation, Divorce, Dissolution of the Bond, and Remarriage: Theological and Practical Approaches of the Orthodox Churches". In *Remaining in the Truth of Christ: Marriage and Communion in the Catholic Church*, edited by Robert Dodaro, O.S.A., 93–128. San Francisco: Ignatius Press, 2014.

Vawter, Bruce. "Divorce and the New Testament". *Catholic Biblical Quarterly* 39 (1977): 528–42.

Vesco, Jean-Paul, O.P. *Tout amour véritable est indissoluble*. Paris: Cerf, 2015.

Virt, G. "Moral Norms and the Forgotten Virtue of Epikeia in the Pastoral Care of the Divorced and Remarried". *Melita Theologica* 63 (2013): 17–34.

Von Balthasar, Hans Urs. *The Glory of the Lord: A Theological Aesthetics*. Vol. 1, *Seeing the Form*, translated by Erasmo Leiva-Merikakis, edited by Joseph Fessio, S.J., and John Riches. San Francisco: Ignatius Press, 1982.

Von Gunten, André-François. "La doctrine de Cajétan sur l'indissolubilité du marriage". *Angelicum* 43 (1966): 62–72.

Von Hildebrand, Dietrich. *Marriage: The Mystery of Faithful Love*. Translated by Emmanuel Chapman and Daniel Sullivan. Manchester, NH: Sophia Institute Press, 1991.

Walshe, Sebastian, O.Praem. "The Formation and Exercise of Conscience in Private and Public Matters". *Nova et Vetera* 16 (2018): 275–309.

Webster, Alexander, F.C. "Icons of the 'Nuclear' Family". In *Glory and Honor: Orthodox Christian Resources on Marriage*, edited by David C. Ford, Mary S. Ford, and Alfred Kentigern Siewers, 171–82. Yonkers, NY: St. Vladimir's Seminary Press, 2016.

Welch, Lawrence J., and Perry Cahall. "An Examination of the Role of Faith in Matrimonial Consent and the Consequences for the Sacrament of Marriage". *Nova et Vetera* 16 (2018): 311–42.

Wenham, Gordon J. "Does the NT Approve Remarriage after Divorce?" *Southern Baptist Journal of Theology* 6 (2002): 30–45.

———. "Matthew and Divorce: An Old Crux Revisited". *Journal for the Study of the New Testament* 22 (1984): 95–107.

———. "No Remarriage after Divorce". In *Remarriage after Divorce in Today's Church: Three Views*, edited by Mark L. Strauss, 19–42. Grand Rapids, MI: Zondervan, 2006.

———. "A Response to Craig S. Keener". In *Remarriage after Divorce in Today's Church: Three Views*, edited by Mark L. Strauss, 121–25. Grand Rapids, MI: Zondervan, 2006.

———. "The Syntax of Matthew 19:9". *Journal for the Study of the New Testament* 24 (1986): 17–23.

Westerholm, Stephen. *Jesus and Scribal Authority*. Lund, Sweden: CWK Gleerup, 1978.

———. *Law and Ethics in Early Judaism and the New Testament*. Tübingen: Mohr Siebeck, 2017.

Witte, John, Jr. *From Sacrament to Contract: Marriage, Religion, and Law in the Western Tradition*. 2nd ed. Louisville, KY: Westminster John Knox, 2012.

Woestman, William H., O.M.I., and Wojciech Kowal, O.M.I. *Special Marriage Cases and Procedures*. 4th ed. Ottawa: Faculty of Canon Law, St. Paul University, 2008.

Wollbold, Andreas. *Pastoral mit widerverheirateten Geschiedenen: Gordischer Knoten oder ungeahnte Möglichkeiten?* Regensburg: Pustet, 2015.

Worgul, George S. "*Amoris Laetitia*: On the Need for a Contextual Theology and Inculturation in Practice". In *A Point of No Return? Amoris Laetitia on Marriage, Divorce, and Remarriage*, edited by Thomas Knieps-Port le Roi, 20–29. Berlin: LIT Verlag, 2017.

Wrenn, Lawrence G., ed. *Divorce and Remarriage in the Catholic Church*. New York: Newman Press, 1973.

Wright, N. T. "Why Christian Character Matters". In *All Things Hold Together in Christ: A Conversation on Faith, Science, and Virtue*, edited by James K. A. Smith and Michael L. Gulker, 157–88. Grand Rapids, MI: Baker Academic, 2018.

Zanetti, Eugenio, ed. *Porte aperte: Accompagnare, discernere, integrare vissuti di separazione, divorzio, o nuova unione alla luce di Amoris Laetitia.* Milan: Ancora, 2016.

Zhekov, Yordan Kalev. *Defining the New Testament Logia on Divorce and Remarriage in a Pluralistic Context.* Eugene, OR: Pickwick, 2009.

Zoghby, Elias. Speech at Vatican II. September 29, 1965. In *Acta synodalia Sacrosancti Concilii Oecumenici Vaticani II*, vol. 4, pt. 3, 45–47. Vatican City: Typis polyglottis Vaticanis, 1980.

Zulehner, Paul M. *Verbuntung: Kirchen im weltanschaulichen Pluralismus: Religion im Leben der Menschen 1970–2010.* Ostfildern: Schwabenverlag, 2011.

———. *Vom Gesetz zum Gesicht: Ein neuer Ton in der Kirche: Papst Franziskus zu Ehe und Familie:* Amoris Laetitia. Ostfildern: Patmos, 2016.

SUBJECT INDEX

SCRIPTURE INDEX